D0212832

FLORIDA STATE
UNIVERSITY LIBRARIES

MAY 24 2000

TALLAHASSEE, FLORIDA

The Native American Oral Tradition

Voices of the Spirit and Soul

Lois J. Einhorn
Foreword by Tamarack Song

Westport, Connecticut
London

PM
217
.E37
2000

Library of Congress Cataloging-in-Publication Data

Einhorn, Lois J., 1952–
    The native American oral tradition : voices of the spirit and soul / by Lois J. Einhorn ; foreword by Tamarack Song.
        p.   cm.
    Includes bibliographical references and index.
    ISBN 0–275–95790–X (alk. paper)
    1. Indian literature—North America—History and criticism.   2. Oral tradition—North America.   3. Indians of North America—Languages—Rhetoric.   4. Indians of North America—Religion.   I. Title.
    PM217.E37   2000
    398′.089′97—dc21   99–045989

British Library Cataloguing in Publication Data is available.

Copyright © 2000 by Lois J. Einhorn

All rights reserved. No portion of this book may be reproduced, by any process or technique, without the express written consent of the publisher.

Library of Congress Catalog Card Number: 99–045989
ISBN: 0–275–95790–X

First published in 2000

Praeger Publishers, 88 Post Road West, Westport, CT 06881
An imprint of Greenwood Publishing Group, Inc.
www.praeger.com

Printed in the United States of America

The paper used in this book complies with the Permanent Paper Standard issued by the National Information Standards Organization (Z39.48–1984).

10 9 8 7 6 5 4 3 2 1

This book is dedicated to the many Native People who have been annihilated and to those who survive.

Their Spirit Lives On

They extend through past and future,
through time and space.
They extend into the past,
in the voices of their ancestors.
Part of them is their philosophy, their teachings, and their traditions.

They extend into the present,
in those they watch grow.
Part of them is their dignity, their courage, and their identity.

They extend through time and space in those who are not yet born.
Through past and future, through time and space,
They gave of themselves.
And parts of them are in all the people they touched.

What is firmly established cannot be uprooted.
What is firmly grasped cannot slip away.
Their spirits will be remembered, honored, and cherished
    from generation to generation.

Lois J. Einhorn

Contents

Illustrations

Foreword

Stuart, a friend, once wrote that he was going to help collect the "myths" of a Native American group in order to help them achieve federal tribal recognition. He explained his belief that hard copy of his People's oral tradition could help legitimize their existence as a tribal entity.

I envisioned Stuart at the door of an Elder, notebook and tape recorder in hand, poised to stick the microphone in her face and ask her to recite some "myths." Hoping to intercept him before that horrid picture could be enacted, I wasted no time in replying.

The term "myth" conjures up in many the image of a paternalistic culture looking upon uncivilized peoples' imaginative attempts to explain their world and quell their fears of the unknown. Stuart's good intention notwithstanding, I feared that he, by projecting this image, along with not honoring the traditional time and way legends are shared, was unwittingly going to heap disrespect upon his interviewees.

I gently explained to Stuart that Native Peoples' oral tradition is their very existence; it is their soul. It is their unique communion with the Circle of Life. It is the web that connects their Ancients with those yet to come. When spoken it is not bounded by the voice or the time of the speaker; it is but the momentary expression of the great flow of a people. Like the flow of a river, it cannot be captured, as it is ever flowing, ever changing.

In our terms it is akin to all our great educational, scientific, political, and religious institutions, all our beliefs and social customs, all our personal and family and national and natural histories and prophecies, all our great bodies of art and craft and literature, and all else that forms our collective consciousness. Can that be conveyed, and that culture thus be validated, by the capturing of a few stories?

And what if there is no one to tell the stories? Does that mean the people are gone as well? Long after the legends of a people are squelched and forgotten, the soul of those people lives on in the way they are with their children, the way they look over the water, the way they feel when an Elder leaves them.

My grandparents, for example, remembered slight few of the traditional legends of their respective people – the HorseRiders of the Steppes, the agrarian Etruscans, the Germanic Seafarers, and the Forest Algonquians; yet, through my grandparents' ways and wisdoms they passed on to me the soul of our Old Ones that I, in turn, may pass it on to those who shall carry it beyond me.

Such is the precious gift of this book; amongst so many books that attempt to toss us the fish, this one guides us in the way of the fish. It gives us not the stories but the tradition of the telling; it gives us not the storytellers but their way of storying. We learn how the Native speaks with a pride that is humility, with a sense of self that encompasses all the relations. Thus we can hear the story within the story – the soul of the people.

Lois Einhorn, the author, whom I have the honor to call friend, was able to craft this guide for us because she has come to know the story within her own story. She is eminently qualified to turn out another collection/dissection of "myths," but she did not do that; she could not do that. The pain that was mashed into her as a child brewed; when rightly aged she poured forth the story within the pain. The pain was a voice; the form and shape of the pain was its story.

She gifts us now with her keen sensitivity for form and shape, so that we too may embrace the soul of story. For soul remains strong even when the voice grows weak.

Tamarack Song
Author of *Journey to the Ancestral Self*

Preface

Imagine yourself living in a world filled with love, peace, joy, cooperation, and unity. People treat you with kindness and respect not because of what you do, but because of who you are. You accept, value, appreciate, and celebrate other people's differences, viewing them as opportunities for you to learn and grow. You see with sensitivity, hear with heart, and speak with sincerity.

You value truth, unity, and peace. You define peace not only as the absence of war, but also as respect and reverence for life and for nourishing, cultivating, and sustaining life. You nurture and cherish your family, friends, and people in your tribal nation, especially Elders, the links to the past, and children, the representatives of the future. You also serve as guardian of the land since the hallowed ground beneath your feet represents your ancestors.

Some violence and crime exist. Occasionally you hear the words rape, murder, and war. But your culture overall stresses love, unity, and living in harmony with nature. You have never heard of alcohol, pollution, or guns or of diseases such as smallpox, cholera, or tuberculosis.

You belong. You belong to your family. You belong to your tribal nation. Most importantly, you belong to the Earth.

You understand your purpose and place on this planet. You nourish and cherish Mother Earth, who, in turn, nourishes you and all her creatures. You believe that everyone and everything possess equal worth. Like all people, you share the exquisite Earth with the shimmering sun, spacious sky, woodland wildlife, and fragrant foliage.

You live each moment in the present to the fullest, in harmony with Mother Earth. You know the past is gone, and the future consists only of dreams. Thus, you savor each moment, feeling gratitude, wonder, and awe for the magnificence and splendor of the universe – the vibrant palette of colors, the harmonies of nature, the rhythms of dance, the way light illuminates leaves, lakes, and landscapes.

You know all things in the cosmos are intrinsically interrelated: affecting one thing means affecting everything. You view the world as a mirror in which you see others as reflections of yourself. You are the sunrise and sunset. You are the stars, shadows, and spirits. Your life is one with everything on Earth.

You love people and nature unconditionally. You see them as real. "What is real?" the Rabbit asks the Skin Horse in the classic children's book, *The Velveteen Rabbit*. "Does it mean having things that buzz inside you and a stick out handle?" "Real isn't how you're made," says the Skin Horse. "It's a thing that happens to you. When a [person] loves you for a long time, not just to play with, but Really love you, then you become Real." "Does it hurt?" asks the Rabbit. "Sometimes," says the Skin Horse for he was always truthful. "When you are Real, most of your hair has been loved off and your eyes droop and you get loose at the joints and very shabby. But these things don't matter at all because once you are Real you can't be ugly, except to people who don't understand." You view people, animals, trees, flowers, and stones as "Real," and you love them "not just to play with, but Really love them." Your love is deep, genuine, and never-ending.

You view spoken words as alive because they carry breath, sound vibrations, and spirits. But you know people are not the only ones to speak. Willows whisper, rains roar, trees talk, hills hum, and spirits speak. You develop an acute awareness, listening to all these languages.

What you have imagined exemplifies how Native Americans say they lived and felt before 1492, when Columbus "discovered" America.

Now envision a different mental picture. Your life consists of isolation, oppression, anguish, torment, and discrimination. People come to this country, most to escape religious persecution. They call you an "Indian" and themselves "Americans." At first, you help the Americans, teaching them how to hunt and how to grow corn, beans, and squash. But rather than thank you, these people use and abuse you.

If you are an Oglala Sioux, you have moved eight times in less than twenty-five years. If you belong to the Cherokee Nation, the federal and Georgia state governments have coerced you to move west, then farther west, then farther west. If you are a Nez Perce, you are forced to live on a cramped reservation, and then thrown off that very same reservation.[1]

In addition to ostracizing, killing, raping, and starving you and your human relatives, the newcomers to this country hurt everything around them – your nonhuman relatives, such as lizards, leaves, and lands. How can they destroy life forms that are spiritually equal to them? You tell them you do not understand. But they continue to ravage and ruin your relatives, their relatives. Their wasteful ways pollute and poison the planet. You watch them pour chemicals into bodies of water, chemicals that neither you nor they can even pronounce. You watch the destruction of the frontier – a rich, forested landscape full of potential and promise. Pristine prairies perish. Verdant valleys vanish. Disgusting debris and devastating destruction abound.

You feel dazed, yet amazed. How can people buy and sell land? The notion is as preposterous as buying and selling the air. Nature belongs to everyone because all people belong to nature.

The newcomers label you a "savage." They call you uncivilized because you do not know how to read and write and because you do not believe in Christianity. But, you do not understand how reading and writing helps a person. These "white men" write treaties, but then break them. You ask yourself, "Why should I want to become an American when Americans lie, steal, cheat, and deceive?"

Clearly these newcomers hold different values than you, and you rapidly watch their values become society's norm. They concern themselves with money and materialism, talking about how external aspects of life bring happiness. But you know happiness comes from inside your heart. They care about logic and rationality including evidence, proof, science, and technology. To you, life is not about logic, but about intuition, dreams, and visions.

The brutal manner in which the new government treats you defies expression. The actions of the "white man" are so grotesque that you would have to invent a new language to explain them; no words in your Native tongue or in the English language come close to expressing their horror and cruelty. These people invade your body and mind, and they try to overtake your spirit and soul.

You no longer belong. These newcomers call this country the "land of opportunity" and "the land of the free." But you feel like a foreigner, a fugitive. You are treated like a trespasser and expelled as an exile from your own homeland.

What you have imagined now exemplifies the ways Native Americans say they have lived and felt since newcomers settled in this country.

Like most readers of this book, I can only imagine the juxtaposition of life for Native Americans before and after Columbus "discovered" America. However, I can empathize with the suffering and pain. I have relatives who were victims of organized massacres in Germany and Austria, and family who died in the Holocaust. Growing up as a Jewish female in the South, I personally endured physical and verbal anti-semitism as well. Most significantly, I am a survivor of severe and sadistic physical and sexual abuse. The acts committed against me were shrouded in secrecy because of their unspeakable and unspoken nature. To survive, I had to shatter myself, numb my feelings, and bury my memories. I have felt the terror, horror, rage, and hate that normally accompany rape. I do not use the word hate often, and I do not mean the word here in the sense of "I hate asparagus." Rather, I mean hate that is red, raw, raging, tormenting, and searing.

In her book, "*My Name Is Chellis and I'm in Recovery from Western Civilization*," Chellis Glendinning explains how the content of her books has mirrored her healing from her own traumatic abuse. She concludes this is not coincidental because "the planetary is personal, the personal planetary." We could add that the personal is political, the political personal. In his book, *Turtle Island Alphabet*, mythologist Gerald Hausman notes the similarities between different forms of suffering; he includes pogroms and the Holocaust among his examples. He criticizes Native Americans who believe only people who have personally experienced events should write about them, concluding that "we all, regardless of our skin color, have felt shame and sorrow, humility and longing, fear and betrayal." Unfortunately, Native People do not possess a monopoly on mistreatment and molestation.[2]

I agree with Hausman. We only further segregate ourselves when we claim that only certain people can identify with certain cultures. We are all people subject to the same emotions. Any of us could have been born as the other. And so I believe it is of utmost importance to see the world through each other's eyes, as best we can.

Hausman continues by explaining how speaking, listening, writing, and reading provide "hope to turn hate into love." Glendinning discusses the need to live in conscious oneness. After recalling extraordinary experiences she and others had as children, she asks, "How do people with no previous environmental knowledge come to feel at home in the natural world and even, in its presence, break through to unintended nonordinary states of awareness?" She answers that some children "sense that something is wrong or missing" because they "have access to the love for life, equanimity, and resilience that are inherent in . . . the rhythms of the Earth." They feel healed by the repeating rhythms of nature, assurances that day follows night and fall follows summer.[3]

As a child, I had experiences similar to those Glendinning describes. I received messages from trees. I saw patterns in the ripples of water. I felt an instantaneous bond when looking into the eyes of an animal. Such experiences consoled and comforted me and made it impossible for abusers to seize my soul. My body and mind were invaded and hurt, but my soul remained pure and untainted.

Like Hausman and Glendinning, I think society's hope lies in people's refusing to be silenced. Only by remembering and speaking out can we hope that the suffering from the horrors the indigenous people of this country endured and are still enduring did not occur in vain. We must speak out, lest from this nothing be learned. My own field, rhetoric, advocates the sharing of many viewpoints, believing truth will triumph in the end if all points of view are exchanged in the marketplace of ideas.

Even though I never knew the Native People or nature beings who suffered and died, their image and meaning have left an indelible imprint on my heart. There is a place in me emptied by their loss and only partly filled by their memory. Yet surely as I live, part of each and every one of the many, many people, animals, trees, plants, and other living beings who were destroyed shall live with me.

The path from degradation to self-respect is arduous. The journey from slavery to freedom is agonizing. From these movements, Native People could have learned bitterness, callousness, insensitivity, and indifference. But that is not the lesson many of them, or I, have learned. I am more convinced than ever of the sanctity of each life – whether it be the life of a person, animal, or tree.

Let us make this a time of memory, celebration, and hope. Let us remember with affection the many lives that were destroyed and celebrate the continuing living presence of these lives in our hearts, now and forever. Let us dedicate our lives to those values, vows, and visions that make living worthwhile. Let us pray that nursery crimes and scary tales become things of the past, that all inhabitants of the Earth shall live in peace, and that all people will respect and revere life. Let us hold hands with our neighbors, regardless of color, religion, or race, and pray together that we shift from swords to speech, from conflict to compromise, and from hostility to harmony. Let each and every person become a messenger of peace for All Our Relations now and for generations to come.

Acknowledgments

I have been blessed by the help of many over the course of this project and over the course of my personal metamorphosis. First, I want to thank nature, one of my earliest and greatest teachers and the deepest source of help on my personal spiritual journey. My close bond with Mother Earth and my knowledge that we are all connected, from the tiniest cell to the greatest mysteries of the cosmos, have brought me to the path of this book, a path I am honored to walk.

The following people have read all or part of the manuscript; to each I am extremely grateful: Joseph Bruchac (Abenaki storyteller and author), Joseph Chilberg (Professor of Communication, State University of New York College at Fredonia), Chellis Glendinning (author), Moon Rainbow (Peace Elder, Wolf Clan Teaching Lodge, Seneca Indian Historical Society), Raven Moon (Wampanoag and Micmac Medicine Woman), Michael M. Osborn (Emeritus Professor of Rhetoric, University of Memphis), Elizabeth Nelson (Area Chair, American Indian Literatures and Cultures, American Culture Association), Tamarack Song (Algonquian Founder and Director of the Teaching Drum Outdoor School), Elizabeth Tucker (part-Cherokee and Professor of Folklore, including Native American, at Binghamton University), Robert W. Venables (Professor of American Indian Studies, Cornell University), and Gerald Vizenor (Anishaabe Professor of American Studies and Native American Literature, University of California at Berkeley). The students in my class on Communication, Ethics, and Social Action (spring 1998) also read most of the manuscript.

This book has benefited greatly from the insightful feedback of so many knowledgeable and talented individuals. However, with multiple critics, at times I was criticized and praised for the same thing. In these cases, I used my best judgment. Thus, it is important to note that the people listed above have not approved of everything in the book and, in fact, some have disapproved of parts.

I also wish to thank the many Native People locally, at pow wows, and elsewhere who spoke with me, answered questions, and allowed me to bounce ideas off of them. Special thanks go to the group where I have had the privilege of immersing myself and participating regularly in sweat lodge ceremonies: the circle that practices Lakota spiritual ways in Vestal, New York, led by James L. Holley (Lakota and Blackfoot Director of the Vestal Public Library).

My deep thanks go to Francene Hart for blessing this book with her inspired illustrations.

Eric Loeb adopted me as his daughter in a Lakota hunka ceremony and gave me the name Oglegleh Ki Iyoyamya Wi (Bright Colors Angel). To him I say "pilamayae" (thank you) for years of unconditional love and support. I love you more than words can express.

Introduction

The fundamental difference in ways of looking at the world, as those differences are reflected in the language of diplomacy, seems to me to constitute the most important issue in Indian-white relations in the past five hundred years.
N. Scott Momaday, Kiowa

Words are gifts, our grandparents say; and they give us many words so that we will remain a nation, a circle of people.
Debra CallingThunder, Northern Arapaho, Shoshone, and Cheyenne

Throughout the over two hundred years of the history of the United States, numerous Native People have given orations, many ranking among the greatest speeches in the world. Storytellers have told stories that listeners have passed on, until generation after generation has heard the same stories with few changes. People have taught prayers and songs to their young ones, preserving the essence of the words spoken by their parents. Native Americans also have passed on historical events, community norms, cultural practices, and views of life. Native People, then, possess a rich oral tradition composed of varying forms of discourse.[1]

Since Native Americans existed without the need to write, for many generations their speeches, stories, prayers, and songs have depended entirely on an oral tradition. They spend an enormous number of hours perfecting the art of public communication and learning methods for memorizing their messages. Not surprisingly, then, Native People value their oral tradition, the body of unwritten principles and teachings handed down orally from generation to generation. This book focuses on this oral tradition as expressed in the discourse of Native People.

Peace for All. Illustration by Francene Hart.

LANGUAGE AS ALIVE

Native People view words as living, breathing, dynamic beings. Living beings create sound vibrations. When people breathe, they exchange spirits, and their breath transforms sounds into words. Uttered sound vibrations possess physical and spiritual energies that find their expression in the voices and visions of all sentient beings. Words vibrate in every vein and crystallize in every capillary. Words carry one's physical totality or state of being and become part of one's being.

Joseph Epes Brown, a friend and pupil of Oglala Sioux holy man Black Elk, elaborates: "When we create words we use our breath, and for people and these traditions, breath is associated with life. And so if a word is born from this sacred principle of breath, this lends an added dimension to the spoken word."[2]

The oral tradition plays more than a prominent position in Native American culture; it is the culture itself. Simon Ortiz, contemporary Acoma Pueblo poet, emphasizes this point:

The oral tradition is not just speaking and listening, because what it means to me and to other people who have grown up in that tradition is that whole process, that whole process which involves a lifestyle. That whole process of that society in terms of its history, its culture, its language, its values, and subsequently, its literature. So it's not merely a simple matter of speaking and listening, but living that process.

Ortiz explains that the "act of language" constitutes this "process": "Our language is the way we create the world. . . . Man exists because of language, consciousness comes about through language, or the world comes about through language. Life – language. Language is life, then."[3]

To Native People, then, words affirm existence. They breathe and beat, pound and palpitate, resound and reverberate. Words pulsate with life, making their use potent and powerful. Sounds re-sound; they react and respond to each other. Their returning rings rebound and ricochet, resulting in a perpetual promenade of timbres and tones. Because words take on a living presence, they possess senses, souls, colors, textures, personalities, and identities. Speakers bring new words to life and new life to words.

Native American speakers rely upon an oral tradition and, hence, accord immense importance to the words they speak. To them a mind incapable of speaking is like a bird without wings. Native Americans talk about spoken words as vigorous vehicles for promoting positive or negative change and as living vibrations that affect the actions and reactions of all sentient beings. Spoken words can unite or divide, lead to cooperation or war. Henri Mann Morton, Cheyenne, emphasizes the potency of language when she says, "There is power in words." In short, without symbols, creation, change, and interchange cannot exist. Spoken sounds represent primitive symbols; words represent more sophisticated symbols.[4]

The life power of words gives the process of speaking a sacred dimension. All words are holy. All bind the past and weave the future. In his poem, "The Oral Tradition," Russell V. Boham, Chippewa, discusses how spoken words represent continual creation:

> The spoken word
> is creation renewed.
> Conceived in the mind
> and born with the breath of life,
> What I say to you
> is sacred.
> These words are my creation,
> but always they are
> My responsibility.
> I choose not beauty nor anger,
> but truth.

Breathing words of truth, communicating in right relationship with self and everyone and everything, and speaking to manifest wholeness – this is the sacred flow of the oral tradition.[5]

As a group, Native Americans say their non-Native counterparts accord little value to words. By frequently breaking treaties and other promises, Native Americans say Americans do not honor their words. In contrast, Native People consider words sacred; the life power of words gives the act of communication a sacred dimension. According to Chief Seattle, Suquamish, "My words are like the stars that never change. What Seattle says the great chief at Washington can rely upon with as much certainty as he can upon the return of the sun or the seasons." A character in a Winnebago story makes a similar comment: "The Indian mind is trained to hunt truth through the mask made by words."[6]

In addition to valuing the words they speak, Native Americans place a premium on words spoken to them. They view listening as a privilege, a responsibility, a sacred act. They take advantage of opportunities to listen and learn. Storytellers sharing the teachings of Medicine People and other wise leaders give the young numerous opportunities. So does attending meetings around council fires where orators well versed in the oral tradition speak.

Native Americans have passed the oral tradition on from generation to generation. The speeches, stories, prayers, and songs that we have today have passed a rigorous test – the test of time. The words have been remembered, collected, integrated, told, retold, enhanced, refined, and tested by human experience over thousands of years, making the words both ancient and living.

A culture that places such importance on the spoken word offers a wealth of potentially useful information to students of rhetoric, a way to better understand the spoken word. Conversely, the field of rhetoric may help us to better understand the oral tradition of Native People.

Rhetoric refers to the use of symbols to influence the beliefs, values, and/or actions of other people. Rhetoric pervades every aspect of life. People's existence within themselves and their ability to extend beyond themselves depend on the gifts of the spoken word – using the voice to talk, listen, laugh, cry, shout, whisper, chant, sing, praise, pause, tell stories, and pass on ways of life from generation to generation.

As a process, rhetoric existed from the moment humans began to communicate. As a study, it was perhaps the first humanistic discipline. Although the study of rhetoric is not limited to the spoken word, the known history of rhetoric began with the oral tradition of Greece and Rome, the Western treatment of communication. Rhetoric deals with discussion in the human forum. It consists of people's choices and, unlike force, it depends on the free will of others to accept or reject these choices. In short, rhetoric forms the foundation of Western civilization.

Especially in recent years, interest in the Native People of this country has grown. Louis Thomas Jones, a scholar of the history and culture of Native Americans, notes, "A mysterious charm has always hovered over the American Indian, this uncomplicated child of Nature who asked no more than life gave him and who thanked the Great Spirit for the privilege of freedom to which he was born."[7]

Despite the importance of the spoken word, and despite increased interest in these people, few thorough studies exist focusing on the Native American oral tradition, the process of communicating from mouth to ear. *The Index to Journals in Communication Studies through 1995* lists only fifteen articles dealing with any aspect of Native American speaking in the title of articles published in communication journals through the year 1995.

An increasing number of books deals with Native American speeches, stories, prayers, or songs. Few books, however, deal exclusively with the oral tradition. Further, many books on Native American speeches, stories, prayers, and songs do not analyze these modes of discourse. I know of none that analyzes them from a rhetorical perspective, focusing on, in the words of rhetorical theorist, Donald C. Bryant, the process of "adjusting ideas to people and people to ideas." In her article on Native American eloquence, Edna C. Sorter points to the need for more analyses of the Native American oral tradition by students of rhetoric and speech communication.[8]

This work seeks to fill this void and provide such an analysis. The chapters examine important aspects of the Native American oral tradition from a rhetorical perspective. They deal with characteristics of the oral tradition of Native People that span individual speakers, nations, and time periods. This book deals specifically with traditional Native American speaking in North America.

My purpose is to examine the Native American oral tradition as presented in its rhetoric. I focus especially on how the oral tradition is inextricably interconnected to their cultural assumptions, principles, values, and beliefs, all of which are reflected in their speeches, stories, prayers, and songs.

In general, I use both a transtextual and a contextual approach. A transtextual approach involves a close reading of many texts, with sensitivity to the subtle nuances and symbolism in the texts. The contextual approach examines the messages in their specific context. I also examine how the Native American oral tradition differs from the "dominant" rhetorical paradigm, requiring changes in both the rhetorical theory and rhetorical practice of Western culture.

By definition, all methods of analyzing the Native American oral tradition oversimplify and overgeneralize complex realities. All Native People do not speak in the same way because they are unique individuals, representing separate, sovereign nations, living on different lands, having distinct histories, speaking different languages, and so forth. With over five hundred separate sovereign nations, not all Native Americans share the ideas discussed, and not all people of Native descent follow traditional beliefs. This book considers the oral tradition of traditional Native Americans, the legacy bequeathed to them by their ancestors, as these ideas are reflected in their messages.

Like all people, not all Native People follow the ideas taught to them. Lenape Jack Forbes, Chairman of the Native American Studies Department at the University of California at Davis, declares, "But I have to say that there are good and bad Indians. There are Native people who are on a traditional path and are keeping their spiritual values, but there are also Native people who have taken a different road, sometimes a very evil road."[9]

A different road does not always equal an evil road. Over the past two hundred years, Native People have incorporated many of the Euro-American ways into their own. Many Native People today are more concerned with finding jobs, raising children, and staying sober than with connecting with nature. This book concerns itself with traditional Native American beliefs, but not because these beliefs are better than some contemporary Native American or North American beliefs.

Native People have benefited in many ways since the coming of the "white man." Like all people, they have reaped the advantages of new technology. The purpose of this book, however, is not to deal with how the dominant society has contributed to the lives of Native People and others. Several books already address this topic.

Some Native Americans object to writing down discourse intended for the ear. In this book I purposely use speeches, stories, prayers, songs, and interviews that are already in print; I intentionally do not include examples from my personal experience. Further, the purpose of this book is not to commit the oral tradition to writing, but to write about the oral tradition.

Some Native People assert that it is impossible to write about the oral tradition because the oral tradition equals the soul and fiber of Native American existence and life. The oral tradition is not one of several parts of Native American culture, it *is* the culture, simultaneously reflecting and manifesting it. Looking at the oral tradition as a separate entity, they argue, constitutes a Euro-American construct that can only result in admiration, adulation, covetousness, or fear. These people may be correct, but what alternative exists? If we are to cross the barriers of cross-cultural or transcultural communication, we must begin somewhere. I agree with the sentiments of the Ojibway prayer: "The more you know, the more you will trust and the less you will fear."[10]

Thus, this book specifically concerns the Native American oral tradition – the words of mouths to ears. The book deals with repeating patterns, principles, themes, symbols, images, and words of Native People, rhetorical elements that transcend speaker, time, and tribal nation. The text identifies and examines aspects of the Native American oral tradition that are pervasive, perennial, and perpetual.

This book is possible because a remarkable consistency exists in the messages of Native People over time and across tribal nation. Although their rhetoric spans hundreds of years, Native American speakers talk about many of the same issues, perhaps because the dominant society continues to threaten their existence. For centuries, Native People have served as spokespeople for survival, suffering, struggle, and serenity. Other common topics include truth, fairness, equality, justice, preservation, life and death, how to co-exist peacefully, the right to protest, and the need to honor the land.

Joseph Bruchac, an Abenaki storyteller, discusses this constancy in Native American rhetoric: "Although the voices would be different over the next two centuries, the sentiments would be much the same. The earth, their mother, gave them life and would always provide for them as long as they remained true to her. Their love for their mother was unchanging and they would protect her with their lives." At another point, Bruchac declares, "The native voices of the twentieth century are often so much like those of the centuries past, their appeals to honor and reason so similar, that only the occasional historical reference or turn of phrase distinguishes them."[11]

DESCRIPTION OF BOOK

The bulk of the book consists of a rhetorical analysis of Native American oral communications.

I begin by examining "Cultural Assumptions Reflecting and Refining the Oral Tradition." This first chapter examines critical differences in the cultural assumptions and values of Native Americans and their non-Native neighbors. Native Americans are not the only people who hold closely many of the beliefs addressed. My purpose is not to identify assumptions unique to the indigenous people of this country, but rather to describe these assumptions, especially as they differ from those of Euro-Americans. The chapter briefly identifies how these differences manifest themselves in the discourse of both groups. Other chapters address specifically how the differences are reflected in their speeches, stories, prayers, and songs.

The second chapter, "Imbuing the Earth with Imagery," examines the major metaphors used in Native American discourse. The communications examined here span subject, time, place, situation, and tribal nation. This chapter also deals with the plethora of images Native People use about nature. Examining the abundance and variety of these images reveals the inextricable relationship that Native Americans see between the soil and the soul.

Chapter 3, "Speeches of Peace and Protest," concerns general characteristics of Native American public speeches. Possession of oratorical ability is prized highly among Native People, in part because the society for many years possessed only an oral tradition, and in part because they have recognized the power of words. This chapter discusses characteristics of nonceremonial Native American orations. Specifically, it identifies frequent themes in these messages, methods of organizing speeches, and recurring rhetorical strategies employed when dealing in councils, committees, and commissions.

The fourth chapter, "Stories Planting Sage for the Soul," examines how Native American stories teach. Specifically the chapter focuses on frequent features of Native American oral narratives including characteristic customs, traditional teachings, recurring rhythms, common characters, and mythical motifs. The chapter looks at how Native American storytelling differs from American storybook reading and television.

The fifth chapter is "Prayers and Songs of Celebration and Purification." This chapter deals with the ceremonial, ritualistic rhetoric of Native Americans, especially aspects of their prayers and songs that differ from those of the dominant Judeo-Christian culture.

The final chapter, "Preserving and Perpetuating the People," focuses again on the significance of the oral tradition to what has been until recently a completely oral society. Specifically, I discuss in a broader way the need to analyze

Native American speeches, stories, prayers, and songs within their culture, a culture where words when spoken take on life and where all living beings create sound vibrations. The chapter also considers how the the the oral tradition may help to account for the survival of Native People.

Because Native Americans have lived in an oral society, many texts were not recorded; these needed translation in order to be understood by non-Native people and Native People of different nations. Translating and recording Native teachings also helps traditional Native People to remember, as Old Man Buffalo Grass, Dine, said in 1928:

I sit as on a mountaintop and look into the future. I see my people and your people living together. In time to come my people will have forgotten their early way of life unless they learn it from white men's books. So you must write down what I tell you; and you must have it made into a book that coming generations may know this truth.[12]

The problems of translation are many. For example, the famous speech by Chief Seattle, a Squamish chief, dealing with treaty negotiations in 1854–1855 was first recorded more than thirty years after it was given by Dr. Henry A. Smith. Seattle probably spoke in Lutshootseed, which was then translated into Chinook jargon, which was then translated into English. Dr. Smith supposedly based his copy on English notes he had taken at the time of the speech. Other versions of this speech also exist, some by non-Native twentieth-century writers.[13]

In selecting texts for this book, I have tried to use ones that Native scholars consider as accurate and authentic as it is possible to be. Still, translation remains an issue since even good translations cannot capture subtle nuances and meanings. By definition, gaps exist in translation as often no parallel words exist in the language being translated into. This is especially the case when translating from an "Old Way" language into a "civilized" language or vice versa. Further, translations of oral discourses cannot convey the rhythms of messages. Translation often destroys subtle aspects of a piece's rhetorical structure. Even the best translations cannot capture stylistic devices such as onomatopoeia. Similarly, standard problems exist when reading words intended for the ear, such as the inability to capture vocal intonation, accent, rate, volume, variety, or emphasis or to see eye movements, gestures, facial expressions, body movements, and pauses.

CONTRIBUTIONS

A book analyzing Native American speeches, stories, prayers, and songs from a rhetorical perspective increases our knowledge of this historically misunderstood group of people. Contrasting how Native Americans have used the spoken word with how North Americans have used it increases our understanding of the rhetoric of both groups and of the differing cultural assumptions underlying the rhetoric.

Not being a Native American myself, I know I miss nuances and subtleties. For these, I apologize in advance. My goal is to illuminate as much as possible the light and love that shine through the rhetoric of our nation's Native People. By learning more about another group's principles and precepts, we may lessen hatred caused by ignorance. To live as a culturally diverse society, we must develop our sensibility of, and sensitivity to, other groups of people and other belief systems. We must accept that we are all flesh and blood, people born from a womb, people belonging to one human family. Let us grow together, learn from the past so as not to repeat its mistakes, and move forward with respect and cooperation.

Let us follow the path toward acceptance and oneness. Let us "listen" to the voices of Native People and learn about them through their own words. By increasing our knowledge about Native Americans, we allow them to take the place they deserve among America's most eloquent speakers.

Cultural Assumptions Reflecting and Refining the Oral Tradition

The language is the heart of the culture, and you cannot separate it.
                                                        Elaine Ramos, Tlingit

The language people use reflects the way they think and reveals the values and attitudes they hold. The speeches, stories, prayers, and songs of the Native People of North America affect and reflect their shared cultural assumptions. In order to understand their discourse, we need first to examine their major principles, beliefs, and values.[1]

By necessity, this chapter oversimplifies and overgeneralizes the cultural assumptions that Native People and North Americans have expressed in their oral messages. Neither Native Americans nor North Americans represent homogeneous populations; therefore, all statements really precede with "many" or "most." Further, the chapter considers the cultural assumptions of traditional Native Americans, the legacy bequeathed to them by their ancestors. Not all Native Americans share these beliefs. Similarly, not all North Americans believe or practice the ideas identified with their group.

To contrast the two groups, I also operate under the dualistic way of thinking characteristic of Western thought. Further, Native American culture and North American culture are not completely separate, nor have they ever been so. For example, Native Americans had a significant impact on the formation of democracy in this country. The Haudenosaunee Confederacy, especially, influenced and inspired the writers of the United States Constitution and the Bill of Rights. Conversely, Native People have benefited from the technological advances accompanying Western civilization. The scientific age has increased efficiency, made life easier, increased pleasure in many ways, and so

Inland Sea. Illustration by Francene Hart.

forth. Native Americans as well as Euro-Americans have profited from these advantages. Finally, one set of assumptions is no better than the other. I distinguish between the sets of assumptions merely to identify the different perspectives that are reflected in and affect the rhetoric of Native People compared to their non-Native counterparts.[2]

CULTURAL ASSUMPTIONS AND VALUES OF NORTH AMERICAN SPEAKERS

Rhetoric as practiced by North American orators has its roots in Greece. In general, American speakers use the paradigm of dominant male discourse found throughout Western civilization. For example, they often use binary language to support their arguments. Throughout the history of Western civilization, many orators have juxtaposed competing ideas. According to Aristotle, opposites constitute a valid line of argument. Today they still function as a standard use of language to support arguments. Traditional rhetoric encourages the use of dichotomous language and the contrasting of ideas and images. Many American speakers, storytellers, preachers, and singers have juxtaposed light and dark, land and water, men and women, winning and losing, and so forth. The contrasts are often simple, consisting of the many moralistic versions of good versus bad, right versus wrong. American speakers generally describe situations as wonderful or repulsive with little room for a middle ground. Other frequent binary opposites include day versus night, human beings versus animals, division versus unity, and the physical versus the spiritual world. When pitting binary opposites against each other, these speakers operate within the realm of assumptions associated with Western civilization.[3]

Through binary oppositions, the first term possesses more power and privilege than the second. Implicitly, American speakers expect listeners to measure the second term by the standards of the first, wanting the second term to catch up and eventually become the first term. Of course, this is not possible, and so prejudice and exclusion occur. Take, for example, white versus nonwhite. In general, white Americans expect nonwhites to assimilate into American culture and accept the principles and precepts of Western thought and European philosophy and religion. The use of binary oppositions creates the impression that the first term (in this case, white) represents the true culture, the only culture that holds value.

In addition to drawing on dualistic divisions, public discourse in North American society often adopts a distant, detached tone. American listeners value rational appeals and consider emotional appeals suspect. They expect and, hence, North American speakers typically provide clearly stated theses and definite introductions, bodies, and conclusions. Generally speakers furnish facts and figures and elaborate on their education, experience, and expertise. For the most part, North American speakers and listeners have little tolerance for ambiguity and uncertainty. Instead, they want to understand and control everything around them. Further, they value external evidence, a mechanistic world view, the scientific method, point- by-point logic, and cause-effect thinking.

By viewing time as linear, Americans orient events at specific times. The use of linear time encourages Americans to equate the history of a family with its lineage and to separate past, present, and future, considering them distinct, separate entities on a continuum. One of the most significant effects of viewing the world in a linear way concerns change. Americans tend to believe all things move in a forward direction; hence, to them all change represents positive progress.

Several factors relate to the mechanistic, rationalistic world view of Americans, including applauding independence, individualism, egocentrism, materialism, possessiveness, and competitiveness. For every winner, there exists a loser. Some common stylistic devices used in American rhetoric foster this either-or thinking. For example, antithesis, contrasting ideas by directly opposing them linguistically, creates tension; speakers help listeners resolve the tension by having one of the ideas "win." Patrick Henry's "Give me liberty or give me death" offers a typical example.

In its oldest and purest form, Western civilization consists of his-story, the story of a patriarchal society concerned with controlling and legislating. History has become the dominant paradigm of North American culture, making Western civilization reflect a male bias, particularly that of the white male.

Legally the United States separates church from state, the spiritual from the secular. Dualistic divisions separate God from people and people from other life forms. Judeo-Christian religions talk about God in patriarchal ways: all-powerful and all-controlling.

As a group, North Americans live increasingly away from the land, surrounded by machinery, and bombarded with information. Many buy polyester clothing using plastic credit cards. Many eat processed, canned, and frozen foods that have been contaminated by pesticides and preservatives, which they "nuke" in microwave ovens. Many live in cloistered, box-shaped, high-rise apartments in busy, bustling cities, where only artificial lights of skyscrapers break through the darkness of night. Many live in a megalopolis and work for a conglomerate. Many surround themselves with the newest technological advances – fax, answering, and photocopying machines. Their telephones connect them to a mass of computerized information. They race and chase, wound up like clocks themselves, trapped in a whirlwind of activity. Their fast-paced, high-pressure lifestyles revolve around clocks, watches, deadlines, calendars, schedules, telephones, and beepers. They move away from a natural state of being with makeup, cologne, deodorant, and hair spray.

In addition to living away from nature, North Americans, as a group, often want to control nature. North American orators sometimes speak about cutting down trees to build roads, buildings, and so forth, in the name of progress.

CULTURAL ASSUMPTIONS AND VALUES OF NATIVE AMERICAN SPEAKERS

The following four cultural assumptions infuse and inform almost all Native American speeches, stories, prayers, and songs: (1) the universe is one circle, moving endlessly and eternally, perpetually and for perpetuity; (2) everything continually changes and moves; (3) everyone and everything are inextricably interrelated; and (4) everything is alive, possessing a physical form and a spiritual vitality, and performing a vital function in the universe. These four principles permeate the oral messages of Native People with remarkable consistency, especially since these oral messages span across speaker, time, place, and tribal affiliation.

The Universe Is One Circle

One of the most important ways the assumptions of Native People differ from those of their non-Native counterparts is their focus on the circle. "Civilized" human beings represent the first living species to measure time in a linear manner. All other life forms deal with the continual ebbs and flows of circular energies. Like these other life forms, Native Americans maintain an intimate relationship with the sun and the moon – circular, primal forms.

Sentiments dealing with this fundamental relationship permeate their discourse. Nez Perce Chief Joseph declared in his now famous surrender speech of October 5, 1877, "From where the sun now stands, I will fight no more forever." "From where the sun now stands" sounds more poetic than "now," but Chief Joseph probably chose the phrase not to sound poetic but because he naturally talked about time in terms of the sun, a celestial body. His statement also illustrates his fundamental sense of connection to the earth – the place from which people experience celestial phenomena.

According to most Native People, creation takes the form of a circle with one solid vibral core in the center. Spirals emanating from the center of circles reveal the depth and mystery of the cultures of Native Americans. Concentric circles spiral outward, rippling, in perpetual patterns.

Since circles symbolize unity, harmony, infinity, eternity, wholeness, and oneness, the different oral discourses of Native Americans frequently concern these qualities – features that follow from seeing the world as a circle. Concerned about their clan, tribe, and community, Native People frequently speak about the idea of all for one and one for all. By seeing the world as a circle, Native Americans view transformation as inevitable. Many speeches, stories, prayers, and songs tell of people becoming animals, animals becoming people, people and spirits moving back and forth between the natural and spiritual worlds, and death and rebirth. Some stories give a sense of unity by making an invisible "circle"; the hero leaves a community at the beginning of the story and returns at the end. Likewise, some speeches create this sense of unity by having the conclusion go back to the introduction. Many prayers and songs deal with the need to give back to the earth as much (or more) than we take from the earth. This idea is so central that the giving usually occurs first – as in prayers concerning laying down an offering before the hunt or harvest.

Native American discourse frequently concerns the circle and creation. In the words of Carter Camp of the Ponca nation:

Indians have always known that our circle extends beyond the present and in a very real way includes the past and future. Ancestors and future generations. . . . Full circle. When we die our atoms once again join the larger circle of Earth. . . . The circle of the eagle and the circle of the human, conjoined in antiquity and mingled as one within the bosom of the Mother Earth. . . . The Great Mystery is the unending circle.

Camp also spoke about the "sacredness to all the universe of the Circle," "circle of the land as one," and the "circle of life on Earth." Similarly, the Lakota Sioux often speak about "standing in the center of the world." The circle, then, represents complete and consummate oneness and wholeness. Words such as *bonds, threads, connections, joining, common, communal, similar, balance, harmony, unity, oneness, wholeness, hoop, together, center, partners,* and *kinship* permeate the oral discourse of Native Americans. Native People frequently say, "What goes around comes around." The notion of the circle seems to reinforce Sioux Vine Deloria's argument that Native Americans operate from spatial schemata whereas Westerners emphasize time schemata.[4]

In a circle, everyone and everything are equal in power and spiritual strength. Unlike the vertical line in Eastern culture that represents hierarchy or the horizontal line in North American culture that encourages people to think in a linear, logical manner, the circle promotes thoughts of oneness and wholeness. All living things stand in sacred spaces, and look at the center from a different spot; all views contain merit. For example, in a circle what is up for one person is down for another person, and both perspectives deserve consideration. Sitting in a circle diminishes height differences. In a circle, everyone can

```
                ONE
            ONE CIRCLE
           ONE PEOPLE
        No beginnings, no ends
        In circles, time suspends
      In the circle, all are One
      Constantly moving, never done
     No boundaries, blocks, or borders
    No confines, crevices, or corners
    Our spirit is both female and male
   This is our truth, by no means a tale
  Circles are the ceaseless cycles of life
   The cosmic womb and the womb of the wife
  You may ask the reason why a circle is round
  The circle is space; nature's energies have sound
 Nature resounds and resonates in rhythmic rotation
 Its sacredness demands preservation and perpetuation
 Its sacredness demands preservation and perpetuation
 Nature resounds and resonates in rhythmic rotation
  The circle is space; nature's energies have sound
  You may ask the reason why a circle is round
   The cosmic womb and the womb of the wife
  Circles are the ceaseless cycles of life
   This is our truth, by no means a tale
   Our spirit is both female and male
    No confines, crevices, or corners
    No boundaries, blocks, or borders
     Constantly moving, never done
      In the circle, all are One
       In circles, time suspends
        No beginnings, no ends
           ONE PEOPLE
            ONE CIRCLE
                ONE
```

One Circle. Poem by Lois J. Einhorn.

see everyone else, also encouraging equality and unity. People sitting in a circle tend to listen to the perspectives of other speakers more than people sitting in rows.

A circle has no borders, boundaries, or blocks, no corners, confines, or crevices. Just as traditionally their homes had no walls or other dividers, Native Americans view their world as one open space with no restraints or constraints. In an open circle everyone belongs. Newcomers make circles larger. Since nothing lives outside a circle, outcasts or disenfranchised members of society do not exist. A circle has no above or below and no in and out, again fostering the idea that no one is better or more important than anyone or anything else.

In their rhetoric, Native People frequently stress the equality of all sentient beings. For example, in speaking about fish, eagles, and other animals, Oren Lyons, a contemporary Onondaga chief and "Faithkeeper," remarked that humans "stand between the mountain and the ant, somewhere and only there, as part and parcel of the Creation." Native American speakers do not seem to portray people as small to down play their importance, but rather to show that all life essences are equal, and each living being possesses a particular purpose, necessary in the order of all things.[5]

To Native People, significant symbols, spiritual forms, and situations also take the shape of a circle. Most importantly, nature takes this shape: The earth, sun, and moon are all circular. Animals use the shape of a circle to mark their territorial space; birds built nests in circles. The growth pattern of trees, flowers, and rocks is circular. All openings to the body are round. People enter and exit the world through the womb, which is circular in shape.

Native Americans often speak publicly in councils sitting in a circular formation, tell stories while sitting around a campfire, and dance in a circle. Hoops, cauldrons, drums, mandalas, and dream catchers, important symbols in many Native nations and used metaphorically by many Native American speakers, storytellers, and medicine people, also use a round shape. Medicine wheels and gourds or holy rattles, used by members of certain Native nations in healing ceremonies, are circular. Purification or sweat lodges represent the Earth or circular cosmic womb. Pipes pass from person to person in a clockwise, sunwise movement. Many Native American houses, such as tipis and wigwams, are circular. At puberty young Mescalero Apache women run around a basket as an indicator of the cycle of life.

According to Native People, time naturally occurs cyclically. Put another way, nature consists of events that, by definition, happen in specific sequences. For example, morning turns to night, which turns to morning, and fall, winter, spring, and summer always occur in that order. The sun rises and sets at appointed times. So do tides rise and fall. People emerge from the womb of the

Earth and at death return to the womb of the Earth. Likewise, lakes, trees, flowers, and stones experience life, death, and rebirth. Nature resonates, resounds, and reverberates in rhythmic rotations. Thus, circles are connected, constant, and continuous. By definition, they eddy endlessly, and for eternity, because they are living entities.

The Native Americans' cyclical view of time differs significantly from the North Americans' linear view of time. Native People, using cyclical time, talk about the many things that transcend time and place, such as truths, principles, totems, stories, prayers, songs, and ceremonies. They blend the past, present, and future into an undivided, unbroken whole. For example, they connect the wisdom of their ancestors with practical problems of today, combining them into a single whole. Whereas North Americans generally believe all change represents positive progress, Native Americans view change as good, bad, or in between.

In their rhetoric, Native American speakers describe the Earth as one circle that is open, vast, free, and without unnatural enclosures. They stress how circles contain no boundaries. They have cherished their ability to traverse the terra firma unencumbered by trammels, and have felt wronged when they have not possessed this ability. Ten Bears, a Comanche chieftain, explained why he wanted to die among his people on the open prairie rather than among white people: "I was born upon the prairie, where the wind blew free, and there was nothing to break the light of the sun. I was born where there were no enclosures, and where everything drew a free breath. I want to die there, and not within walls."[6]

Everything Continually Changes

According to Native Americans, everything continually vibrates and, thus, fluctuates and changes. In the ever-moving universe, nothing stands still. Operating beneath the threshold of awareness, energies act and react in dynamic and dramatic ways with other energies. The dynamic inner forces by which people create and animate their world relate to the belief that everything constantly moves and continually evolves. As soon as you, the reader, finish reading this sentence, the experience is past. Rereading the sentence constitutes a slightly different experience. All living things belong to a web of connections, and each part of the web constantly moves, changes, and exchanges energies. Rather than fight against inevitable movements, in their rhetoric Native Americans generally advise people to flow with the changes. Whereas North Americans are generally pro-active, interested in changing things and making them better, Native Americans are generally reactive, expressing interest not in changing things, but in living in harmony with things as they are.

Consistent with the general needs North Americans have to define, delineate, and classify things, the English language centers around nouns, relatively stable and fixed words. Conversely, consistent with the Native People's belief that things constantly change, most of their languages center around verbs or transitory words. Many Native languages leave definitions open-ended to allow for the unexpected or forgotten. Many have no word for "goodbye." The Hopi language contains no verb tenses, no words to differentiate past, present, or future; everything occurs in the perpetual, perennial present. Wa'na'nee'che' (also known as Dennis Renault), a Native American teacher, explains, "For the logical mind something is either a chair or it's not a chair. But in a world seen in constant flux, a chair is a tree on its way to becoming broken pieces of firewood."[7]

Both North American and Native American cultures embrace change, yet the emphasis differs. Americans focus on progress, problems of nature, and controlling whereas Native Americans focus on process, conditions of nature, and cooperating.

To Native People things exist in relationship to other things. Whereas North Americans tend to focus on text, Native Americans tend to focus on context. For them context includes the unseen as well as the seen.

Movements around circles occur slowly and gently, unifying all things. To Native People, circles represent perfect paragons, consummate communications, and equality for eternity. In short, circles represent rhythms and the ceaseless cycles of life.

Everyone and Everything Are Related

Native People view all things in the universe as related to the unified whole of the circle. Unlike North American speakers, who, reflecting their Western roots, tend to dissect, categorize, and analyze objects, Native Americans look at the whole. Almost every Native American speech, story, song, and prayer express in some way how people and other sentient beings are inextricably interconnected, interdependent, and interactive at the deepest levels. The fact that most Native languages have no word to differentiate between human beings and other animals serves as powerful testimony of the equal relationship that Native People see between themselves and other living creatures. People, animals, flora, fauna, and other natural parts of the cosmos must interrelate, working together to convert cacophony into harmony. Wub-e-ke-niew, of the Ahnishinahbaeojibway nation, explains with an example:

Rather than acting upon the world, in *Ahnishinahbaeojibway* one acts in concert with the other beings with whom one shares Grandmother Earth. There are no objects of verbs in the *Ahnishinahbaeojibway* language. A person harmoniously "meets the Lake," rather than "going to get water."

Speech after speech and prayer after prayer underscore the importance of universal unity and planetary peace: All living beings belong to one Earth; another Earth does not exist. All Relatives in Creation breathe the same air and drink the same water.[8]

The holistic perspective of most Native Americans contrasts with the dualistic thinking of most Euro-Americans. Generally Native People do not separate people and nature, the secular and the spiritual, or the body, mind, and spirit. They talk about how the body gives and receives energetic vibrations, allowing people to communicate with trees and rocks.

Native People frequently speak of the physical body as a sacred vessel. They say painting their bodies expresses sacredness and adorning their bodies marks rites of passage. They talk about accepting the body, owning it, belonging to it, living in it, coming home physically. Traditional Native Americans talk about the physical body as the first sanctuary. It provides a place for spirits to dwell.

Most Native languages contain no word for religion. Unlike their Judeo-Christian neighbors, as a group Native People view religion not as a part of life, but rather as life itself. The mundane and the mystical naturally commingle. The Judeo-Christian tradition teaches that people are created in God's image. This view differs from the Native American view that people and God – whom they refer to by many names including the Great Spirit, Great Mystery, Creator, Manitou (Cree and Algonquian), Orenda (Haudenosaunee), and Wakan Takan (Lakota) – are one. Especially in their prayers, Native People speak about the divine and sublime stature of all living beings.

Everything Is Alive and Necessary

By living things, Native Americans do not mean just people, trees, and plants. To them everything lives both physically and spiritually. Mountains move. Winds whirl. Seas swirl. Trees, plants, and other elements in nature live, possess souls, and communicate. John Trudell, Santee Sioux activist, said in an interview in 1997, "We're just a different shape from uranium or from a tree, just a different shape, but we all have the same DNA. Truly what happens to the Earth happens to us."[9]

Because nature lives, traditional Native People tend to appreciate, honor, and cherish it. Extremely observant of their environment, they sometimes make predictions based on configurations of stars and clouds. They are especially attuned to the rhythms of nature with its continual ebbs and flows, whirls and swirls. They consider themselves custodians and caretakers of the cosmos who have the privilege of preserving and protecting its splendor and delicate balance. They talk about how the Earth belongs to everyone. People cannot buy or sell land any more than they can buy or sell air. In the words of Suquamish Chief Seattle, "How can you buy or sell the sky, the warmth of the land? The idea is strange to us. If we do not own the freshness of the air and the sparkle of the water, how can you buy them?"

Traditionally, Native Americans speak about every part of nature as sacred and hallowed. Since they believe the Great Spirit gave them the land to care for, and people should strive to live in harmony with nature, they expressly speak about not tampering, tainting, defiling, contaminating, or polluting nature. North American orators, on the other hand, generally view humans as having dominion over nature.

Specific beliefs and behaviors accompany the Native Americans' view of the Earth. For example, they believe Mother Earth gives people life and supplies everything people need to survive. Because they trust the Earth will supply sufficient resources, as a group they do not hoard; generally, they take what they need and nothing more.

Native People talk about living air, living water, living earth, and living fire. They explain how each plant, each tree, each rock, each mountain, each animal, and each person play an intrinsically valuable part in the Creator's plans, unfolding as they should. Each serves particular purposes. There is no such thing as a weed. Each part of creation tries to form a physically and spiritually harmonious relationship with all other parts. Harmony and balance equal survival and happiness. Lack of harmony and balance causes sickness and death or, in short, dis-ease.

Focusing on interdependence has led the Native people of this country to concern themselves with group identity more than with individual identity. In 1988, then-President and Executive Director of Americans for Indian Opportunity LaDonna Harris commented: "One cannot be 'an Indian.' One is a Comanche, an Oneida, a Hopi. One can be self-determining, not as 'an Indian,' but as a Comanche, an Oneida, etc. We progress as communities, not as individuals." Significantly, these tribal names are mainly post-contact. Native Americans usually called themselves some variation of "the People." The general focus of Native American nations on people in the plural rather than on individual in the singular fosters the conception of community as the core or center of creation, crucial for its continuation. The Lakota word *Tiospaye,* meaning strength through the extended family or the community, emphasizes the importance of the good of the group. Not surprisingly, frequent words found in Native American discourse include *community, communal responsibility,* and *communal unity.*[10]

All parts of creation, then, depend on and are pieces of all other parts; all are relatives, and all are necessary. What one creature exhales, another creature inhales, and vice versa. The predator is related to the prey. Likewise, the Earth needs both grass and grass eaters; both serve a purpose in the web of life. Native Americans frequently talk about how the heart of people and the heart of the Earth reciprocally reflect, resound, resonate, and reverberate off each other. The interdependent nature of life and of everything in the cosmos forms the backbone of the cultural assumptions of Native People.

CONCLUSIONS

Native American speakers hold to the four truths discussed in this chapter unwaveringly and seem undaunted when other people criticize them. They talk about how these truths are as rigid as a rock. Dagmar Thorpe, citizen of the Sauk and Fox nations, puts it this way: "We are all interconnected, we are all co-equal. Those basic philosophies, I believe, are universal and natural laws that transcend and cut across our differences. It is there. It is a reality." The four principles and the tenacity with which Native American speakers argue these principles result in a rhetoric marked by moderation and humility.[11]

Rhetorical theorist Richard Weaver claimed that speakers who argue consistently from first principles, maxims, and truths are conservative or moderate in nature. Although I do not consider arguing from first principles definitive proof that speakers are moderate, I agree with Weaver that Native Americans present themselves as moderates; frequently arguing from firmly anchored truths provides one proof of this conclusion.

The Native American use of imagery (discussed in more detail in the next chapter) advances the vastness of their viewpoint. They choose figures of speech that are particularly broad, sweeping, and inclusive.

The moderation of Native American rhetoric manifests itself also in their extensive use of the passive voice when compared to North American speakers. Tamarack Song, Algonquian Founder and Director of the Teaching Drum Outdoor School, explains, "In the Civilized languages, the *subject* of the sentence usually appears first, as in '*I* made Venison stew,' whereas in the Native languages, the object of the sentence usually appears first, as in '*Venison stew* was made by me.'" Placing the subject first, Song continues, emphasizes the speaker, consistent with the people-centeredness of cultures like the American culture. Placing the object first "allows for more intimate, less intellectually-based involvement by the listener."[12]

The holistic way Native Americans look at the world results in "both/and" thinking rather than "either/or" thinking. Traditional Native Americans do not admonish or judge directly. Respect for all and value of interdependence require that people not try to control or dominate. Problems with others or others needing counsel are achieved through allegory (stories) or appropriate ceremony.

One of the primary ways Native People express both/and thinking in their oral messages is by frequently using the word *and,* especially where Westerners would generally say *but.* Native Americans demonstrated this inclusive mentality before Columbus "discovered" America. Different nations possessed different customs, rituals, and languages; yet, in general, the different nations coexisted relatively peacefully. Rather than the North American ideal of this country becoming a melting pot with each group giving up its identity and individuality in order to adapt to American ways, Native Americans all along have advocated that each nation retain its cultural differences and all people respect these special qualities. They laud and applaud atypical aspects, treating them not as obstacles or obstructions but as opportunities. To them new sights add strength. Harris gives this explanation:

The tribal concept as regards differences is quite contrastive to the Euro-American one. Differentness, rather than being seen as a problem to be eradicated, is seen as a contribution to the whole. In tribal society the group does not dominate the individual, it nurtures individuals, so that strong, idiosyncratic individuals contribute to the strength of the group. . . . Difference does not equate to good/bad, better/best, hierarchy, domination, and conflict. Difference is coordinated in terms of contributions made toward the good of the whole.

Cheyenne Henri Mann Morton titled one of her speeches "Strength Through Cultural Diversity." In it she quotes a Native American philosopher who declared, "It is not necessary for eagles to be crows." In other words, Native Americans do not have to mask, mesh, and mix their differences. Rather, by retaining their cultural contrasts and comprehensive completeness, the whole attains potency and power.[13]

The idea of unity through diversity affects the way Native Americans view their speaking. In general, they advocate cooperation and consensus, but they also uphold the right to dissent. This right assumes an exchange of ideas among equals and a reciprocal respect for others' ideas. In his 1974 speech on "Urban Indian Education," Ojibway Dennis Banks explained by using an example: "Just this week Peter MacDonald won the Navajo tribal election, 23,000 to 17,000 votes. They asked him for comments, and he said, 'Even though I won the election, it is the 17,000 who are dissatisfied with my services that I must deal with.'"[14]

To Native Americans, speaking equals cooperation, listening, and respect. In practice, this view of speaking encourages viewing all sides of an argument and making decisions by consensus rather than by majority rule. Whereas generally North Americans prefer a conflict management process of dispute resolution to reach decisions, Native People use an interactive management model that provides collaborative and consensual techniques to create composite vision. Harris elaborates on the differences between competitive and cooperative views of discourse:

Majoritarian forms of discourse emphasize adversarial relationships and consist of debates where each person argues their own position and tries to persuade other people to come over to their position. Consensus-building discourse occurs in a learning environment in which points of view are shared in order for a mutual vision to emerge. Participants in the discourse strive to articulate their understanding of the situation as clearly as possible and at the same time to listen carefully to everyone else's understanding. It is only after incorporating all these perceptions that a decision adequate to a total comprehension of the issue at hand and appropriate to the community can be made.[15]

The light and love that shine through the Native People's rhetoric provide a blueprint for living in a pluralistic society where people accept, value, appreciate, and celebrate ways in which they are the same and ways in which they differ. In the words of Hiamovi, a chief among the Cheyennes and the Dakotas,

There are birds of many colors – red, blue, green yellow – yet it is all one bird. There are horses of many colors – brown, black, yellow, white – yet it is all one horse. So cattle, so all living things – animals, flowers, trees. So men: in this land where once were only Indians are now men of every color – white, black, yellow, red – yet all one people. That this should come to pass was in the heart of the Great Mystery. It is right thus. And everywhere there shall be peace.[16]

Star Woman. Illustration by Francene Hart.

Imbuing the Earth with Imagery

Indians live and think in metaphor – consequently even the most mundane of their speeches are like brightly colored pictures reflected in the minds of their listeners.

Louis Thomas Jones

Rhetorical theorist I. A. Richards contended, "The mind is a connecting organ. It works only by connecting and it can connect any two things in an indefinitely large number of ways." Metaphors are common linguistic devices used to establish connections. Because of the limitless choices available, the metaphors and other images and symbols that dominate the messages of a people provide insights into the ways in which these people view themselves and their world.[1]

This chapter first discusses how Native Americans talk about symbolism. Second, it examines the most common metaphors used by American speakers, and, finally, it discusses how these differ from the most common metaphors used by Native American speakers. Of course, since no one homogeneous Native American culture exists, this chapter generalizes; the ideas discussed apply to most, but not all, Native speakers.

HOW NATIVE AMERICAN SPEAKERS TALK ABOUT IMAGERY

In order to understand how Native American speakers use imagery in their discourse, we need first to examine what they mean by images. As the last chapter explained, Native People talk about the Earth as animate and all parts of the Earth as equal and interrelated. They say an inextricable relationship exists between the physical and spiritual worlds. They believe all things possess a spirit, including things that Euro-Americans consider inanimate. Given these cultural assumptions, Native Americans talk about everything as symbolic and metaphorical.

For people reared in the Western tradition, the Native view of symbolism, as expressed in their discourse, may be difficult to understand. When a North American speaker uses the word *sun* as a metaphor, the speaker means the sun represents light or some other quality. But when a Native American speaker uses the word sun metaphorically, the speaker is saying the sun represents light, becomes one with light, and is light. The sun and light are one with the speaker, listeners, and people who read the speech. And since everything in the cosmos is connected, the speaker is saying the sun is one with everyone and everything.

For Native Americans, metaphors, symbols, and images are not just figures of speech to add eloquence and interest to messages. Joseph Rael, Picuris Pueblo writer, directly states that "a metaphor is not simply a figure of speech: "Metaphor is how God is present in our lives. . . . Metaphor is energy that is in a state of action, breathing life into ceremony." Instead of figures of speech, Native People speak of metaphors, symbols, and images as another indication that everything is inherently interrelated and one. For example, Native People speak of the image of a spider's web to represent the invisible threads that weave everything together.[2]

John Lame Deer, a Sioux medicine man, and Paula Gunn Allen, a contemporary Laguna Pueblo and Sioux writer, identify important differences between how Americans and Native Americans perceive symbolism:

We Indians live in a world of symbols where the spiritual and the commonplace are one. To you, symbols are just words, spoken or written in a book. To us, they are a part of nature, part of ourselves — the earth, the sun, the wind and the rain, stones, trees, animals, even little insects like ants and grasshoppers. We try to understand them not with the head but with the heart, and we need no more than a hint to give us the meaning. (John Lame Deer)

Symbols in American Indian systems are not symbolic in the usual sense of the word. The words articulate reality — not "psychological" or imagined reality, not emotive reality captured metaphorically in an attempt to fuse thought and feeling, but that reality where thought and feeling are one, where objective and subjective are one, where speaker and listener are one, where sound and sense are one. (Paula Gunn Allen)[3]

Pulitzer Prize–winning Kiowa writer N. Scott Momaday frequently discusses the living vitality of language in a culture immersed in an oral tradition. He clearly illustrates how sound, symbols, and images bring words to life with his telling of the metaphorical story of the arrowmaker. The story passed down through many generations goes as follows:

Once there was a man and his wife. They were alone at night in their tepee. By the light of a fire the man was making arrows. After a while he caught sight of something. There was a small opening in the tepee where two hides had been sewn together. Someone was there on the outside, looking in. The man went on with his work, but he said to his wife, "Someone is standing outside. Do not be afraid. Let us talk easily, as of ordinary things." He took up an arrow and straightened it in his teeth; then, as it was right for him to do, he drew it to the bow and took aim, first in this direction and then in that. And all the while he was talking, as if to his wife. But this is how he spoke: "I know that you are there on the outside, for I can feel your eyes upon me. If you are a Kiowa, you will understand what I am saying, and you will speak your name." But there was no answer, and the man went on in the same way, pointing the arrow all around. At last his aim fell upon the place where his enemy stood, and he let go of the string. The arrow went straight to the enemy's heart.[4]

Momaday discusses how language determines the identity and reality of the arrowmaker: "Language is the repository of his whole knowledge, and it represents the only chance he has for survival." The metaphorical qualities of the story, says Momaday, are obvious since "The arrowmaker is preeminently the man made of words. He has consummate being in language; it is the world of his origin and of his posterity, and there is no other."[5]

Momaday's discussion of language illustrates how images for Native Americans are more like holograms than pictures. They possess multiple dimensions, they change constantly, they reflect off themselves. The parts are separate but they work together. Only when seen together, each part in relationship to each other part, do they take on a life of their own.

Listeners in any culture may experience symbols on many levels, but Native symbols seem to possess many more layers and levels than the symbols used in western cultures. Tuscarora Chief Elias Johnson explained, "And when you have learned all that language can convey, there are still a thousand images, suggestions, and associations recurring to the Indian, which can strike no chord in your heart. The myriad voices of nature are dumb to you, but to them they're full of life and power." For Native People the number of layers and levels of symbolism seem limitless; they talk about imagery as complex and multifaceted.[6]

For the purpose of gaining insights into the oral discourse of Native Americans, I discuss metaphors, images, and other forms of symbolism in this chapter as entities separate from their context. But, I urge readers to remember that for Native Americans these images are animate and alive, fluid and forceful, spiritual and sacred, and interconnected and integrated.

THE USE OF METAPHOR BY AMERICAN SPEAKERS

Generally American speakers, storytellers, singers, and other spokespeople choose figures of speech that are what rhetorical critic Michael M. Osborn has labeled "archetypal." These are associations that are timeless, cross-cultural, grounded in experiences common to all human beings, and symbols of fundamental human motivations. Osborn's research has revealed that categories of archetypal metaphors include the following: light/darkness, water and the sea, the family, the human body, war/peace, disease/cure, structures, and the sense of space (vertical and horizontal). Many of the archetypal metaphors, as used by the great speakers discussed by Osborn, reflect the binary way of thinking (see Chapter 1) that has permeated Western culture and civilization and the accepted theories of rhetoric.[7]

Understanding how people believe the universe was formed provides insights into their views of the world as these are reflected in their word choices. Author Marie-Louise Von Franz calls creation stories "the deepest and most important of all myths." The Judeo-Christian tradition, which is accepted by many Americans, includes several stories about the creation of the world. Despite some differences, significant similarities exist. Many Americans accept some literal or metaphorical version of the story of creation as told in Genesis. The story consists of a poetic narrative about images, usually in opposition. On the first day, God created *light* and *dark* and contrasted the two. On the second day, He *divided* the *sky above* from the *waters below.* Day three involved dry *land* versus *water,* continents versus oceans. The words *earth* and *nature* appear frequently here. The first mention of *day versus night* occurs on day four as God created the sun, moon, and stars. Day five followed from day two: God created *birds* (in the sky *above*) and *fish* (in the sea *below*). On the sixth day, God created all other *animals,* including *people* whom He created in His image and to whom He gave dominion over the world. The emphases are added here to demonstrate how the primal images of the biblical creation story correspond remarkably to the images used by many North American speakers. Even many of the divisions correspond, such as light versus dark and day versus night. Of special importance, too, are the continual separations and divisions and the fact that many Judeo-Christians cite the story of creation as giving them permission to rule over animals and nature.[8]

Osborn has explained how frequent use of light and dark metaphors nurtures and nourishes an elemental, black/white view of the world. He writes, "When light and dark images are used together in a speech, they indicate and perpetuate the simplistic, two-valued, black-white attitudes which rhetoricians and their audiences seem so often to prefer," and "The situation has been simplified until there are two – and only two – alternatives, one of which must become the pattern for the future."[9]

Most great American speakers have used light-dark image combinations in precisely the way Osborn explains. They clearly present the world as a place of opposing tensions and conflicts. Then they express optimism that good will triumph over evil by using light and related metaphors such as day, sun, star, brightness, dawn, and waking up. These speakers equate light and related metaphors with life, change, power, knowledge, freedom, strength, justice, truth, and hope, while darkness and related metaphors such as night and sleep equal death, silence, hate, oldness, despair, ignorance, and stagnation. In books of great speeches in American history, examples abound. Below are a few typical ones from speeches spanning speaker, time, and subject matter:

Knowledge, in truth, is the great sun in the firmament. Life and power are scattered with all its beams. The prayer of the Grecian combatant, when enveloped in unnatural clouds and darkness, is the appropriate political supplication for the people of every country not yet blessed with free institutions: – "Dispel this cloud, the light of heaven restore; Give me to see – and Ajax asks no more." (Daniel Webster, "Bunker Hill Monument Oration," 1825)

Onward, comrades, all together, onward to meet the dawn . . out of darkness, out of silence, out of hate and custom's deadening sway! Onward, comrades, all together, onward to the wind-blown dawn! With us shall go the new day, shining behind the dark. With us shall go power, knowledge, justice, truth. . . . There are bright lights ahead of us, leave the shadows behind! . . . Meteor-like through the heavens flashed the golden words of light. . . . Words sun-like piercing the dark . . . bidding the teeming world of men to wake and live! Onward, comrades, all together, onward to the bright, redeeming dawn. . . . To the life-giving fountain of dawn . . . onward to the spirit's unquenchable dawn. (Helen Keller, "Onward, Comrades," 1920)

Live beyond the pain of reality with the dream of a bright tomorrow. . . . Weeping has endured for the night. And, now joy cometh in the morning. (Jesse Jackson, "The Rainbow Coalition," 1984)

The optimistic tone of these speeches probably contributes to their effectiveness. The orators help people believe they can succeed by *turning on the light*.

The light/dark and related images above and the other archetypes identified by Osborn reflect a constructed binary ideology that permeates Western civilization. Western culture values absolutist language, linear thought, either-or patterns of organization, choosing between alternatives, people as controllers of their environment, and speakers as agents of change. These values promote a dichotomous orientation to the world where people perceive life as consisting of tensions between fundamental oppositions and conflicts.

Many of the most famous lines of American speeches exemplify these dialectical oppositions. For example, Patrick Henry ended his famous speech with the words, "Give me liberty or give me death!" Two of the most popular statements in John F. Kennedy's Inaugural Address use antithesis, a stylistic device that, by definition, pits words and ideas against each other in direct clashes: "Let us never negotiate out of fear. But let us never fear to negotiate" and "Ask not what your country can do for you – ask what you can do for your country."

One of the most prominent characteristics of successful American speeches is consistent use of archetypal metaphors in opposition. The tensions and conflicts created contribute to the successes of the speeches because they touch a human cord central in mainstream American culture. For example, Lincoln began the peroration to his First Inaugural Address with words that separated him from part of his audience: "In your hands, my dissatisfied fellow-countrymen, and not in mine, is the momentous issue of civil war. The Government will not assail you. You can have no conflict without being yourselves the aggressors. You have no oath registered in Heaven to destroy the Government, while I shall have the most solemn one to 'preserve, protect, and defend' it."

THE USE OF METAPHOR BY NATIVE AMERICAN SPEAKERS

Native American speakers use metaphors, images, and symbols much more frequently than do their non-Native counterparts. Almost every speech, story, prayer, and song is replete with imagery. Sometimes entire prayers and songs involve metaphor. For example, "Nicely, Nicely," a prayer spoken at the Zuni Corn Ceremony, is structured as one major metaphor with minor metaphors also included:

> Nicely, nicely, nicely, away in the east,
> the rain clouds care for the little corn plants
> as a mother cares for her baby.

Put differently, the prayer says that nature behaves in an identical way to a mother.[10]

Generally Native speakers use figures of speech that fit Osborn's label of "archetypal": light/darkness, water and the sea, the family, the human body, disease/cure, war/peace, structures, and the sense of space (vertical and horizontal). Three groups of images that Osborn does not mention but that certainly fit his definition of archetypal are images dealing with masculine and feminine, those dealing with animals, and those dealing with nature. The latter includes images concerning the land, trees, flowers, climate, harvest, earth, and so forth.[11]

American speakers use archetypal metaphors in ways that promote a binary way of thinking characteristic of Western civilization and thought. Although Native American speakers often use the archetypal metaphors identified by Osborn, they do so in ways that encourage thoughts of wholeness and oneness, ideas discussed in the last chapter as central to their worldview. Instead of using contrasting terms as opposites, Native American speakers generally use them as natural parts of ongoing circles or cycles: One part naturally turns into the other. Rather than polarities, the parts live and work together.

Given the hundreds of Native nations in North America, it is not surprising that Native People possess numerous stories of creation. The book *American Indian Myths and Legends* contains twenty-one different tales of human creation and another seventeen tales of world creation. Although different Native American nations have different creation myths, almost all end with Mother Earth and Father Sky. Other similarities include the cultural commonality that parts work together and that the Great Mystery created every part of the Earth. In contrast to the Judeo-Christian belief that "we are created in God's image," most Native People believe all entities are living, and all contain the divine inside themselves. As Picuris Pueblo writer Joseph Rael says, "God is present in the land; the soil, the sky, the clouds, the seasons, the climate."[12]

The Dine "Song of the Earth" deals almost exclusively with what most Americans would view as opposites. Although opposites, they do not oppose. Instead, they unite, working in unison. The song begins with Mother Earth and Father Sky "meeting, joining one another, helpmates ever they." Each stanza continues explaining how two images are "meeting, joining one another, helpmates ever, they." The images include Sisnajinni (the sacred mountain of the East) and Tsodsichl (the sacred mountain of the South), Doko-oslid (the sacred mountain of the West) and Depenitsa (the sacred mountain of the North), night of darkness and dawn of light, Hastyeyalti (God of Sunrise) and Hastyehogan (God of Sunset), white corn and yellow corn, corn-pollen and the Ripener, and life-that-never-passeth and happiness-of-all-things. Likewise, "The Four Corners of the Universe," the Mescalero Apache song for young girls, refers to "where the land meets the big water; to where the sky meets the land." Native American speakers, then, employ many of the same metaphors as their non-Native counterparts, but in ways that unite rather than divide, that champion cooperation rather than competition or opposition.

Subtle word differences may allow two images to work in contention or in concert. Great American speakers often use words such as *but* and *instead*. For example, Martin Luther King, Jr.'s, "I Have a Dream" speech begins in the following manner:

Five score years ago, a great American, in whose shadow we stand, signed the Emancipation Proclamation. . . . *But* one hundred years later, we must face the tragic fact that the Negro is still not free. . . . It is obvious today that America has defaulted on this promissory note insofar as her citizens of color are concerned. *Instead* of honoring this sacred obligation, America has given the Negro people a bad check; a check which has come back marked "insufficient funds." *But* we refuse to believe that the bank of justice is bankrupt.

Where American orators generally use words such as *but* and *instead,* Native American speakers generally use words such as *and, also, too, along with,* and *add.* The following examples are typical:

The fish live, they have blood *also.* The animals, *too,* have red blood (Phillip Deere, Muskogee-Creek, 1978)

I *add* my breath to your breath. . . . (an old Keres song)

American speakers, then, perceive planes of polarities whereas Native speakers conceive of cosmic cycles, a union of natural forces.[13]

Light-Dark Metaphors

The oral messages of the Native People of this country often include light and light-related metaphors such as day, sun, star, brightness, and dawn. However, Native speakers rarely use dark metaphors or light and dark metaphors together.

In his article "Archetypal Metaphor in Rhetoric: The Light-Dark Family," Osborn discusses the significance of a preference by Euro-Americans for light/dark metaphors. His explanation may lend insight into why Native People frequently use light and related metaphors, but rarely use dark and related metaphors or light and dark metaphors together:

Light (and the day) relates to the fundamental struggle for survival and development. Light is a condition for sight, the most essential of man's sensory attachments to the world about him. With light and sight one is informed of his environment, can escape its dangers, can take advantage of its rewards, and can even exert some influence over its nature. . . .

In utter contrast is darkness (and the night), bringing fear of the unknown, discouraging sight, making one ignorant of his environment – vulnerable to its dangers and blind to its rewards. One is reduced to a helpless state, no longer able to control the world around him.[14]

Generally Native People do not fear the dark or fear death; these facts may help to explain why they use few metaphors dealing with the dark. When their speeches, stories, prayers, and songs do deal with death, they portray death as a continuance of the cycle of life. Out of life comes death; out of death comes life. Every end also marks a beginning. When people die, say Native People, they return to the Earth Mother in order to nourish her. Life-death-rebirth – an ongoing, continuous cycle. Native Americans revere life, and when death approaches, they fight fervently. But if it is their time, they let go, knowing their spirit lives on forever. Before going into battle, many Native speakers have said, "Today is a good day to die." In the peroration of his now-famous speech, Seattle, chief of the Suquamish and Duwamish tribes, stated, "At night when the streets of your cities and villages are silent and you think them deserted, they will throng with the returning hosts that once filled them and still love this beautiful land. . . . The dead are not powerless. Dead, did I say? There is no death, only a change of worlds."[15]

Concentrating on cultivation and growth also fosters an acceptance of death as a natural part of the cycle of life. For example, a flower becomes compost, which then becomes food for fresh flowers. The flower and compost are physically and spiritually equal, both needed in the never-ending cycle of nature. Native American speakers often talk about cultivating flowers and foliage. Words such as *seeds, roots, flowering, harvesting, cultivating,* and *growing* permeate their discourse.[16]

Certainly the Native People of this nation have struggled strongly and stalwartly for survival. Coupling this with their constant and continual images of nature make light metaphors almost inevitable. The beginning of Seneca Red Jacket's famous 1792 speech "Brother, The Great Spirit Has Made Us All" exemplifies this: "[The Great Spirit] has taken his garment from before the sun and has caused the bright orb to shine with brightness upon us. Our eyes are opened so that we may see clearly." The second of two stanzas in an Eskimo song is another of a nearly endless supply of examples:

And yet, there is only
One great thing,
The only thing:
To live to see in huts and on journeys
The great day that dawns,
And the light that fills the world.[17]

The Native People of this country speak almost habitually about the voices of nature. They talk about sibilant sounds, voices of vireos, and night chants of owls. In an interview, Mary Leitka of the Hoh nation talks about living by the river. Her description exemplifies the use of dark images in a positive way:

I go down by the river. I say to myself that I will not stay till dark. Then, what do I do? I stay anyway. I end up heading out on my trail home in the dark. Since this is part of the rain forest, the growth is so thick, it's hard to see. It's a trail of darkness. I always get home. I can sense the way.

Leitka continues to explain how she understands and identifies with the river: "My knowledge is the river. I know its moods, I feel comfortable with the river, even when it gets rough and the river is pushing all the trees down. It is alive.[18]

Water and the Sea

Leitka's comments also illustrate the use of water metaphors, another of Osborn's archetypal images. Osborn has discussed the rhetorical significance of the frequent use of images of water and the sea for Euro-American speakers. In tracing the changes in the meanings of these images, he has written at length about how the technology of the Industrial Revolution caused speakers with poetic minds to use water and sea imagery to represent freedom, moral beauty, and a sense of renewal. Osborn wrote, "As the day of technology dawned, and workers swarmed into the cities to provide human grist for its machines, the urban experience . . . quite soon seemed intolerable." According to Osborn, the Industrial Revolution contributed to the sea offering "the most total and symbolically satisfying escape from the new urban existence." Osborn's words seem remarkably similar to the words Native People use in their speaking: Sources of water serve as refuges, places to escape the oppression of the new urban life.[19]

In an essay comparing how American male and female speakers have used archetypal metaphors, Osborn found that men use water metaphors frequently: "The sea metaphor," he concludes, has "long belonged to the rhetorical domain of men, who return to it often for dramatic depictions of personal and social conditions." American women orators, on the other hand, use water and sea metaphors infrequently. When they do choose this imagery, they generally opt for serene images such as pools or fountains rather than stormy ones.[20]

In examining speeches, stories, prayers, and songs by Native American male and female speakers, I found both groups regularly use a plethora of water and sea metaphors, usually in tranquil ways. The verse of a Dine song is typical:

> From the top of the great corn-plant, the water gurgles, I hear it;
> Around the roots the water foams, I hear it.
> Around the roots of the plants it foams, I hear it;
> From their tops the water foams, I hear it.[21]

Even water imagery like thunder and lightening that many Americans associate with turmoil are used by Native speakers in calm, nonstormy ways. The following example from a Zuni prayer illustrates this:

Cover my earth mother four times with many flowers.
Let the heavens be covered with the banked-up clouds.
Let the earth be covered with fog; cover the earth with rains.
Great waters, rains, cover the earth. Lightening covers the earth.
Let thunder be heard over the earth; let thunder be heard;
Let thunder be heard over the six regions of the earth.[22]

Family

Both North Americans and Native People frequently refer in their speeches to family, another of Osborn's archetypal metaphors. For example, both American and Native American speakers frequently talk about their fathers, but the references differ qualitatively. In general, American orators view the Founding Fathers as a group of great men who lived and formed our government. These speakers sometimes refer to the Founding Fathers as representing the beginning of democracy. In contrast, to Native People, fathers and grandfathers are spirits. Although dead, they live eternally because spiritual life is everlasting. That is why, for example, Native People put food out for spirits and receive visits from them. Further, Native American society is Elder centered; age represents knowledge, wisdom, and prudence.

A related difference exists: In youth-centered American society, speakers frequently talk about children in an emotional appeal to listeners' love of children. Native American orators also often mention children, but generally as a means of emphasizing perpetuity rather than as a pathos appeal. Native orators also frequently speak about unborn children and future generations. For example, in 1988, President and Executive Director of Americans for Indian Opportunity LaDonna Harris stated, "The ultimate criterion on which decisions were made for most tribal groups was a simple concept. Would such a decision allow the people to continue, not just in the present generation, but to the children's children's children's generation?" Around A.D. 1000, the Peacemaker, Founder of the Confederacy of the Haudenosaunee, made a similar comment: "Think not forever of yourselves, O Chiefs, nor of your own generation. Think of continuing generations of our families, think of our grandchildren, and of those yet unborn, whose faces are coming from beneath the ground."[23]

Another difference in how American and Native American orators use metaphors about family concerns the meaning of family. American speakers generally focus on people's immediate families and sometimes on the world as belonging to one human family. References to family in Native American discourse include these groups, but also more. Native speakers talk about our country, the physical world, the natural world, and the spiritual world. To them, family includes the deceased, living, and unborn; family also encompasses creatures in the visible and invisible worlds. Given their holistic perspective, Native People do not talk about the deceased, living, and unborn or the visible and invisible worlds as separate entities, but rather, as existing together and mutually involved with each other. At any moment, we are born, dead, and reborn at the same time; these perpetual rhythms create the Hoop of Life.

To Native Americans, then, family relationships stretch across time and distance, and include flora and fauna as well as people. Carter Camp, Ponca, offered this example: "Just as our grandfathers are us, we are our grandchildren. In this way the grasshopper, the sweetgrass, the rabbit, the clover and the sage are part of us." He illustrated his point, continuing, "As when my brother Crowdog came home from prison. He stepped from the car and went to the trees around his homeplace. He put his arms around each and told them he was home. He spoke to his grandfathers, his separation from them had hurt."[24]

Given the belief that all things interconnect with all other things, it is not surprising that Native People speak about relationships, sometimes on topics that Americans do not perceive in terms of relations. For example, Hopi Vernon Masayesva commented, "To me, math is about relations, pattern, and symmetry, ... Two plus two equals four is a statement of symmetry, because it's simply saying, what's true on this side is also true on the other side." Camp used an example in his speech to prove the interrelatedness of all things: "The corn and tobacco we use are the relations of many generations, there is a common resonance between our very cells. The circle of each contained within the circle of the land as one, then born as differing children of the same ancestors. Future tree, past turtle, present Medicine Man."[25]

Personification

In Chapter 1, we learned that Native Americans talk about all things as alive and interconnected with all other things. Given this assumption, the idea of personification does not exist as a separate entity in Native American discourse, but rather is an inherent part of their discourse. Personification, by definition, means the attribution of human characteristics to nonhuman forms. Native People always personify what many Americans consider inanimate objects because Native People believe these objects are alive, possess a soul, and are imbued with a personifying spirit. They often speak of other forms as people in their own right, on an equal plane with human people. For example, Native Americans sometimes refer to the Stone People or the Wolf People. Again, almost every Native American speech, story, prayer, or song contains a host of examples of what Americans consider personification. The following speech by Cheyenne Henri Mann Morton is typical: "The land you strive to protect is my grandmother – my mother. She is the oldest woman – first woman. She is sacred; she is our beloved earth woman . . . who must be revered and protected; she upon whom we walk and live; she who supports our feet and gives us life; she who nurtures us, her children."[26]

In contrasting how male and female speakers use archetypal metaphors, Osborn found that male speakers "appear to prefer more precise synecdochical references to specific anatomical features as representative of some whole (such as "the arm of the empire"), while women speakers prefer more holistic representation by personification (Kansas pictured as heroine, the church viewed as "digging its own grave," etc.)." Both male and female Native speakers refer to specific anatomical features, but much more literally and in much more detail than do their non-Native counterparts. In addition to standard parts of the body, both male and female Native American speakers talk about the skin, hair, eyes, ears, breasts, and bones. The following examples are typical:

Our eyes are opened so that we may see clearly. Our ears are unstopped so that we have been able to distinctly hear the words which you have spoken. (Red Jacket, Seneca, 1792)

You ask me to plow the ground. Shall I take a knife and tear my mother's breast? Then when I die she will not take me to her bosom to rest.

You ask me to dig for stone. Shall I dig under her skin for her bones? Then when I die I cannot enter her body to be born again.

You ask me to cut grass and make hay and sell it and be rich like white men. But how dare I cut off my mother's hair? (Smohalla, Nez Perce, 1850)[27]

In addition to dealing with detailed parts of the body, sometimes Native American speakers devote discourse almost completely to body parts. The following Dine prayer deals with pollen, a sacred element used in Dine rituals. In the prayer pollen symbolizes peace. The prayer is itself an example of personification, as well as an example that deals almost exclusively with parts of the body:

Put your feet down with pollen.
Put your hands down with pollen.
Put your head down with pollen.
Then your feet are pollen.
Your hands are pollen.
Your body is pollen.
Your mind is pollen.
Your voice is pollen.
The trail is beautiful.
Be still.[28]

Generally Native speakers talk about body parts more openly and explicitly than do their neighboring non-Natives.

In addition, they speak openly about bodily functions. For example, Suquamish Chief Seattle said, "Continue to contaminate your bed and one night you will suffocate in your own waste."

An abundant amount of Native American rhetoric "personifies" the Earth, comparing specific parts of the land to specific parts of the body. Generally, the soil refers to the Earth's flesh, the grass to her hair, and the wind to her breath. Kee Shay, grandson of female Dine Elder Asa Bazhonoodah, says the following when discussing his grandmother's teachings about the bond between the body and the soil: "My grandmother told us that the coal at Black Mesa near Cactus Valley is the lungs. And Navaho Mountain is the head of 'she' mountain, and Big Mountain, the most prominent on Black Mesa, is the liver to that female mountain, and where the fingernails are, that's the Hopi mesas." In general, Native American speakers often use graphic metaphors to paint a picture of the future of the Earth unless people change their ways. They talk about how the Earth is weak and weary from wretched wrongs. They talk about how people in the dominant culture have raped and ravaged her. Since everything interconnects, pouring poison into the Earth pours poison into ourselves.

Disease and Cure

In dealing with disease and cure metaphors in American oratory, Osborn explains, "Images of disease arouse strong feelings of fear, images of remedy focus that emotional energy towards the acceptance of some reassuring recommendation. . . . The fears and remedies have a universal and timeless appeal because most people fear their own mortality."[29]

The discourse of Native People contains many disease and cure metaphors, but speakers use the metaphors in completely different ways and for completely different reasons than Osborn explains. Whereas Americans focus on symptoms and speak of disease as sickness, Native People focus on the imbalances that cause the symptoms and speak of disease as malaise or dis-ease. Whereas Americans speak of cures as remedies, Native People speak of cures as healing, making whole, restoring balance. Further, Americans speak about medicine as separate, patented products coming from an array of external sources such as pharmacies whereas Native People talk about medicine as healers coming directly from nature. Medicine People especially, men and women appointed and sanctioned by their nations, use plants from the Earth to restore the physical, emotional, and spiritual well-being of the individual and the community. Some plants serve as aphrodisiacs, others cleanse the blood, others stimulate the liver, others heal grief, and others eliminate negative thoughts. Many Native prayers ask plants for their assistance and thank them for offering their lives. Communicating with plants is a primary part of Native doctoring.

When Native Americans talk about illness, they mean not only physical ailments, but spiritual ailments as well. They frequently use disease metaphors to refer to the illnesses of Euro-Americans including greed, possessiveness, and indifference about the Earth. Sitting Bull, a Sioux warrior, talked in a speech in 1877 about how "the love of possession is a disease": "These people have made many rules that the rich may break but the poor may not. They take tithes from the poor and weak to support the rich who rule. They claim this mother of ours, the earth, for their own and fence their neighbors away; they deface her with their buildings and their refuse." More than one hundred years later, in 1997, Santee Sioux activist John Trudell made a similar comment:

In a way I feel like it's a disease, it's like some kind of cancer came into what was the Western Hemisphere. . . . We have to look at what they're doing to the environment, the life-support systems. The water, the earth, the land. Just look at what they're doing to the physical, necessary life-form providers – total disregard for it.[30]

Like Trudell, Native People often discuss damages already done to the Earth. Several speeches, stories, prayers, and songs use highly descriptive language and intense, passionate metaphors to address how the land has been deadened, defoliated, and destroyed. The only cure for the ills of the Earth, Native People say, is for all people to live in right relationship with her. Gkisedtanamoogk, of the Wabanaki nation, for example, said in 1993, "The Mission, then for all who are Spiritually Conscious/Awake is to restore Balance/Harmony where Imbalance/Disharmony prevail."[31]

War and Peace

Before Europeans came to America, Native People fought among themselves. Native nations did not engage in large scale warfare, but intertribal aggression existed, based on various cultural values, customs, economic systems, and so forth. Stealing horses to enhance wealth and prestige and achieving honor through revenge were consistent sources of threats to survival and well-being.

The amount of fighting, however, was relatively little when compared to the abundant amount of fighting in the two hundred plus years since newcomers have come to North America. Steven Crum, member of the Tosa Wihi or White Knife Band of the Western Shoshone Nation of the Great Basin, states, "Back in 1490 in the Great Basin, you would find no warfare. We had family squabbles and differences before the coming of the white man, but there was no such thing as mass-scale war between the tribes in the Great Basin. Warfare emerged at a later date for some tribes." And, of course, a massive amount of warfare has occurred in the over two hundred years since newcomers have come to this country, since at various points in America's history the government has implemented policies of extermination toward various Native nations.[32]

An abundant amount of Native American discourse concerns how the living land that once belonged to them gave way to naked brown Earth – mile after mile of sacred land was defoliated and destroyed. Native American speakers discuss how women, crying for husbands and sons, fill the air with their wails; and orphans, the helpless flotsam and jetsam from leveled villages, wander homeless through the country. Wars reaped their crimson harvest of collapsed corpses, bloody bodies, and lost limbs. The discourse of Native People chronicles how day after day, month after month, and year after year, newcomers to this continent have wrenched their lives because of their sin of being born.

In this quagmire of madness and mayhem, Native nations became warrior societies. The historical fate of the Native People made images of war and peace almost inevitable in their discourse. Yet, despite the many attempts by newcomers to exterminate Native People and their culture, surprisingly images of peace occur far more frequently in their discourse than do images of war.

One of the most famous examples of peace metaphors in Native American rhetoric is the Tree of Peace, a symbol of the Haudenosaunee model of a democratic confederacy. The confederacy was a response to intratribal and intertribal acts of aggression. The Haudenosaunee used warfare to dominate tribal people; yet their dominion of control also brought a state of intertribal peace. According to the Haudenosaunee "Roots of Peace," the Peace Maker "planted a pine tree, and called it the Tree of Peace; and four roots spread out, to the four directions. Then he uprooted the tree, and took all the weapons of war and threw them in the hole under the tree, and then he planted the tree again. In the topmost branches he placed an eagle, to watch and cry out if any evil approached the people."[33]

In addition to discussing peace with their invaders and those conquered, Native American speakers use images of peace to talk about living in harmony with the natural and spirit worlds. Peace is an important part of Native American life. For example, the word *Hopi,* a Pueblo Nation in northern Arizona, means the peaceful ones, and the Haudenosaunee use the same word for peace and law. Common metaphors for peace among Native American speakers in general are the pipe of peace and the hand of friendship.

To Native Americans, peace means more than just the absence of war. Peace means living in harmony and right relationship with everything in the natural and spiritual worlds. Living in harmony and right relationship involves mutual respect, generosity, compassion, and caring. Inner peace within the heart comes when people keep themselves deeply rooted in nature, when the rhythms of their lives become one with nature's cosmic rhythms.

Structures and Buildings and Sense of Space

Whereas Osborn identified metaphors dealing with structures and buildings as a group of archetypal metaphors used frequently by great American orators, metaphors of this type are rare in the rhetoric of Native Americans. A frequently quoted example of the "house" as metaphor comes from the Dine "Nightway Prayer":

House made of dawn
House made of evening twilight,
House made of dark cloud,
House made of male rain,
House made of dark mist,
House made of female rain,
House made of pollen,
House made of grasshoppers, . . . [34]

The materials that make up the house are clearly not standard materials for domestic dwellings. Using elements of nature in the prayer rather than expected building materials emphasizes the importance of people's homes becoming one with nature or in relationship to nature.

The peculiarity and rarity of structural and building images in the discourse of Native People relate directly to cultural assumptions discussed in Chapter 1: Americans encourage expansion and create sophisticated technology to change the environment; they are terrified of change unless it is change they create, such as permanent structures. Native People see permanence in the process; they encourage harmony with the Earth and its features and abhor defiling the natural terrain. In short, Americans build on the land; Native People live within the land. When the "white man" came to this country, Native Americans literally could not comprehend how people could buy or sell land. Doing such a thing seemed as preposterous as buying and selling air. An enormous amount of Native American discourse discusses the dishonor done by desecrating the Earth and treating her as a commodity or object. Native People also speak about not understanding the need for walls, floors, ceilings, fences, or other unnatural dividers. The Earth, they say, provides all the materials necessary to create a home.

Some Native American discourse even discusses the absence of structural imagery. For example, in protesting land sales in 1810, Tecumseh, a Shawnee orator and warrior, pronounced, "Houses are built for you to hold councils in; Indians hold theirs in the open air."[35]

Arthur Amiote, Lakota teacher, relates the virtual absence of structural images to the transparent, transcendent, and transient nature of all things. He explains the uninstitutionalized Lakota sacred traditions:

They formally and consciously reject permanent sacred architecture as suitable or as having any lasting significance. The transparency of the world of matter and the transmutability, birth-lifetime-death, of all things including the earth itself, precludes the thought that material permanence has very much to do with sacred space. Rather, by not being in a structure, one is in the sacred temple – templum – which is the world itself, with the actual dirt of the earth as the floor and the vast blue dome of the actual sky as the ceiling.[36]

Traditional Native People, then, talk about the entire Earth as holy ground.

Native Americans speak about spaces and places as important, not structures and buildings. Many of the differences between Native nations stem from each adapting to the peculiar qualities of the space or place where they live. The climate, crops, animals, clothing material, makings of shelter – all become part of the people living on the land as the land becomes part of the people. Native People not only know the plants in their area, for example, but they also know which part of the plant to use for which medicinal purposes – the whole herb, the seed, the leaf, the flower, the twig, the root, the wood, the bark, the rhizomes, the fruit, the resin, the needle, the bud, and so forth. The continual displacement of Native People becomes even more tragic when we understand the importance they accord space and place. George Tinker, a part-Osage pastor and professor, explains how many Osage people died when relocated from Missouri into Kansas and then into Oklahoma. "That's the story of many, many tribes that were relocated in Indian territory," he says, "where they had to learn to live in relationship to a new land."[37]

OTHER ARCHETYPAL IMAGES

Three groups of images that Osborn does not mention but that certainly fit his definition of archetypal metaphors are images dealing with male and female, images dealing with animals, and images dealing with nature – the land, trees, climate, and so forth.

Male and Female

For many years American speakers have pitted males against females. Various forms of discourse of Native Americans over scores of years reveal that they recognize differences between the sexes, but they also believe all things possess both male and female attributes that need to work in unison to exist in balance. Gerald Hausman, a contemporary Dine medicine man, explains how the union of male and female stems from creation stories:

Geologists like to tell us that the basic components of earth, air, water and fire, fused in the crucible of primordial time, formed our world. Native Americans, however, speaking through their religious myths, tell a different tale. Their version of the origin story speaks of a mythical creator, like an energy force, who, in concert with Earth and Sky, created our universe. The result may be the same – out of chaos is born order – but the difference as seen through Indian eyes is not a matter of boiling and cooling and the interchange of light, heat and mass. Rather, it is the bonding of two principles, male and female, mother and father.

Native People speak about the Great Mystery or Creator as formless and shapeless. I have seen no attempts to personify the Creator either in words or in pictures. To Native Americans, the Creator is not a he or a she, but rather contains both male and female attributes.[38]

Native American speeches, stories, prayers, and songs continuously refer to the Earth Mother and Great Father. The paired images of Mother Earth and Father Sky may be frequently found in their discourse. The Tewa "Song of the Sky Loom" is typical, highlighting these image pairs at the beginning and end of the song:

O Our Mother the Earth, O Our Father the Sky
Your children are we and with tired backs
We bring you the gifts you love. . . .
That we may walk fittingly where the grass is green.
O Our Mother the Earth, O Our Father the Sky.[39]

Although specific meanings vary with different nations, generally Native speakers talk about the dynamic interaction between the sun, a masculine figure who protects and acts, and the moon, a feminine figure, a womb, who gives life and nourishes that life. Many Native People call a woman's menses her "moon time" because it happens at each cycle of the moon. Like most of their non-Native counterparts, Native People talk about the masculine as depicting strength, courage, and action and the feminine as representing creativity, intuition, receptiveness, and compassion.

Unlike their neighbors, Native People frequently talk about how all people and other sentient beings possess both masculine and feminine qualities and about how both sets of qualities possess value and power. Instead of discussing male and female as opposites, they talk about how one set of qualities cannot exist without the other; they are complementary opposites. Both perform vital functions that work together in the cycle of life. The masculine constantly seeks union with the feminine, and the feminine constantly seeks union with the masculine. Working together in harmony is key.

The striving for unity of male and female applies to minute details of Native American life. For example, Native People talk about feathers as having both masculine and feminine energies and the need in ceremony to align these energies in perfect balance.

Native People of the North American plains talk about the pipe, an especially sacred symbol, and discuss how the pipe perfectly combines masculine and feminine energies. The stem of the pipe is masculine; it transmits prayers, performing the action. The feminine bowl is the cauldron where the tobacco or herbs become transformed into smoke. The joining of pipe and bowl represents the sexual completion of the male-female circle.

Discussions of the balance between male and female energies permeate the oral rhetoric of Native People. The following examples are typical:

So we look for the balance in life, the male-female balance of life which is in the universe, which is trapped in these trees, those grasses. All of life is a male-female balance, even you. (Russell Means, Lakota, 1988)

Native Americans/American Indians believe in the dualities of life, such as sky-earth; sun-moon; love-hate; wisdom-ignorance, etc. Of them all, however, the most powerful is: man and woman. Together they make the perfect whole, and are part of the great sacred circle of life. . . . The most powerful of all pairs in the universe are men and women working together. (Henri Mann Morton, Cheyenne, 1989)[40]

Animals

Native American speakers often talk about animals metaphorically. They revere animals, often referring to them as conduits to the spirits. They talk about animals as their relatives, stressing the equality of animals and human beings. The following statement is typical:

[I speak] the truth on behalf of people, of the world, of the four-footed, of the winged, of the fish that swim. Someone must speak for them. We forget and consider ourselves superior, but we are after all a mere part of the Creation. And we must continue to understand where we are. And we stand between the mountains and the ant, somewhere and only there, as part and parcel of the Creation. (Oren Lyons, Onondaga, 1977)

In Native American discourse, some animals receive more frequent mention than others. For example, Native People often talk about eagles as especially revered animals because they fly higher than other birds and, thus, serve as messengers of people's prayers to the Creator. They often talk about bears as healers, beings who bring medicine. Deer, buffalo, and fish, depending on the Native nation, are often connected to survival. These animals sacrifice their lives so that two-legged creatures can live.

Some Native American public speakers also frequently talk metaphorically about salmon, perhaps because the salmon is a dramatic type of fish. As it grows up, a salmon swims from fresh water such as a lake or stream to the ocean, and when it is time to spawn it swims upstream, against the flow of the water, back to the fresh water of its birth – a good example of the Native awareness of the circular form of things. A very acrobatic fish, a salmon jumps high and readily. In a speech in 1967, Dan George, chief of the Coast Salish nation, commented, "But in the long hundred years since the white man came, I have seen my freedom disappear like the salmon going mysteriously out to sea."[41]

Animal characters appear in many Native American stories. Coyotes, known as tricksters because of their cunning, devious ways, frequently appear in these tales, sometimes disguised as other animals until the end.

Nature

Perhaps the most distinctive feature of the oral rhetoric of Native People is the pervasiveness of images involving nature. Almost all Native American speeches, stories, prayers, and songs contain a plethora of such metaphors. The abundance and variety of these images reveal the importance they accord their nature friends. The following example helps to explain this:

Every part of this soil is sacred in the estimation of my people. Every hillside, every valley, every plain and grove, has been hallowed by some sad or happy event in days long vanished. Even the rocks, which seem to be dumb and dead as they swelter in the sun along the silent shore, thrill with memories of stirring events connected with the lives of my people. (Chief Seattle, Suquamish, 1853)

Whereas Americans talk about people as living on the land or off the land, Native Americans talk about people as living in the land and allowing the land to live in them.

Many of the nature images of Native speakers concern rhythmic cycles such as the four seasons. The following examples, all from Shawnee Tecumseh's speech "Sleep Not Longer, O Choctaws and Chickasaws" typifies this:

We will be driven away from our native country and scattered as autumnal leaves before the wind.

They have vanished before the avarice and oppression of the white man, as snow before a summer sun.

You, too, will be driven away from your native land and ancient domains as leaves are driven before the wintry storms.

Using images of natural cycles might lessen tensions created by a speaker because, no matter what happens, autumn, winter, spring, and summer always occur in that order.[42]

The seasons comprise just one of many ways that Native American speakers give special attention to the number four. They often refer to the four directions – west, north, east, south. They talk about the four stages of life – birth, puberty, maturity, and death. They talk about those who fly, crawl, walk on four legs, and those who walk on two legs. They address the four parts of the universe – earth, air, fire, and water. John Lame Deer, a Lakota Holy Man, declares that "*four* is the number that is most *wakan,* most sacred." He continues explaining the power of the image: "It represents the unused earth force. By this I mean that the Great Spirit pours a great, unimaginable amount of force into all things – pebbles, ants, leaves, whirlwinds – whatever you will. Still there is so much force left over that's not used up." Thus, many Native nations use the number four in their ceremonies, such as taking four puffs from a peace pipe and adding holy water four times over hot rocks in a sweat or purification lodge.[43]

In their speeches, stories, prayers, and songs, Native Americans refer to nature in more detailed ways than do their Euro-American counterparts. Their descriptions often involve vivid vocabularies, picturesque phrases, and familiar figures of speech. Native American speakers frequently question how a field or a firefly feels. Their discourse concerns cornfields chattering, mountains murmuring, and hills humming. They often voice marvel at the miracles of the world. By listening to the sounds of nature, Native Americans say they hear and talk about the heartbeat of life itself.

USE OF SENSORY IMAGES

Overall the detailed descriptions of Native American speakers use more sensory images and fewer intellectual images than do their non-Native counterparts. Sensory images refer to words and phrases that evoke images that listeners can see, hear, smell, taste, or feel; intellectual images refer to all images that are not sensory. According to rhetorical critic Carroll C. Arnold, "Sensory images tend to stimulate listeners to experience vicariously; to that extent the linguistic form invites them to become experientially, hence feelingly, involved in what is said."[44]

Compared to North American rhetoric, traditional Native American rhetoric is a veritable feast for the senses. Some sensory images are exotic, but most are familiar, making their use a means of identifying with audiences. Examples abound for each sense; they literally may be found in almost every speech, story, prayer, or song, no matter the speaker, year, or Native nation:

The armies of the whites are without number like the sands of the sea. (sight – Shabonee, Potawatomi, 1827)

You heard the voice of the Red Man. You have heard their cries. (hearing – Phillip Deere, Muskogee-Creek, 1978)

And as I snuffed up the smell of their blood from the earth, I swore eternal hatred – the hatred of the avenger. (smell – Tecumseh, Shawnee, 1812)

They were not sweet like sugar, but bitter like gourds. (taste – Ten Bears, Comanche, 1867)

Having never stepped from our circle we could feel the thrum of the life force around us. We could touch and understand the circles of those we invaded, from the termite to the tree to the deer. (touch – Carter Camp, Ponca, 1988).[45]

Often Native speakers appeal to more than one sense, and they frequently combine sensory images with other forms of imagery, especially archetypal images. Consider, for example, the Zuni prayer for rain:

When our earth mother is replete with living waters,
When spring comes,
The source of our flesh,
All the different kinds of corn,
We shall lay to rest in the ground.
With their earth mother's living waters,
They will be made into new beings.
Coming out standing into the daylight
Of their sun father,
Calling for rain,
To all sides they will stretch out their hands.
Then from wherever the rain makers stay quietly
They will send forth their misty breath;
Their massed clouds filled with water will come and sit with us, . . .
The clay-lined hollows of our earth mother
Will overflow with water,
Desiring that it should be thus,
I send forth my prayer.

This portion of the prayer appeals to listeners' senses of sight, hearing, and touch and to at least the following categories of archetypal forms: light, water, personification, the human body, family, animals, and nature. A person presenting this prayer speaks directly to listeners since the extensive imagery and vivid, descriptive language involve listeners.[46]

The use by Native American speakers of sensory and archetypal images also contributes to their effectiveness because their images are generally more vivid and vigorous than the images of North American speakers. Paiute Sarah Winnemucca Hopkins criticized the white Christian takeover of Native American land using powerful, persuasive images: "Your carbines rise upon the bleak shore, and your so-called civilization sweeps inland from the ocean wave; but, oh, my God! leaving its pathway marked by crimson lines of blood, and strewed by the bones of two races, the inheritor and the invader; and I am crying out to you for justice."[47]

In general, sensory forms of figuration are difficult to refute because they involve the listener and appeal to the imagination. The Native People's reliance on sensory images, forms of figuration that, by definition, encourage listeners "to experience vicariously what is being discussed," make them especially difficult to refute since listeners need to criticize themselves and/or not identify with images common to all human beings.

Generally Native speakers choose images that are more broad, sweeping, timeless, and inclusive than the images used by American speakers who more frequently choose images that are specific to particular situations or audiences. The wide use of figures of speech by Native speakers often brings abstract and complex ideas into the immediate ken of varying audiences. The images help the speakers to identify with audiences. In short, the images add to the persuasive and poignant power of their rhetoric.

ELEMENTAL FORCES

Another way to examine the imagery in Native American rhetoric is to consider the four elements contained in all things – earth, air, fire, and water. These constitute especially useful archetypal forms for examining Native American discourse because Native American speakers constantly discuss these elemental forces, in general far more often than do their non-Native counterparts. They talk about these elements as coming from the breath of the invisible, the breath that gives living energy to all things. These four natural, elemental forces permeate and actuate everything. According to some Native speakers, air, fire, water, and earth correspond to the breath, energy, blood, and body of the Mother. Although discussed separately below, the elements are interrelated; one could not exist without the others, and nothing could live without all four.

Earth

My addition of nature to Osborn's list of archetypal images deals largely with the importance in Native American rhetoric of images concerning the Earth. The images include humans, animals, plants, minerals, herbs, mountains, rocks, valleys, and so forth. Mother Earth provides the foundation for the other elements. Earth concerns the world of matter, perceived by the senses of sight, hearing, taste, touch, and smell. The Earth is similar to a large stable container. Traditional Native American speakers talk about protecting the Earth, saving it as a condition of survival and respect. All the images dealing with different land forms, different things that live on the Earth, cultivation, climate, and planting would fall under this category. So too would images concerned with the need for universal harmony and natural balance. Examples of Earth imagery abound even in titles of stories such as "Creation of the Animal People" (Okanogan), "Yellow Jacket and the Ant" (Nez Perce), "Why Mosquitos Bite People" (Spokane), and "Stone Boy" (Brule Sioux), and in titles of songs such as "Song of the Earth" (Dine,) and "Song to the Earth-Maker" (Winnebago). The first half of the "Song of the Vigil" (Osage) provides a typical example of the frequency of the use of Earth in Native American discourse:

The touching of the earth is an act divine – Greetings,
The touching of the earth is an act divine – Greetings,
The touching of the earth is an act divine – Greetings,
I have come – Greetings,
The touching of the earth is an act divine – Greetings.[48]

Fire

Fire deals with the core of energy at the center of the Earth. Metaphorically speakers often use fire imagery to discuss destruction, renewal, and rebirth. A renewal can arise from ashes (destruction) into new creations (rebirth). Fire ignites and consumes. It can bring about dramatic changes. It energizes. Native Americans and other people associate fire with the sun, the great ball of energy from which everything obtains its light and energy. Fire imagery covers all radiant and electrical phenomena. It often relates to the spirit and is associated with intuition. Smoke carries prayers upward to the Creator. In addition to obvious terms like camp fire and council fire, other fire images that appear frequently in the discourse of Native People include the following: ashes, blaze, burn, bright, candle, desert, energy, flame, fuel, heat, illumination, light, melt, power, purify, radiate, reflect, rekindle, smoke, spark, sparkle, star, sun, sunlight, and warmth.

Many stories, prayers, and songs of Native People use the word sun in the title. Representative examples include the following stories: "Children of the Sun" (Osage), "The Hopi Boy and the Sun" (Hopi), "Sun Creation" (Brule Sioux), and "Coyote Steals the Sun and the Moon" (Zuni). "Song of the Sun" (Winnebago)and "Prayer to the Sun" (Blackfoot) provide other typical examples.

Water

Bodies of water constitute one of Osborn's archetypal forms. Water is like the blood of people and of Earth. Most of the human body consists of water, and most of the surface area of the Earth is covered with water.

Water cleanses and dispenses. It is fluid and adaptable. It constantly flows and changes, taking the shape of whatever it contains. Therefore, images dealing with different bodies of water (bogs, brooks, lakes, marshes, oceans, ponds, pools, rivers, seas, springs, and streams) fit under water imagery. Animals who live primarily or completely in the water are in the same category. Water imagery also deals with absorption, adaptability, flexibility, indestructibility, and malleability. Native American discourse frequently concerns going with the flow of nature rather than trying to dominate nature and control the flow, a typical trait of speakers steeped in Western civilization.

"Song of the Rain Chant" (Dine) and "Rain Prayer" (Sia) provide typical examples. Consider also a brief portion of "Rain Song" (Sia): "Clouds like the plains come and water the earth. . . . Medicine bowl, cloud bowl, and water vase give us your hearts, that the earth may be watered."[49]

Air

Air concerns the breath of people, of all sentient beings, and of Mother Earth. Air is invisible; no one can see it, but we can feel its presence and track its movements. Air is a transforming element because it moves constantly. Air stimulates. It can be gentle like a breeze or dramatic like a hurricane.

Air imagery appears in Native American discourse in discussions about winged creatures who fly such as eagles and in talk about the wind and about weather patterns. Much of the rhetoric of Native People concerns keeping the air clean, uncluttered, and free of pollutants. Frequent air images found in their speaking include breath, breeze, cloud, cool, fog, gust, power, rainbow, snow crystals, soar, sway, thunder, weather, and wind.

"A Gust of Wind" (Ojibway) is a typical story full of wind/air imagery. Representative songs include "Wind Song" (Pima), "Song to Bring Fair Weather" (Pima), and "Song of the Thunder" (Objibway).

Combinations of the Four Elements

A large amount of oral discourse of Native People deals with more than one of the four elements — earth and water or fire and wind or all four. The examples below come from different Native cultures:

> We are the songs that sing,
> We sing with our light.
> We are the birds of fire,
> We fly over the sky.
> Our light is a voice;
> We make a road for spirits,
> For the spirits to pass over.
> Among us are three hunters
> Who chase a bear;
> There never was a time
> When they were not hunting.
> We look down on the mountains,
> This is the Song of the Stars. ("The Song of the Stars," Algonquian)

Ho! Sun, Moon, Stars, all that move in the heavens, . . . Ho! You Winds, Clouds, Rain, Mist, all you that move in the air, . . . Ho! You Hills, Valleys, Rivers, Lakes, Trees, Grasses, all you of the earth, . . . Ho! You Birds, great and small, that fly in the air, . . . Ho! All you of the heavens, all you of the air, all you of the earth. ("Prayer to Introduce a Child to the Cosmos," Omaha)[50]

CONCLUSION

I contend that the archetypal metaphors identified by Osborn are thematically cross-cultural, but the ways speakers use the metaphors reflect the culture that shapes them. Since Western culture divides, segments, and categorizes experiences, great American speakers use archetypal metaphors in ways that likewise divide, segment, and categorize experiences, resulting in messages that reflect a binary way of thinking and that are fraught with oppositions and tensions. Most of the images used by Native American speakers fit into Osborn's archetypal categories, but the ways the speakers use the metaphors differ significantly from Osborn's explanation. Although they employ many, but not all, of the same metaphors as their non-Native counterparts, and some that their non-Native counterparts may not use as often, Native People speak about the metaphors as ways of creating unity, harmony, cooperation, and wholeness. At least as used by Native American speakers, Osborn's archetypal metaphors are not cross-cultural, but rather emerge organically from the culture.

Understanding the archetypes of a culture allows for a deeper and richer understanding of the beliefs, values, and actions of the people. Examining the archetypal metaphors of different cultures and looking at the creation stories of these cultures provide fruitful areas for future research.

Like all words, Native People speak of images as living, flowing, dancing, and connecting. The images they use in their oral rhetoric have a rhythm and life of their own. They breathe, pulsate, and vibrate. They possess colors, textures, and scents. Their extensive use of imagery creates messages that teem with life, energy, and vitality. Rather than static symbols, they are living processes, more similar to verbs than to nouns.

Native People talk about how spoken words breathe life into things. Through imagery, people relate, sharing the breath of life with all sentient beings. For Native People, images constitute important energies of life, creative forces of the universe that permeate and animate us all.

Perhaps primordial energies, living symbols, resonating vibrations, or holographic relationships are more precise terms than images when considering how Native People speak of imagery and how the imagery is reflected in their oral rhetoric. Or given their stated view that human beings have a primal relationship with nature, perhaps we can conclude, as Lame Deer did, that images "are part of nature, part of ourselves."

Speeches of Peace and Protest

The heartfelt eloquence of Native American oratory – which so astonished and bemused white negotiators at treaty talks – arose from a culture in which a word, once spoken, never died.

Neil Philip, Author

The ability to make a good speech is a great gift to the people from their Maker.

Saying of the Oglala Sioux

Because the written word is used infrequently in their culture, Native Americans cherish the spoken word. They value highly people who possess oratorical ability, and these people often become their leaders. In part because their societies for many years possessed only oral traditions, they view words as special gifts and the ability to speak publicly as a powerful weapon. Leaders exert influence through words, not force.[1]

TOPICS OF NATIVE AMERICAN SPEECHES

Much speech of Native People concerns rhetoric, contrasting the Native American view of the word with the Euro-American view, known since the arrival of the "white man." Native People say they consider the word sacred whereas they say Euro-Americans pay little attention to the words they use. Native People often make statements in their speeches about the veracity of their messages not because of their credentials as speakers but because they understand that words, by definition, have value and should not be misused. For example, Yakima George Meninock said, "This is all true. . . . These words

Protecting Mother Earth. Illustration by Francene Hart.

are mine and they are true." Often Native People end their speeches with the words, "I have spoken," as Creek Muskogee, Speckled Snake did in a speech in 1830. Concluding speeches in this manner again stresses the inherent sanctity of words.[2]

In a speech in 1879, Nez Perce Chief Joseph criticized the use of words by his non-Native neighbors:

I have heard talk and talk, but nothing is done. Good words do not last long unless they amount to something. Words do not pay for my dead people. They do not pay for my country, now overrun by white men. They do not protect my father's grave. They do not pay for all my horses and cattle. Good words will not give me back my children. Good words will not make good the promise of your war chief General Miles. Good words will not give my people good health and stop them from dying. Good words will not get my people a home where they can live in peace and take care of themselves. I am tired of talk that comes to nothing.[3]

Lakota tribal judge Four Guns indirectly justified the oral tradition when he criticized the written word as used by the "white man": "We are puzzled as to what useful service all this writing serves. . . . The Indian needs no writings; words that are true sink deep into his heart where they remain; he never forgets them. On the other hand, if the white man loses his papers, he is helpless."[4]

Public persuasion by Native Americans often concerns sustaining the tribal ways of their ancestors. Many of their orations record their struggles and sufferings as the "white man" has encroached upon their homes. Native People have been displaced again and again and again from lands they know so well. They have become aliens in their own society, stuck in a reservation of spiritual starvation. Many of their speeches to non-Native audiences contain a brief history of the injustices committed against Native People. For example, in 1966 Earl Old Person of the Blackfoot nation gave the following historical summary in his testimony before Congress:

In the past 190 years, the U.S. Government has tried every possible way to get rid of the troublesome Indian problem he feels he has on his hands. First the Government tried extinction through destruction – where money was paid for the scalps of every dead Indian. Then the Government tried mass relocation and containment through concentration – the moving of entire tribes or parts of tribes to isolated parts of the country. . . . Then the Government tried assimilation – where reservations were broken up into allotments . . . and Indians were forced to try to live like "white men."[5]

The historical overview provided in many Native American speeches often consists of a reminder to listeners of the friendliness and generosity of the original inhabitants of this country to the first newcomers. The following examples, separated by more than 150 years, are typical:

Your forefathers crossed the great waters and landed upon this island. Their numbers were small. They found friends and not enemies. . . . We took pity on them. . . . We gave them corn and meat. (Red Jacket, Seneca, 1792)

Many winters ago your forefathers came to our country. They were poor, weak, and feeble. They asked for a little land to plant corn on for their women and children, a place to spread their blankets. We took pity on them. . . . Our forefathers taught them how to live in America. They showed them many things. (Indians of the St. Regis Reservation, Mohawk, 1948).[6]

Debunking the myth that Columbus discovered America also constitutes a common topic of speeches. John Echohawk, Pawnee, asserts, "Hopefully the great American myth about Columbus discovering America, which every school kid learns, will be buried. Native Americans discovered it a long time before that. The myth assumes no one existed on this land and that's totally wrong. We were here since time immemorial . . . we're still here and we're growing stronger and stronger."[7]

Native American speakers talk not only about past persecution, but also about how the oppression of Native People continues. They explain how attempts to conquer and colonize Native Americans continue and how Native People are still subjects of suppression and oppression.

Another frequent topic in the speeches of Native Americans is their continued life and vitality. Here they react to some people in the dominant society who think of Native People as part of America's past, museum pieces, or antiquated fossils out of touch with the rest of civilization. In several speeches Native speakers declare unequivocally that they are not the vanishing Americans. Rather, they live and will continue to live.

Unlike other groups in this country, such as people of color, Native Americans in general have not tried to assimilate until recent times. The Old Ways ask that they be allowed to maintain their identity, beliefs, customs, and languages; in turn, they would respect the principles and practices of non-Native people. But newcomers to this country viewed America as a melting pot, and a melting pot could not exist with one group refusing to give up its ways. Discourse of Native People often concerns this lack of desire to assimilate, to become part of the American melting pot. Cheyenne Henri Mann Morton succinctly comments on the lack of need for her to become a white American clone: "An American Indian philosopher once said, 'It is not necessary for eagles to be crows.'" Muskogee-Creek speaker Phillip Deere proudly declares, "I want to continue to be who I am. . . . You cannot change the color of my eyes. Neither can you change my hair. I was born a Native American Indian and I will die an Indian." Richard Erdoes, the person asked by Lakota Lame Deer to write his life story, quotes a Native American who explained the difference between Native People and other minority groups: "'Us Indians and the Blacks have the same problem living under the White Man, but there is one big difference: they want *in,* we want *out.*'"[8]

Perhaps the most frequent topic in the speeches of Native People is nature. Repeatedly speakers talk about how land cannot be bought, sold, or owned. They describe how an umbilical cord connects them to Mother Earth. They contrast the eternal treasure of nature with the ephemeral glitter of gold. They talk about the natural world as not only where we live but also as the very reason we are alive. Specifically, orators try to thwart dam construction, bulldozers, and concrete; they oppose opening land to obtain minerals, gold, copper, tin, coal, uranium, and oil. With rhetoric, they fight for hunting and fishing rights. Their words reveal a deep passion and sincere reverence for nature. In 1896, Lakota Gertrude Simmons summed up how the Native person views land as sacred by referring to the land as "a priceless legacy to be sacredly kept."[9]

Native Americans talk about nature very differently than their North American counterparts. In general, Native Americans talk about nature while North Americans speak about the environment and ecology. Native American orators speak about nature in simple terms. They talk about the difference between experiencing the Earth as a breathing, boundless Being rather than as an immobile, motionless mechanism. They discuss people's primal unity with the Earth, and the need for people to be attuned to the minute meanings and messages of the Earth. They speak about nature without what purports to be scientific flooring. They deal with the Earth's problems on an affective basis — how people become powerless and paralyzed, depressed and distressed when the Earth hurts. They discuss people's relationships with other natural forms. In other words, they talk about trees, for example, not as symbols but as others in I–Thou relationships.

In criticizing Americans' treatment of the Earth, Native speakers stress again and again that the Earth is alive; it has feelings and possesses a soul. In several speeches Native People question how the Earth feels or what their nature friends hear. For example, in 1855 Young Chief, of the Cayuses nation, asked rhetorically, "I wonder if the ground has anything to say? I wonder if the ground is listening to what is said?" He continued saying he could hear what the ground, water, and grass say. In 1925, Wintu medicine woman Kate Luckie spoke on behalf of the trees and the rocks: "The tree says, 'Don't, I'm sore. Don't hurt me.' But they chop it down and cut it up.... That hurts them.... The rock says, 'Don't. You are hurting me.' But the white people pay no attention."[10]

Environmentally conscious American orators usually give facts, figures, and other forms of evidence to prove that people are depleting the earth's resources. They generally deal with the earth's problems on a reasonable basis, giving an abundance of information, especially facts and figures. They employ technical words and concepts such as ozone layers, biospheres, acid rain, insecticides, population controls, and global warming.

The reasons for preserving the Earth differ markedly between traditional Native People and their non-Native counterparts: Americans generally speak about preserving the earth for their use; they do not talk about the earth as a living being. In contrast, traditional Native Americans talk about preserving the Earth because of its intrinsic value; many stress the sanctity of the Creator's handiwork. Preserving something sacred follows. Native Americans view people as temporary visitors or guests on the Earth. In short, Native Americans begin by viewing Mother Nature as a living, viable Being. Animals, trees, plants, and stones have souls and communicate. People, referred to by many Native Americans as two-legged creatures, are intrinsically connected to the Earth and to her other creatures such as the four-leggeds, no-leggeds, and one-leggeds, and to creatures that fly, swim, and crawl.

Because they strive to become one with nature, the messages of Native People often concern universal balance, the fusion of people and nature. The following statement by Pete Catches, a Sioux medicine man, exemplifies: "As I get older, I burrow more and more into the hills. The Great Spirit made them for us, for me. I want to blend with them, shrink into them, and finally disappear in them. As my brother Lame Deer has said, all of nature is in us, all of us is in nature." Repeatedly Native People express this sentiment of how the Earth exists in people and how people exist in the Earth or, as Suquamish Chief Seattle put it, "The earth does not belong to man; man belongs to the earth." Native speakers repeatedly express the need for people to bend and blend with the Earth rather than intrude and dominate her.[11]

Frequently Native American orators criticize Americans for treating the Earth as a possession. Native speakers express bewilderment at the wanton destruction of nature, the gouging of the Earth, and the desire of Americans to tame the wilderness. They seem genuinely perplexed and mystified that Euro-Americans do not perceive these problems, at least not enough to solve them at their core, which to Native Americans means cooperating with nature rather than trying to dominate nature. They talk with horror at how Americans have misused fire to make bigger and bigger weapons of destruction such as thermonuclear bombs that risk instantaneous and mass annihilation. Much of their rhetoric expresses outright confusion; viewing the Earth as their mother, they do not understand how people can purposefully hurt her. For example, in 1877 Sitting Bull, a Sioux warrior, expressed horror at how Americans treated the Earth: "They claim this mother of ours, the earth, for their own and fence their neighbors away; they deface her with their buildings and their refuse. That nation is like a spring freshet that overruns its banks and destroys all who are in its path."12

Cheyenne Henrietta Mann, Professor of Native American Studies and in 1986 the first woman Director of the Office of Indian Educational Programs of the Bureau of Indian Affairs, explains the idea of the Earth as our mother: "This concept of earth as giver of life, therefore, is a sacred relationship of a mother to her child or as children to their mother. In return for her gift of life, we keep her alive through our ceremonies, and we return time and again to our sacred sites to renew and strengthen our spirits and the spirit of the earth." In a speech to the World Council of Churches in Seoul, Korea, in 1991, Osage-Lutheran scholar George Tinker elaborated on the subtle, deep meaning of Mother Earth:

The Indian understanding of creation as sacred, of Mother Earth as the source of all life, goes far beyond the notion of such Western countermissions as Sierra Club or Greenpeace. It embraces far more than concern for harp seals or a couple of ice-bound whales. It embraces all of life, from trees and rocks to international relations. And this knowledge informs all of the community's activity, from hunting and dancing and even to writing grant proposals or administering government agencies.

It especially concerns itself with the way we all live together. Perforce, it has to do with issues of justice and fairness, and ultimately with peace.13

Asa Bazhonoodah, a Dine Elder, translates general discussions of the Earth as mother to a specific discussion against strip mining. At the 1971 Senate Hearings in Washington, D.C., she testified, "How much would you ask for if your Mother had been harmed? There is no way that we can be repaid for the damages to our Mother."14

Consistently Native Americans express confidence that the Earth will continue even if humans do not. Two-leggeds in their arrogance, they say, cannot destroy the Earth. She has been around for billions of years and has billions of years to heal Herself. The question is, Will the human race endure?

Native American speakers sometimes extend their discussions about concern over the growing alienation of people from the Earth to the growing alienation of people from their inner selves. N. Scott Momaday, Kiowa, makes this point succinctly when he says, "We may be perfectly sure of where we are in relation to the supermarket and the next coffee break, but I doubt that any of us knows where he is in relation to the stars and to the solstices." The following statements, made nearly fifty years apart, provide further illustrations:

The white man does not understand the Indian for the reason that he does not understand America. He is too far removed from its formative processes. The roots of the tree of his life have not yet grasped the rock and soil. (Luther Standing Bear, Lakota, 1928)

We're all wounded, not just Indian people, but all of us have been wounded by the culture that has split us from the natural world, from our inner lives. Linda Hogan, (Chickasaw, 1992)

Specifically, Native People frequently speak about the human consequences of America's fast-paced society and growth juggernaut including crime, drugs, alcohol, disease, and domestic violence. Alcohol, drugs, gambling, and poverty particularly represent the painfully human side of Native American life today.[15]

Many speeches by Native speakers concern the loss of tribal roots and the pain of displacement. Forced assimilation and trying to live in two worlds at once have created identity problems for many contemporary Native People. Because of intermarriage, most Native People are mixed-bloods, adding further to identity crises that many Native speakers address: They talk about how neither the Native world nor the dominant society will accept them completely. Ben Black Elk, son of Sioux chief Black Elk, talks about the difficulty of being a Native American today: "We who are Indians today live in a world of confusion. . . . We are Indians, and we love the Indian ways. We are comfortable in the Indian ways. But to get along in this world the white man tells us we must be white men, that we cannot be what we were born to be. . . . Today there are Indians who are ashamed they are Indians."[16]

Many speeches concern the rights of animals. For example, Luther Standing Bear, Oglala Sioux chief, identified the rights of animals, "the right of man's protection, the right to live, the right to multiply, the right to freedom, and the right to man's indebtedness." Oren Lyons, an Onondaga chief, spoke about how the furred, finned, and feathered depend on two-leggeds for a voice in an international forum in 1977 before the United Nations: "Someone must speak for them. I do not see a delegation for the four-footed. I see no seat for the eagles."[17]

Many speeches by traditional Native American orators concern opposition to war. Generally, the speakers advocate peaceful coexistence, non-aggression, and harmony. Kahkewaquonaby, an Ojibway minister, spoke about how it made no sense to engage in war:

"I do not see any good that it would do me to put a bullet through your body – I could not make any use of you when dead; but I could of a rabbit or turkey. As to myself, I think it more wise to avoid than to put myself in the way of harm; I am under apprehension that you might hit me. That being the case, I think it advisable to keep my distance."[18]

Several Native speakers express frustration at the many misunderstandings people of the dominant society have about Native Americans and war, as Lakota Elder Mathew King explains in detail:

He [the white man] says we're warlike when we're peaceful. . . . See, he calls this head-dress a warbonnet. Sure, we used it in war, but most of the time it was for ceremony, not war. . . . When we sing songs he calls them war songs. But they're not war songs, they're prayers to God. We have drums, so White Man calls them war drums; but they're not for war, they're for talking to God. There's no such thing as a war drum. He sees our warriors paint their faces, so he calls it war paint. But it's not for war, it's to make it so God can see our faces clearly if we have to die. So how can we talk to the White Man of peace when he only knows war?[19]

In a speech at the Cooper Institute in New York in 1870, Oglala Sioux Red Cloud spoke about how Native People wanted peace and love rather than riches, materialistic things, and possessions. He used himself as an example: "Look at me, I am poor and naked, but I am the chief of the nation. We do not want riches but we do want to train our children right. Riches would do us no good. We could not take them with us to the other world. We do not want riches, we want peace and love." In addition to wanting peace rather than war, generally the messages of Native orators express preference for conservation and collectivism to consumption and competition, protection and preservation to production and profit.[20]

RHETORICAL STRATEGIES

Research has shown that generally people portray enemies as subhuman, vermin, dispensable beings. Exterminating and extinguishing enemies logically flows from portraying them as expendable. Because Native People say all created beings possess equal worth, they, not surprisingly, portray the enemy in ways that Euro-Americans would consider atypical.

Like all human beings, Native People sometimes want revenge. Even then, however, their rhetoric generally discusses revenge without portraying the enemy as subhuman. For example, Shawnee Tecumseh wanted the enemy killed when he said in a speech in 1811, "They seize your land, they corrupt your women, they trample on the ashes of your dead! Back whence they came, upon a trail of blood, they must be driven."[21]

Usually Native Americans talk about the dominant people as ignorant rather than as subhuman. They portray abstract groups such as countries, governments, or institutions as bad rather than people as bad. For example, Russell Means, Lakota, declared in a speech in 1977, "I talk for a people who live in the belly of the monster. The monster being the United States of America and every country in the Western hemisphere and in the Western world who follows the lead of that monster." Rather than portraying the enemy as a lower life form, some Native American orators present the enemy's ideas as wrong.[22]

When Native Americans directly confront their non-Native counterparts, their speeches still contain a disproportionately small amount of conflict, blame, or bitterness. Some traditional Native Americans seem to believe that they will not affect change by belittling their listeners or telling them they are wrong. Rather, these orators earnestly try to befriend their non-Native neighbors, even after countless lies and broken promises. Perhaps, they seem to reason, if they love their enemy, they will not have an enemy anymore.

Even Santee Sioux activist John Trudell, former national chairman of the American Indian Movement (AIM), advocates treating the enemy without hatred. In a speech at the Black Hills Survival Gathering in 1980, just one year after his wife, three children, and home were burned while he was demonstrating in Washington D.C., Trudell concluded,

And no matter what they ever do to us, no matter how they ever strike at us, every time that they do it, we must never become reactionary. The one thing that has always bothered me about revolution, every time I have seen the revolutionary, they have reacted out of hatred for the oppressor. We must do this for the love of our people. No matter what they ever do to us, we must always act for the love of our people and the earth. We must not react out of hatred against those who have no sense.[23]

In 1997, almost twenty years later, Trudell made a similar comment: "I see the white man society as diseased. The spirit is diseased and can't see reality clearly. But unless that poses an immediate physical danger to me, I have more pity than hatred or anger."[24]

One technique of Native American orators that makes their speeches seem less confrontational is the use of the third person when referring to their "white" audiences. For example, in his speech in 1805, Red Jacket, of the Seneca nation, used third person plural pronouns (their, they, and them) rather than the second person you:

Your forefathers crossed the great waters and landed on this island. *Their* numbers were small. *They* found friends and not enemies. *They* told us *they* had fled from *their* own country for fear of wicked men, and had come to enjoy *their* religion. *They* asked for a small seat. We took pity on *them,* granted *their* request and *they* sat down amongst us. We gave *them* corn and meat. *They* gave us poison in return. *The white people* had now founded our country. (Emphases added. This was the speech as given.)

Note how much more fractious and confrontational this message sounds if we substitute you for their, they, and them:

Your forefathers crossed the great waters and landed on this island. *Your* numbers were small. *You* found friends and not enemies. *You* told us *you* had fled from *your* own country for fear of wicked men, and had come here to enjoy *your* religion. We took pity on *you,* granted *your* request and *you* sat down amongst us. We gave *you* corn and meat. *You* gave us poison in return. *You* had now founded our country. (Emphases added. This is the speech as rewritten.)

In the example below from an 1830 speech by Creek Muskogee Speckled Snake, consider how much more confrontational the message sounds if the third person pronouns and other words for the audience such as *palefaces* and *white man* are changed to second person pronouns and if the speaker refers to Native Americans by using the first person *we* rather than the third person *(him, their, Indians):*

When the *white man* first came to these shores, the *Muskogees* gave *him* land, and kindled *him* a fire to make *him* comfortable; and when *the palefaces* of the south made war on *him, their young men* drew the tomahawk, and protected *his* head from the scalping knife. But when the *white man* had warmed *himself* before the *Indian's* fire, and filled *himself* with the *Indian's* hominy, *he* became very large. (Emphases added. This is the actual message.)

When you first came to these shores, we gave *you* land, and kindled *you* a fire to make *you* comfortable; and when *you* of the south made war on *us, we* drew the tomahawk, and protected *your* head from the scalping knife. But when *you* had warmed *yourself* before *our* fire, and filled *yourself* with *our* hominy, *you* became very large. (Emphases added. This is the rewrite of the message.)[25]

Many Native speakers use the third person in human examples; it is a way to humanize their messages without directly confronting their audiences. Their speeches sound like little stories. For example Ponca Susette LaFlesche recited several examples/stories in a speech in 1879:

Let me relate one or two instances which serve to show how powerless we are to help ourselves. Some years ago an Omaha man was missed from one of our tribes. No one could tell what had become of him. Some of our people went to look for him. They found him in a pig-pen, where he had been thrown to the hogs after having been killed by white men. Another time a man of our tribe went to a settlement about ten miles distant from our reserve to sell potatoes. While he stood sorting them out two young men came along – they were white men, and one of them had just arrived from the East; he said to his companion, "I should like to shoot the Indian just to say I shot one." His companion badgered him to do it. He raised this revolver and shot him.[26]

Native speeches often seem less confrontational also because of their inductive organization. Whereas most American speakers follow the old maxim, "Tell them what you're going to tell them, tell them it, tell them what you told them," Native American speakers often wait until near the end of a message to state their thesis. That is what Dine Elder Asa Bazhonoodah did in her testimony in 1971 before the Senate concerning the Peabody Coal Company's mining on top of Black Mesa: After an in-depth discussion of how "the Earth is our mother" and how "our Mother is being scarred," Bazhonoodah concluded, "I want to see the burial grounds left alone. . . . I want to see the mining stopped."[27]

Leslie Marmon Silko, Pueblo writer, discusses how English structure generally takes listeners "from point A to point B to point C." By contrast, she explains how the structure of the oral tradition "resembles something like a spider's web — with many little threads radiating from the center, crisscrossing one another. As with the web, the structure emerges as it is made, and you must simply listen and trust, as the Pueblo people do, that meaning will be made."[28]

Some Native American speakers directly adapt to their audiences, using the language of American culture to explain their points. Lakota Russell Means did this skillfully in 1977 in the example below:

> Well, let me put it to you in the white man's terms. Instead of asking you to respect life we are going to ask you to respect capital. Look upon the natural resources of this world as capital. No longer look upon them as income that has to be flushed out immediately because if you continue to look at our relatives and our sacred Mother as income you will waste all the non-renewable resources in this country, in this world. But if you look on them as capital then you might find some respect. . . . Our oil, our petroleum, our uranium, our coal, our timber, all of these natural resources are capital. And if you look on them as capital, then maybe you will think of the future.

Similarly, in 1971 Dine Asa Bazhonoodah identified with her listeners by talking about things with which they were familiar, a rhetorical technique common in American oratory: "Black Mesa is to the Navajo like money is to the Whites. . . . Black Mesa is my billfold. . . . The staff that I prod my donkey with is like the pencil the whites use."[29]

Like American speakers, Native American speakers sometimes use humor to identify with their listeners. Four Guns, an Oglala Sioux, concluded his 1891 speech explaining why Native People did not need writing by saying, "I once heard one of their preachers say that no white man was admitted to heaven, unless there were writings about him in a great book." Eighty years later, two Native American orators spoke before the Speech Communication Association, now called the National Communication Association, a professional organization composed primarily of university professors of speech communication. Both chose to begin their speeches with a dose of humor:

> The Crow tribe has an annual event. . . . Every night there was a dance in a great big circular arbor. And surrounding this arbor were little concession stands all run by Indians. . . . Every one of these stands had one feature. It was called the Watergate cocktail. It was a glass of water with a bug in it. It was very reasonable, too, because it had no price tag, just whatever you could alibi, cover-up, or get away with. (Dr. Barney Old Coyote, Crow, 1973)

> We Indians have accepted many things right from the beginning of our ancestors. First of all, we accepted the name "Indians." I presume it was Columbus who called us that. I understand also that Columbus went looking for India. . . . It is often said, "If he were

out looking for Turkey, I wonder how would we be referred to today? (Earl Old Person, Blackfoot, 1973)

Native People seem to use more self-deprecatory humor in their speeches than do their non-Native counterparts, a quality related to the value Native People place on being humble.[30]

Both in direct parlays with American audiences and in speeches to their own or other Native groups, Native American speakers frequently invite audience participation by asking regular questions or rhetorical questions; with rhetorical questions, the correct answers are implicit in the questions. By definition, questions involve listeners, encouraging them to think of their own answers and seeing if their answers match the speaker's. American orators ask questions also, but Native American orators seem to do so more frequently than do their non-Native counterparts. For example, one of the first published speeches of Native Americans, a plea in 1699 by Wahunsonacock, leader of the Powhatan Confederacy, begins with a series of questions: "Why should you take by force that from us which you can have by love? Why should you destroy us, who have provided you with food? What can you get by war?" In his famous speech in 1811, Tecumseh, a Shawnee orator, pleaded with the Choctaws and Chicasaws to join in a common fight against the white man. Much of his speech consists of a series of questions:

But have we not courage enough remaining to defend our country and maintain our ancient independence? Will we calmly suffer the white intruders and tyrants to enslave us? Shall it be said of our race that we knew not how to extricate ourselves from the three most dreadful calamities – folly, inactivity, and cowardice? But what need is there to speak of the past? It speaks for itself and asks, Where today is the Pequod? Where the Narragansetts, the Mohawks, Pocanokets, and many other once powerful tribes of our race?[31]

Sometimes the rhetorical questions contain ridicule and irony. In replying to the white people's offers to bring their religion to the Native People, Seneca Red Jacket offered the following reply in 1792:

Brother! You say there is but one way to worship and serve the Great Spirit. If there is but one religion, why do you white people differ so much about it? Why not all agree, as you can all read the same book? . . . Since [the Great Spirit] has made so great a difference between us in other things, why may we not conclude that he has given us a different religion, according to our understanding?

Almost two hundred years later, Audrey Shenandoah, Onondaga Clan Mother, said in a keynote speech in 1990 at the Global Forum on Environment and Development for Survival, "It is foolish arrogance for humans to think themselves superior to all the life-support system. How can one be superior to that upon which one depends for life?"[32]

The tendency of Native People to involve their listeners helps speakers to identify with audiences. Frequently Native American speakers try to get their listeners to see them as human beings. They stress the similarities between Native Americans and Euro-Americans. In 1870, for example Chief Red Cloud, Oglala Sioux, proclaimed to a Cooper Union audience, "You have children. We, too, have children." In 1879, Oglala Sioux Standing Bear tried to prove he was a person. Lifting his arm he declared, "That hand is not the color of your hand, but if I pierce it I shall feel pain. The blood that will flow from mine will be the same color as yours. I am a man. The Great Spirit made us both." Also in 1879 Ponca Susette LaFlesche declared, "We are human beings; God made us as well as you" and "I tell you we are human beings, who love and hate as you do."[33]

In addition to seeing Native People as human, Native orators try to make listeners realize that they too could be the object of prejudice. For example, Muskogee-Creek Phillip Deere tried to get his listeners to realize that they could be the next minority when, as part of the Longest Walk demonstration in 1978, he declared in his speech,

A few years ago, Black people fought for what they wanted. They could see the signs in many states. On the doors was written, "No Coloreds Allowed." We don't see that anymore. . . . Today we see another sign on there that doesn't have anything to do with your color. . . . On that door that "no colored" sign is not there, but there is a sign that says, "No Shirt, No Shoes, No Service." It doesn't say anything about color any more. But in the future, you will probably be the next Indian. If you are not careful, you are going to be the next Indian. After a while, we are going to walk up to that door and we are going to read a sign that says, "All the People with Moustaches, Stay Out!"

The sentiment in this example is remarkably similar to the words of Pastor Martin Niemoller, a Protestant theologian. Shortly after his release from a Nazi concentration camp, Pastor Niemoller said the following words:

In Germany, they first came for the communists, and I didn't speak up because I wasn't a communist. Then they came for the Jews, and I didn't speak up because I wasn't a Jew. Then they came for the trade unionists, and I didn't speak up because I wasn't a trade unionist. They came for the Catholics, and I didn't speak up because I wasn't a Catholic. Then they came for me. And by that time, there was no one left to speak up.[34]

Like American orators, Native American speakers sometimes emphasize the personal perspective by including detail. Giving detail helps to ground their messages in reality. As discussed in the last chapter, they also infuse their messages with an abundance of descriptive language and sensory images, more than are found in public speeches by American orators. The extensive use of details, descriptive language, questions, rhetorical questions, and sensory imagery helps the speakers establish rapport with their listeners by drawing them into their messages.

To Native Americans, listeners of speeches are never limited to those immediately present. Since they view everything as alive and ensouled, listeners of speeches always include the deceased, the unborn, and all the elements of nature. They also speak about the self and the Great Spirit as listeners.

Many speeches of Native Americans have a moral overtone. Often orators talk expressly about people's need to communicate truthfully and authentically. They speak about the need to be true to themselves, to have integrity and dignity as human beings. The emphasis of Native cultures on the group rather than on the individual is reflected in their oratory by drawing attention away from the speaker's credentials and towards the veracity of the message. For example, in the introduction to his 1879 speech, "An Indian's Views of Indian Affairs," Nez Perce Chief Joseph talks about honest speech, "The white man has more words to tell you how they look to him, but it does not require many words to speak the truth. What I have to say will come from my heart, and I will speak with a straight tongue. Ah-cum-kin-i-ma-me-hut (the Great Spirit) is looking at me, and will hear me."[35]

Showing humility constitutes another frequent way Native American orators downplay their own credentials. In 1974, Kiowa Allen C. Quetone stated how expressions of humility are expected: "No talk is ever given without first indicating your humility. 'I am an ignorant man; I am a poor man' – all the talks start this way – 'I don't know nearly as much as you men sitting around here, but I would like to offer my humble opinion.'" In 1912, Black Elk, medicine man of the Oglala Sioux, gave a typical example of this expression of humility, "Grandfather, Great Spirit, once more behold me on earth and lean to hear my feeble voice." In their orations, Native American speakers seem to make almost deliberate attempts to detach themselves from their listeners. For example, they rarely use the pronoun "I," placing emphasis on the message rather than on them.[36]

Like female American speakers, female Native American orators tend to downplay their credibility more often and more seriously than do their male counterparts. For example, an orator known as Wyandotte, Little Beaver's wife, said in a speech to President Washington, "I am but a woman, yet you must listen. . . . But I am ignorant. Excuse, then, these words, it is but a woman who speaks."[37]

Whereas Western rhetoric celebrates the individual, Native American rhetoric celebrates the group. Most Native American nations make decisions affecting the entire tribe in councils held around council fires, campfires specially positioned and ceremonially lit and tended. Members of councils represent the people. They sit on the council because they have proven themselves wise, brave, compassionate, and fair. Individual views are encouraged. After considering differing perspectives, the good of the whole takes precedence over the good of the individual.

In these participatory councils, speakers continually change. Sitting down puts listeners on an eye-to-eye level with the speaker and with other listeners. Sitting in a circle reminds listeners of the equality of all beings. Sitting on the Earth reinforces the sanctity of nature.

A talking stick is a tool unique to Native People. Held by the orator when speaking in council, it allows the speaker to talk without interruption. When one person finishes speaking, the talking stick is given to the next speaker. The talking stick teaches people to honor all ideas and fosters the view that many perspectives exist on any topic. It allows exploration of perhaps otherwise unconsidered points of view. The talking stick also gives all participants an equal voice, again emphasizing the group over the individual. Speakers are also supposed to tell the truth when holding a talking stick.

Generally Native orators prepare their speeches thoroughly and use language that is simple, familiar, direct, and concrete. They employ a concise style, weighing words rather than wasting them. They almost never use sugar-coated language or euphemisms.

Most Native American orators speak peacefully and calmly. They usually seem nonthreatening in tone. A few, however, possess vibrant voices, sounding like roaring thunder. Red Jacket, a famous Seneca orator, credited his deep resonant voice to his practice of standing next to Niagara Falls and trying to speak over the roar. He is also known to have breathed purposefully from his diaphragm, a practice used by all good orators.

CONCLUSIONS

Some scholars have criticized the protest rhetoric of the American Indian Movement for its failure to sway authorities of the dominant culture. Many Native American protesters, however, purposely speak to other activists and especially to Native youth caught between the spiritual traditions of their ancestors and the chance of a "better" life by assimilating and accepting the technology of "white" culture. They do not attempt to influence American decision makers because they realize the inherent impasse caused by fundamentally different cultural assumptions.[38]

The incompatible world views of Native People and the dominant culture doom their rhetoric to failure by traditional rhetorical standards of immediate success. The ideas and ideals of Native Americans are so different from those of their non-Native counterparts as to make one group's views virtually incomprehensible to the other. Rappahannock Dr. Kevin Foley, a clinical psychologist and Director of the Leo Camp Alcohol Program of the Sacramento Urban Indian Health Project, explains,

Columbus met people he could not understand. His cognitive thinking and reductionism were not capable of relating to the red race, whose wisdom comes through the heart. . . . It's difficult for Indian people to understand alienation as a part of a world view. For us the Western type of thinking is so foreign it would involve a painful psychological process to adopt it.[39]

I contend that the Native American oral tradition has contributed to the immediate failure and the long-range success of the rhetoric of Native People. The oral tradition does not possess a concept of public, at least not in the way Western rhetoricians have defined the term. Rhetoric in the United States, with roots stemming from ancient Greece and Rome, focuses on the ability of speakers to sway their immediate audiences. By using sufficient evidence, bolstering their credibility, and appealing to listeners' emotions, American speakers gradually try to alter the beliefs, values, and actions of their audiences. American speakers adopt a paradigm of conversion – one speaker tries to convert the ideas of many listeners. Typically speakers stand in front of listeners, who usually sit in rows. Listeners look up which bolsters the credibility of speakers. Large numbers of people sitting in rows in auditoriums, churches, and so forth further foster the view of speakers as active and of listeners as passive.

By contrast, when Native People speak within their groups, they follow a paradigm of dialogue, conversation, and negotiation. In councils around council fires, speakers continually change as the people deliberate strategies, proposals, and courses of action. Without tape recorders, minutes, or other types of records, listeners must be active and attentive. The circular formation encourages participants to express differing viewpoints without fear of judgment. Sitting down further emphasizes equality and the right of all speakers to share their views. Councils meet for the purpose of making decisions for the group, decisions that will affect unborn generations. Decisions require unanimity. Individual speakers downplay their own importance, focusing on the group instead of on themselves. They appeal to values such as the family and tribal nation and talk about how people do not live for themselves but for the benefit of all sentient beings. Many Native groups base their decisions on what is best for the next seven generations.

The focus on the group rather than on the individual gives a new definition of *public*. Gkisedtanamoogk, Wabanaki nation, uses the pipe as an example:

How does one Keep something? In terms of the Pipe – and all Sacred Articles handed to us – we are told to Keep these for the People. They don't belong to us; the Pipe that I may carry doesn't belong to me. In that sense I belong to the People of an area because I have the Pipe and the Pipe belongs to the People. We are no longer our own person. We become a Public Person.[40]

The moderation of the Native American oral tradition complements its cooperative rather than conversionary quality. The abundance of metaphors discussed in the last chapter adds to the moderation of their rhetoric. Sarah Hutchison, Elder of the Oklahoma Cherokee people, states, "Indians speak in metaphor. Metaphor is gentle and indirect." The various ways Native speakers make their messages less confrontational also contribute to their moderate quality as does the usual softness of their voice while speaking.[41]

The belief in the interconnectedness of everything also encourages caution. Words and actions reverberate affecting everyone and everything. Terry Tafoya, a Taos Pueblo psychotherapist and healer, puts it this way: "You always have to be careful because everything you do causes this ripple that goes out in all directions, to the furthest star. If a spider web wiggles in one place, the ripples go throughout the web."[42]

Often Native speakers address the cosmic perspective rather than the specific situation. They incorporate the cosmic perspective in their orations in a variety of ways. For instance, they explain time as entailing the entire past, present, and future, and they expound on how the future encompasses eternity. They rarely mention dates or count years. Instead they say, "many moons ago" or "spirits will blow across the plains and prairies until the sun rises no longer." Their cosmic view extends also to place; for them place encompasses the entire Earth. They seem to speak for all living beings for whom the present represents but the passing vexation of a generation.

In 1993, Dr. Gregory Cajete, Tewa, commented powerfully on the importance of a cosmic perspective to Native thinking:

The elders remind us of the importance of the long view when they say, "pin peyeh obe" – look to the mountain. They use this phrase to remind us that we need to look at things as if we are looking out from the top of a mountain, seeing things in the much broader perspective of the generations that are yet to come. They remind us that in dealing with the landscape we must think in terms of a ten-thousand, twenty-thousand, or thirty-thousand year relationship.

Taking a cosmic perspective makes speeches sound poetic, but takes away from the potential ability of the speeches to sway particular listeners at particular times.[43]

The oral tradition, by definition, is conservative. N. Scott Momaday,

Kiowa, explains, "It is in the nature of oral tradition that it remains relatively constant; languages are slow to change for the reason that they represent a greater investment on the part of society."[44]

Other factors contributing to a moderate and humble rhetoric include talk about the need for balance and harmony and talk about the need to move with the flow of nature rather than try to control nature and change this flow. In Chief Seattle's words, "Tribe follows tribe, and nation follows nation, like the waves of the sea. It is the order of nature, and regret is useless." These words are very different from the typical words of the great North American orators who often try to change and control the world with their rhetoric.[45]

Despite continual struggles, Native orators generally speak in ways that are tender, sensitive, gentle, compassionate, and upbeat. They affirm life and love. Despite starvation, slaughter, and suffering, they generally speak with integrity, dignity, and pride, focusing on faith and belief rather than on skepticism and cynicism. In a speech in 1854, Suquamish Chief Seattle talked about our "common destiny," asserting, "We may be brothers after all. We shall see." Similarly, in 1977, after talking about the oppression of the Red people, Russell Means, Lakota, concluded his speech in a compassionate and generous way: "I hope, I foresee, that maybe with the cooperation of the international community, just maybe, twenty-five years from now, the Red people will be helping other indigenous peoples gain their liberation."[46]

In sum, the orations of traditional Native American speakers are generally marked by consideration, benevolence, humility, sincerity, and gentleness. Despite unspeakable acts of abuse inflicted on their people, Native American orators generally express more bewilderment and impassioned sadness than anger. In general, they devote their orations to pursuing good deeds and to restoring balance to the world. Hope, harmony, and humility characterize their speeches. Their valiant voices generally speak from the heart, focusing not on eloquence, but on truth, dignity, and right action.

Story Circle. Illustration by Francene Hart.

Stories Planting Sage for the Soul

We know we can still hold on to those things because we know we all come from story. We know we all come from places of emergence. They may not all be the same story but there is a sameness. There is a oneness in it all and it comes from language. It comes from places where the word was sacred, and is sacred, and will remain sacred.

Harold Littlebird, Laguna/Santo Domingo Pueblo

Language *is* story.

Leslie Marmon Silko, Laguna Pueblo

Harold Littlebird and Leslie Marmon Silko speak about the sanctity of the story for Native People, sacred because they are composed of words and words are sacred. The story – narrative – is the oldest rhetorical form in recorded communication. Old myths, sagas, and poems of Native Americans and other cultural groups make use of this structure. Historically stories illustrate moral principles in ways others can understand and remember. They contain lessons that other modes of communication cannot teach as well.[1]

Communication scholar Walter R. Fisher argues that human beings are inherently *homo narrans,* or storytelling creatures. This means that people instinctively share narrative stories to explain occurrences that happened to them or to others.[2]

First, this chapter briefly summarizes North American stories, the stories told by people in the dominant American culture. Then the chapter examines Native American stories especially as these differ from American ones.

NORTH AMERICAN STORIES

Most North American stories are associated with the young. Told usually at night by one parent, bedtime stories lull children to sleep. Parents read stories to their children out of a book that usually has beautiful pictures to accompany the text.

American stories often focus on competition, domination, individualism, and beauty. Most characters in American stories are strong, self-reliant, handsome, and powerful. They know what they want, and they pursue these goals. Many stories deal with people's drives to be the best, people pushing to get ahead, or people going boldly where no one has gone before. Often characters have extraordinary abilities such as Superman's X-ray vision. The stories are generally action-oriented (See Jack run).

American stories are based on problems and solutions. They set up a situation, create a conflict resulting in a climax, and then resolve the crisis.

In many Euro-American fairy tales and some other stories, nature is a dangerous place. Consider the woods in "Hansel and Gretel" or "Little Red Riding Hood." The untamed wilderness is dark, scary, and fraught with dangers.

Most American stories depict good battling evil with good triumphing in the end. They often include opposites, contrasting ideas and images. They paint people and situations as wonderful or repulsive. The good versus evil theme makes stories easy to follow and predict.

Most American stories are also easy to follow because they flow logically. Clarity and consistency characterize the stories. They have a definite purpose and story line. They are organized coherently with a pronounced beginning, middle, and end. They almost always end in a positive way, sometimes with the words, "And they lived happily ever after."

NATIVE AMERICAN STORIES

Native American stories help people answer the fundamental questions: "Who am I?" and "Where did I come from?" Stories join people to their past, giving them a sense of identity and a sense of belonging. American stories have these goals also, but storytelling is more important to Native Americans than to their non-Native counterparts.

Native People use stories primarily to teach. In the last chapter, we learned that Native American public speeches are marked by gentleness. The Native People's way of educating the young is likewise gentle. Rather than didactically telling children, "Do not lie, do not steal," Native Americans usually impart these and other teachings through stories. Native American stories give little direct advice. Instead, individuals need to glean the answers to stories to answer their own questions and solve their own problems. Although Native American stories do entertain, their primary purpose is to teach. Most of the stories possess one or more morals.

The oral narratives of Native Americans also possess a sacred dimension, a healing purpose. They literally have helped Native nations survive. Abenaki Joseph Bruchac, a famed storyteller today, declares, "I believe that in those old stories and in the more recent stories . . . we can find the real roots of survival." In the same vein, Kiowa N. Scott Momaday quotes writer Isak Dinesen, "All sorrows can be borne if you put them into a story or tell a story about them."[3]

The Introduction and other chapters already discussed how Native People view words as alive. Likewise, Native Americans speak about stories as having a living presence. Bruchac uses examples to explain how the words in Native stories live and breathe in a way foreign to most Westerners:

When you say "drum," do you see something to be played in a band or something, *some thing* to be made by an elementary school student in a crafts class in a "Native American Unit"? Or do you see a living creation, and does the word "drum," in whatever language it is spoken, mean to you the heartbeat of the Earth? When you say the word "dog," is it a word which just means an animal or a word which is an insult? Or does it refer to one of the animal people, an honorable being, even a relative? The animals, you see, are seen as ancestors.[4]

Because Native stories get passed from generation to generation, no one owns the stories. Although storytellers transmit stories, the stories do not belong to them. Rather, the stories belong to no one and everyone. They have a life of their own.

Storytelling is one of the most important ways Native American children learn the lessons of their elders – their rich heritage, central values such as truth, respect, and love, and the important part played by each creature, whether the creature walks, flies, crawls, or swims. Through stories children learn about creation and planetary peace and about the need for two-leggeds to be responsible stewards of the Earth. Teaching stories illustrate the consequences of ethical and nonethical behavior. Stories often deal with everyday dilemmas. Some expose human foibles by poking fun at various aspects of life. According to Native storytellers, one purpose of storytelling is to let people know indirectly that their behavior is inappropriate.

Within tribes, elders often take on the role of storyteller, sharing their sage advice with younger members. Some storytelling consists of sharing personal experiences. For example, Lakota warriors were expected to boast about their exploits; they commonly did this through telling a story. Native Americans use storytelling to pass on heroic exploits, tribal history, cultural beliefs and values, societal roles and norms, and humorous human foibles. Some storytellers travel from tribe to tribe telling of heroic deeds, prophesying future events, and relaying news of births and deaths.

In an oral tradition, listeners remember only some stories. Some tales die with the storyteller. By definition, stories that get passed from one generation to another are especially engaging and enchanting. They usually deal with timeless themes or with themes that different people can adapt in different ways.

Because Native Americans tell stories orally, the act of storytelling involves direct communication with audiences. Stories are meant to be told to audiences consisting of several people rather than read aloud to one or a few children or read silently by oneself. Listeners usually sit in a circle, often on the Earth. The circular formation helps to make listeners an active part of the story. Whereas many American stories try to lull listeners to sleep, Native American stories try to keep listeners engaged and involved. The personalized, individualized type of communication involved in the storytelling of Native Americans strengthens the oral tradition and the messages passed on through it. Stories draw people closer, creating communions between adults and children, adults and adults, and children and children.

Stories are impersonal enough so children will listen and personal enough so they speak directly to the hearts of audiences. Listeners can imagine what characters look like and hear in their own minds the sounds of people, animals, and nature. They temporarily transport themselves into the characters, feeling the emotions of the characters as if the events in the story were happening directly to them. Stories are like borrowing other people's eyes, ears, and bodies. They connect listeners with males and females, old and young, animals and spirit beings, and beings of different times and cultures. Through stories people reach across race, gender, and religious creed. They travel the world in human and nonhuman form. They become animals, trees, oceans, and rocks, and each of these creature beings speaks with each other with ease.

Stories introduce the full range of human emotions. They invite listeners to laugh, to cry, to awaken, to journey with others. Often listeners of stories think about how they would handle situations similar to those of the main characters and then check how close their thinking parallels that of the the central figures. Stories possess enormous persuasive power in part because they involve listeners' entire beings.

Storytelling encourages the imagination. It expands the mind, allowing it to picture characters, backgrounds, and sounds. Native American stories are also rendered active by frequent inclusion of dialogue; almost all their stories involve characters who talk. The dialogue form invites listeners to participate in the stories. As the stories progress, listeners can follow each twist and turn of logic. They can engage in imaginary verbal banters with the interlocutors, and, in general, participate in the interplay of the stories. Since most stories not only effect but also reveal popular roles, ideas, and values, they allow listeners to see parts of themselves reflected back upon themselves, thereby confirming and amplifying these roles, ideas, and values.

Whereas most American stories are written for young children, listeners to Native American stories vary in age from very young to very old. Adults form an important part of storytelling audiences. Stories help older Native People stay in touch with their inner child. Most Native American stories have multiple layers of understanding, which is why they speak to all ages.

Some listeners have never heard the story while others have heard it or a similar story many times before. Hearing the same story several times and memorizing it add to the power of stories to seep into the consciousness of listeners. Many Native People have written about how they would think about stories long after they were told; the stories resonated and reverberated in their minds and souls.

Stories are magical, in part, because listeners can understand and appreciate them on different levels and because listeners can hear them over and over. Many stories of Native People intentionally include ambiguous terms, multiple meanings, several levels of symbolism, abstract morals, and subtle nuances, innuendos, and rhythms. Unlike most American stories that state points directly, many Native stories purposely encourage listeners to infer meaning.

Stories serve as springboards for curious minds, striving to facilitate discovery as children apply the lessons learned to their own lives. Michael J. Caduto and Abenaki Joseph Bruchac, two famed storytellers today, explain how stories help children become "Keepers of the Earth":

Tell children a story and they listen with their whole beings. Lead children to touch and understand a grasshopper, a rock, a flower, a ray of sunlight and you begin to establish connections between children and their surroundings. Have them look at a tree – feel it, smell it, taste its sap, study its many parts and how they work. Help them to understand how it is part of a forest community of plants, animals, rocks, soil and water. . . . how all things are intertwined. Keep the children at the center of their learning encounters. Build on these experiences with activities that help them to care for, and take care of, the Earth and other people.[5]

Native American stories generally encourage listeners to find their own answers to life's everyday problems. For example, most American children's stories end "happily ever after," directly stating or implying that the lives of the good characters will be perfect forever. They will not age, become ugly or fat, or experience want, doubt, frustration, or pain. Good and evil differ sharply; little gray area exists. By contrast, many Native American teaching stories possess no ending, in order to encourage children to become self-sufficient, to think for themselves, and to turn inward to discover their own resources rather than depending on the views of other people. Allowing children to find solutions themselves makes the learned knowledge belong to them. Since the solutions represent choices they make as listeners, they now "own" the knowledge.

Some stories of Native People have unhappy endings, mimicking real life experiences. The Nez Perce story "Yellow Jacket and Ant" typifies stories with unhappy endings. Coyote turns Yellow Jacket and Ant into stone, and they are "locked in each other's arms" when they refuse to stop fighting. The story also deals with other lessons, including the negative consequences that occur when two living beings refuse to get along. Since the fight concerned Yellow Jacket's refusal to eat anywhere except on the rock where he always ate, the story further supports the idea that no one can possess or own rocks and encourages sharing and cooperation.[6]

Native American stories deal with a plethora of topics. Ojibway George Copway states, "There is not a lake or mountain that has not connected with it some story of delight or wonder, and nearly every beast and bird is the subject of the storyteller." A large number of stories talk about creation, giving listeners a sense of where they came from and who they are. Numerous stories explain peculiarities of nature such as "Why Trees Lose Their Leaves." Many, if not most, stories include animals, often explaining why animals look or behave in the ways they do. The following story names exemplify this: "Why the Chipmunk Has the Black Stripe" (Haudenosaunee), "How Mosquitoes Came to Be" (Tlingit), "Why Mole Lives Underground" (Cherokee), "How Coyote Got His Cunning" (Karok), and "Why the Owl Has Big Eyes" (Haudenosaunee). Other common topics of stories include the coming of corn; the changing of seasons; the sacred four directions; the four elements of nature (earth, water, fire, air); the birth, death, and rebirth of people and nature; and the celebration of war heroes.[7]

Native American stories affect and reflect their beliefs that people and the natural world are related and that no being is superior to any other. In story after story, the sun, moon, stars, trees, rocks, clouds, and animals are alive, possessing a soul, and endowed with feelings. They often interact in stories with people. In some stories, people change into animals or animals change into people.

Stories provide insights into the fears, values, and feelings of a people. All people have a story to tell, and all people's stories involve pleasure and pain. But what constitutes pleasure and what constitutes pain vary across different people and different cultures. For example, whereas American stories often portray nature as frightening and dangerous, most stories of the Native People present nature as gentle and accommodating. Almost all Native stories include nature since almost all stories take place outdoors.

The values generally advanced in Native American stories differ from those usually put forth in American stories. Whereas American stories may be compared to report talk, Native stories may be compared to rapport talk because they often focus on cooperation, compromise, sharing, interdependence, pride in the success of the community, and connections between the personal and the planetary. They stress the importance of establishing, nurturing, and negotiating relationships with oneself, other people, and everything in the world. They reinforce the importance of people, Earth, and place – even when the stories are not about such matters.[8]

The Cherokee story "How the Milky Way Came to Be" shows neighbors concerned with one family's problems. The people meet and give everyone an equal chance to speak. They find a solution without hurting the dog in the story. Cooperation and community triumph.[9]

In the Onondaga tale "The Earth on Turtle's Back," a duck, beaver, loon, muskrat, and turtle all work to bring up the Earth and place it on the back of the turtle. The determination of the muskrat is especially noteworthy; he succeeded where others had failed.[10]

The Spokane story "Speela and Wood-Tick" advises listeners to act carefully, warning that if people treat people and animals without kindness and respect, they will suffer negative consequences in the end. The Winnnebago story "How Skunks Came to Be" has a similar message, but puts it in a form similar to Aesop's Fables: The last line of the story tells the moral. Thus, this story ends, "Moral: Don't be vain."[11]

While the heroes in American stories tend to be large and powerful, the heroes in Native American stories are often the small and powerless. For example, in the Pawnee story "Song of the Wren," a priest feels enchanted by the beautiful sound of a bird. He then discovers that the bird is a wren, "the smallest, the least powerful of birds, that seemed to be most glad and to pour out in ringing melody to the rising sun its delight in life." The priest concludes, "Here is a teaching for my people. Everyone can be happy; even the most insignificant can have his song of thanks."[12]

The stories of Native Americans often show listeners new ways to view situations. They are more likely than their American counterparts to start and end from a position of curiosity. The purpose of several stories is to encourage listeners not to think like the storytellers, but just to think. Therefore, many stories lack definite solutions; some end in an open-ended manner.

The Hopi story "Maybe" exemplifies a story without an ending. The story begins with a poor, elderly main character whose horse runs away. When his neighbors say, "This is indeed a great misfortune," the elder replies, "Maybe," and smiles. The elder continues to reply "maybe" when his neighbors react to his horse's returning with other horses, when his grandson breaks his leg while trying to tame one of the horses, and when this broken leg keeps the grandson from going off to war. By the end of the story, even the neighbors say "maybe" to each other.[13]

The Brule Sioux story "Remaking the World" typifies a story that advocates peace and leaves the ending of the story up to the actions of the listeners. The Creator told how he made and then destroyed the first and second worlds because the people behaved badly. Then he gave the following sage advice: "Now, if you have learned how to behave like human beings and how to live in peace with each other and with the other living things – the two-legged, the four-legged, the many-legged, the fliers, the no-legs, the green plants of this universe – then all will be well. But if you make this world bad and ugly, then I will destroy this world too. It's up to you."[14]

Native Americans do not shield themselves or their children from the stark realities of life. Their stories deal with the hungry and homeless and with the despair and desolation of the downtrodden. In stories they deal with bodily parts, bodily functions, and sexual acts much more directly and explicitly than do their non-Native counterparts. No dirty words exist in the Native tongues; the concept of obscene is foreign. Native Americans openly use the words *rape, penis, vulva, make love, intercourse, copulation, urinate, defecate, breast, anus, naked* and *fart* in their stories, not considering them obscene. For a good laugh, try to imagine the White River Sioux story "What's This? My Balls for Your Dinner?" being read at a local public library or elementary school in the United States! Iktome invites his friend Coyote for dinner. As he leaves to hunt some additional game, he warns his wife, "Don't let him stick his hands under your robe. He likes to do that." And when Coyote arrives, he is soon found "quickly sticking his hand under the woman's robe and between her legs. . . . He joked, he chucked the woman under the chin, he tickled her under the arms, and pretty soon he was all the way in her, way, way up inside her." Afterward, Coyote asks Iktome's wife what's for dinner. She responds, "'Why, you *itka,* you *susa,* your eggs, your balls, your big hairy balls! We always have the balls of our guests for dinner.'"

Similarly, try to imagine an American mother reading the Zuni story "Teaching the Mudheads to Copulate" to her children at night. The Mudheads were not bright people. After trying to teach them other things, the instructor said, "'I'll try one thing more. I'm going to show you how to copulate.'" A fat woman volunteered. First, the instructor "copulated with her in the simplest way – from the back, as dogs do." The Mudheads could not "find the right opening. One did it in the anus . . . another in the navel."[15]

In addition to dealing candidly with bodily functions and the act of love making, the stories of Native People openly discuss death and rebirth, topics rarely found in American stories. Native American stories talk about death and rebirth as inherent and natural parts of life. Some emphasize that the soul never dies but eventually becomes another creature as people die and become animals, animals die and become people, and so forth. In a typical story from the Inuit in Canada, a human became a dog, seal, wolf, caribou, walrus, and then seal again. In *Wisdom of the Elders: Sacred Native Stories of Nature,* David Suzuki and Peter Knudson continue the story:

This time the seal decided to sacrifice itself willingly to a hunter, whose wife happened to be barren. As she flayed the seal's lifeless carcass, its wandering soul passed into her body, and she became pregnant at last. In time, she gave birth to a healthy boy, who became a hunter and was very skilled, partly because of the wisdom his soul had accumulated during the course of its challenging, interspecies journey.[16]

Many Native American stories demonstrate the consequences of poor behavior. The Cochiti story "The Neglectful Mother" does this while also conveying the message that families are about love and caring, not about blood. The plot seems like some American films: Mother Crow leaves her eggs in the nest. Mother Hawk hatches the eggs, gets food for them, and watches them grow up. Mother Crow returns, wanting her children. She takes Mother Hawk to court before the king of the birds. He decides in favor of Mother Hawk and says to Mother Crow, "Don't cry. It's your own fault." Most similar American tales side with the birth mother.[17]

Native American stories often deal with experiences that actually happened to members of the tribe. Stories give children real heroes, something sorely lacking in contemporary society for most American children whose heroes are fantasy characters on television such as Batman, Superman, Wonder Woman, Power Rangers, and so forth. By dealing with actual events, Native American stories provide realistic positive role models whose virtues children try to emulate.

Whereas in most American tales, women are described as helpless and pretty, women in Native American tales often exhibit qualities of strength and courage. Wood-Tick, the female in the Spokane story "Speela and Wood-Tick," is strong and knowledgeable. "The Sick Buzzard" – a story found in the Seneca, Konawa, and Cherokee nations – also portrays a positive woman hero. In fact, one of the most popular cultural heroes in a Native American story is the heroine White Buffalo Calf Woman, who brought the sacred pipe of peace to the Lakota people.[18]

Not all people in the prose tales of Native People, however, are all good or all bad. Many are like most people – they have a mixture of good and bad qualities. For example, in the Abenaki story "Gluscabi and the Game Animals," Gluscabi tricks animals into his game bag, and afterward he releases them when his Grandmother tells him that if he keeps all the animals in a bag they will get sick and die. Listeners can relate to characters in stories who are similar to themselves, characters who make mistakes, characters who learn some things the hard way, characters composed of good and bad characteristics. Listeners can identify with these characters on a gut level.[19]

The coyote, a central character in many Native American prose narratives, is an example of a character who conjoins good and evil; he sometimes plays a trickster and he sometimes plays a hero. Often cunning and devious, he sometimes appears in the guise of another animal. He often surprises and acts in spontaneous and unpredictable ways, warning of the folly of surrendering to limits and human vulnerabilities. Often he provides comic relief.

Like other Native American stories, coyote stories usually make an effort to teach. Most obviously, a coyote often tells listeners how not to act; when he behaves inappropriately and irreverently, people do not want to behave like him. A typical example is the Jicarilla Apache story "Coyote Steals Tobacco from Crow." When Coyote would not share the tobacco, the people in his camp played tricks on him to get it. The story ends, "That's how he lost his tobacco. He went away ashamed." In another typical story, "Coyote and Buffalo," Buffalo Bull gives Coyote a cow with the following instructions, "'Never kill this cow, Coyote. When you are hungry, cut off a little of her fat with your flint knife. Rub ashes on the wound. The cut will heal. This way, you will have meat forever.'" Coyote disobeys these instructions and kills the cow. Crows and magpies come and eat all the meat, an old woman takes the marrow, and the bones turn into sticks. Buffalo Bull refuses to give Coyote another cow. Rather than "happily ever after," the story concludes, "Coyote went back to his village. When he got there he found everyone had moved. They had heard what he had done and were ashamed to be in the same place with him."[20]

Using stories as a primary way of educating young people differs significantly from using television as a primary means. Because children only hear stories, they must imagine what characters look like, how they sound, and other relevant details. Rhetorical theorist Marshall McLuhan discussed how different media affected messages. According to McLuhan, television is a cool medium because it shows a picture and requires little participation on the part of viewers. Stories, on the other hand, are hot media because they play on the imagination and require a high degree of participation on the part of listeners. Television fills the mind. Television guides and previews of episodes give viewers hints of what to expect. Commercial advertisements interrupt the flow of thoughts. Stories, on the other hand, summon the mind and encourage expansiveness of the mind. They leave more room for the inner imagination.

Across the country people watch a television show at exactly the same time. After an episode, a person in New York can talk to a person in Florida comparing reactions to "who shot J. R." By contrast, even if the same story is told at the same time in two different places, the stories are not exactly the same.

Storybooks also give the exact same story over and over again. Even before children can read, many know when to turn the page because the story is the same each time. The book distances the storyteller from the listener. Knowing the story is written down and can be read again and again makes attentive listening less important. Illustrations in storybooks tell children what characters look like, leaving less to the imagination. Almost all people in this country, for example, instantly recognize Cinderella, Snow White, and the Cat in the Hat.

Stories in capitalist societies such as the United States also have an economic imperative. They are functional commodities. With mass media and technology, American story characters do not remain in books. They come to life in movies, audiotapes, and videotapes. They become commercialized; children may own a Cinderella lunch box, a Snow White doll, or some Superman sheets. Certainly society has commercialized Pocahontas, but this story belongs to Americans more than to Native People.

Reading storybooks and watching television occur in solitude or sometimes in familial settings. By contrast, storytelling is a communal experience, linking storyteller to listeners and listeners to each other. Storytelling also links all to past generations who have heard the same story and to future generations who will hear the same story. Stories, then, bond generations together in an oral tradition. Shared histories, hopes, fears, legacies, and safe harbors get passed along in whispers.

Another significant difference between Native American stories and American television or books is the element of time. On television, all problems are resolved before the end of the program. The size of a book indicates the length of the story. Since children do not know how long a story will last, they also do not know if central characters will resolve their problems in the next two minutes or in the next two hours. And, since all stories do not have a happy ending, listeners do not even know if the central characters will resolve their dilemmas at all. This suspense gives stories a spellbinding quality, seizing listeners like a good suspense novel.

A related issue is that all elements in a story occur in the moment, encouraging listeners to focus on the present. Abenaki Joseph Bruchac explains, "When Native People speak of the time when animals could talk, they are speaking in the present tense."[21]

The stories of Native People usually include structural markers. Typical beginnings include "Would you like to hear a story?" (Haudenosaunee), "When the world was new" (Seneca), and "They say it happened long ago" or "Long ago" (Pima and Papago). Typical endings include "That is all" (Haudenosaunee), "That is the end" (Abenaki, Pima, and Papago), "And so the story goes" (Abenaki), and "That is the center of the basket" (Pima and Papago). This last phrase means that the different parts of the story have been woven together.

Sometimes storytellers use beginnings that involve the audience by asking them to respond. Zuni storytellers typically begin by saying, "Now we are taking it up." Audiences reply, "Yes, indeed." Storytellers continue, "Now it begins to be made." Audiences again reply, "Yes, indeed." More simply, Yakima storytellers usually begin, "This is the way it was," and listeners respond, "Yes."

Involving the audience by having them participate often occurs during the story. For example, storytellers may tell listeners to say "Hey" every time the storyteller says "Ho." Having audiences respond throughout stories helps to keep them awake, aware, and involved.

Native American stories are rich with commonplace details, vivid imagery, and short, straightforward thought units. The simplicity of stories makes them easier to digest. They often use the techniques of exaggeration, distortion, and caricature. Although many stories employ humor, few are uproariously funny; rather, they seek to make listeners smile while understanding a serious point. The language of Native American stories is usually concrete and colorful, and, according to American standards, is often off-color.

Many of the details in the stories of Native People concern place — specific geographical locations, remarks about the terrain, comments about the climate, and so forth. Whereas American stories, like American culture, seem to emphasize time, Native American stories, like Native American culture, seem to focus on place. In his foreword to Barry Lopez's book on Coyote, Barre Toelken ascribed this characteristic to the live contexts of the original stories. He wrote,

A sense of locality, a feeling for place — both geographic and sacred — infuses these dramatic narratives. Small details of geography, seemingly minor references to the color of a feather, the direction of the wind, the smell of grass or water, are all signals which awaken memories, trigger recognition, and allow for the re-experiencing of the texture and quality of a life locally known as it becomes a context for Old Man Coyote's universal adventures.[22]

In order to maintain interest and survive through the ages, most Native American stories use poignant, descriptive language and a plethora of metaphors, allowing listeners to see and hear the messages. Like imagery in the rest of their discourse, most of the metaphors come from nature. Because they are delivered orally, the language is more colloquial and informal than in most American stories. Circuitous trains of thought and ungrammatical sentences, especially in their original languages, often creep into stories. Listeners take for granted gaps in logical reasoning.

Many Native American stories involve the number four – do things four times, do things over four days, carry four bundles, and so forth. Native People consider the number four sacred since there are four directions, four stages of life, and four elemental forces – earth, air, water, and fire. Lame Deer declared, "We Sioux do everything by fours."[23]

Storytellers communicate large portions of their messages nonverbally. Some include American sign language as part of their presentation. Rate, volume, pitch, emphasis, intonation, inflection, rhythm, pace, pronunciation, and articulation constitute just some of the ways storytellers communicate with their voice. They also use eye movements, facial expressions, hand gestures, and body motions to engage their audiences. Speaking stories forces words to come alive. The words carry the storytellers' breath, tone, mood, and feelings.

Storytellers communicate messages not only through words and nonverbal behaviors, but also through silences. The placement of pauses and the duration of pauses are important rhetorical tools. Dennis Tedlock, Professor of Anthropology and Religion at Boston University, claims, "The spoken word is never delivered in the gray masses of boxed-in words we call prose; indeed, according to Frieda Goldman-Eisler, as much as half the time spent in delivering spontaneous discourse is devoted to silence, and 'pausing is as much a part of the act of speaking as the vocal utterance of words itself.'"[24]

CONCLUSIONS

Storytellers are crucial members of tribal communities. They serve as conduits of the oral tradition from one generation to the next. They are rememberers, educators, entertainers, historians and carriers of tradition.

In the Native American way of thinking, where the physical and spiritual worlds are one, the concept of "myth," as most Americans understand the term, does not exist. Native People do not distinguish between stories, myths, legends, fables, parables, and tales. No story of any sort is considered fictitious. All tell the truth.

As a group, Native People follow the adage, "There are only two things we can give our children. One is roots. The other is wings." Stories give children a firm foundation of roots in the Earth from which to grow. Allowing children to determine the outcome of some of the stories gives them wings to fly like eagles, soaring higher and higher. Just as learning is a never-ending process, so too, people can never stop learning from stories. Stories deal with timeless topics, varied vistas, infinite choices, and expanding horizons.

Native People say the act of storytelling constitutes a ceremony. Taos Pueblo Terry Tafoya, Executive Director of Tamanawit Unlimited, an international consulting firm, puts it this way: "Every time we tell a story it's a ceremony. In English, we translate it that when you tell a story you 'wet it with your breath.' You give it life, just as when you give water to a seed it blossoms."[25]

Stories continue to live long after they are told. People ponder their purposes, meditate about their meanings, and study their symbols. They interact with the stories as if the stories were close friends. Greg Sarris, Miwok and Pomo, and Professor of English at the University of California, Los Angeles, says, "The way Western man is taught to read is to find the meaning, the symbols. Instead I say no, a story is not something you figure out the meaning of, but something you carry with you the rest of your life to talk back and forth with."[26]

In their book, *Storytelling: Art and Technique,* Augusta Baker and Ellin Greene say, "Storytelling brings to the listeners heightened awareness — a sense of wonder, of mystery, of reverence for life." They quote Lewis Carroll who "called stories 'love gifts.'" I conclude this chapter by thanking Native People for imparting so many "love gifts."

Prayers and Songs of Celebration and Purification

The oldest human ceremony is that of giving thanks to the earth, the mother of us all.

Saying of the Iroquois

It is as important to me to sing as to draw breath.

Orpingalik, Netsilik Inuit

Rituals play a powerful role in the oratory and life of Native Americans. Many of their speeches deal with ceremonial cycles, unchanging rituals that help preserve the history and heritage of their ancestors. The purposes of most ceremonies are to celebrate, praising the Great Spirit for all of creation, and to purify, restoring harmony and balance to both the individual and the universe. In general, ceremonies help Native People create a covenant with all creatures, reconnecting themselves to every part of the world. Native American ceremonies often involve expressing gratitude, singing, chanting, dancing, fasting, and feasting.[1]

As in the other chapters, I need to oversimplify and overgeneralize; not all Judeo-Christians and not all Native People share the ideas attributed to each group. My purpose also is not to say that any group of spiritual beliefs is better than any other; I try merely to point out similarities and differences between the beliefs of traditional Native People and the Judeo-Christian beliefs that are dominant in the United States as expressed in prayers and songs.

By definition, religion and spirituality deal with ethical and moral behaviors, ideals toward which humans can only strive. In reading this chapter, we might remember the words of former congressman and minister Adam Clayton Powell, Jr., "No one can say that Christianity has failed. It has never been tried."

Forest Cathedral. Illustration by Francene Hart.

In order to contrast the spiritual beliefs expressed in Native American prayers with those of the Judeo-Christian religions, it is necessary first to summarize some Judeo-Christian beliefs and practices.

JUDEO-CHRISTIAN SPIRITUAL BELIEFS AND PRACTICES

Judeo-Christian religions speak of God as an anthropomorphic being who dwells apart from people in the heavens above. Separations exist, dividing God from people and people from animals. Christians believe in the Holy Trinity – the Father, Son, and Holy Spirit; when Christians pray, they do so to all three parts of the Trinity.

According to many Judeo-Christian prayers, people represent the climax, the crown of the cosmic story of creation. The birth of man is the central event in the creation story and in the history of the cosmos.

Judeo-Christian religions speak of God in authoritarian and patriarchal ways: all-powerful, all-knowing, all-controlling. God directs the course of human destiny. Judeo-Christian prayers often use the language of royalty such as king, kingdom, crown, and glory and military language such as conquer and overpower. Frequently prayers use the language of competition such as victory and triumph. The role of people is to serve and praise God, again emphasizing God's power; He is master, the people are His servants. In general people are passive, acted upon by God. Consider, for example, the words of the Lord's Prayer:

Our Father, who art in Heaven, hallowed be Thy name. Thy kingdom come, Thy will be done, on earth as it is in heaven. Give us this day our daily bread, and forgive us our trespasses as we forgive those who trespass against us, and lead us not into temptation, but deliver us from evil. For the kingdom, the power and the glory are Yours now and forever. Amen.

Some Christians state their religion is the True Way. They send out missionaries to convert other people. For many years missionaries went to various Native nations to convert those whom they viewed as "heathens" or "pagans," to salvage the savage, so to speak.

Most Christians and some Jews believe in original sin. All people are born sinful. Because of the fall of Adam and Eve, human beings are imperfect and flawed. Often words in prayers talk about people's sins and ask for forgiveness. Consider, for example, the popular Christian hymn "Amazing Grace": "Amazing Grace, how sweet the sound that saved a wretch like me."

God judges the actions of people. Christians say He uses a system of rewards and punishments. Put simplistically, when good people die, they go to heaven; when bad people die, they go to hell. People spend their lives trying to achieve eternal salvation, making the purpose of life future oriented: People spend the present preparing for the future.

Most Judeo-Christian ceremonies take place indoors. Sometimes elaborate cathedrals and majestic stained glass windows honor God. Most prayers are read from prayerbooks. A liturgy exists; much ceremony is codified in print. Priests, preachers, rabbis, and other members of the clergy usually stand on bemas higher than the members of the congregations, who sit in rows.

Judeo-Christian religions talk about God and the world as a fundamentally finite place. Things change and cycles occur, but within a framework of an inanimate, static system. God is a noun. Miracles are separate from the normal course of events. They happen infrequently; something is not considered truly miraculous if it happens often.

NATIVE AMERICAN SPIRITUAL BELIEFS AND PRACTICES

A large amount of rhetoric of Native People concerns the importance of prayer. Santee Dakota Ohiyesa's statement in 1911 applies to almost all Native nations in almost all periods of time: "In the life of the Indian there was only one inevitable duty, – the duty of prayer – the daily recognition of the Unseen and Eternal. His daily devotions were more necessary to him than daily food. . . . He sees no need in setting apart one day in seven as a holy day, since to him all days are God's."[2]

Blackfoot Betty Cooper, Director of the Pikuni Family Healing Center, also expresses how for Native People religion is not separate from life, but life itself: "Being in touch with the Great Spirit is not just something you do on Sunday, it's not just when you get up in the morning or kneel by your bed at night. It's every moment of your life. . . . Every day, every hour, everywhere, through all living things." When religion occurs all the time, even the most mundane tasks become sacred. It is as if Native People are familiar with the Zen Buddhist saying, "After the ecstasy, the laundry," or the opposite, "After the laundry, the ecstasy." Terry Tafoya, Taos Pueblo psychotherapist and healer, explains, "In our tradition, every time you take a sip of water it's a religious act, because it's a form of purification. It's not big and fancy, but it still has the same spiritual meaning: to make those small everyday occasions of life into sacred ones."[3]

Native People frequently talk about the oneness of everyone and everything. No separation exists between people and God, often referred to as the Creator, Great Spirit, and Great Mystery. The Great Spirit lives in all that is, ever was, and ever will be. God and the self are one. God exists everywhere, hiding behind every leaf, every blade of grass, every weed. The Great Spirit interpenetrates ordinary life, speaking to people through beauty, truth, nature, and relationships. Native American scholar Carlos Cordero explains how the Judeo-Christian-Islamic spiritual beliefs are not only different and incompatible with Native ones, but are antagonistic: "The Judeo-Christian-Islam tradition established a hierarchical relationship between the Creator and humans. The Creator is above and the humans are below." Native People were "never defined as being out of a state of grace with the universe. We weren't kicked out of paradise." Rather, he says, Native people believe "in a reciprocal relationship between humans and the Creator."[4]

Just as no separation exists between people and the Creator, no separation exists between people and other sentient beings. Whereas Judeo-Christian religions speak of humans as the only life form possessing mind and soul, Native People say trees, rocks, mountains, and animals also possess a mind and soul. In his book, *Crying for a Dream*, Richard Erdoes talks about a panel discussion involving him and Sioux medicine man Lame Deer:

> A missionary priest turned to Lame Deer and said, "Chief, I respect your beliefs. My church is built in the shape of a tipi, my vestments are beaded, the Sacred Pipe hangs next to the cross on my wall. I participate in Indian ceremonies. I tell you – The Great Spirit and God are the same. Sweet Medicine and Christ are the same. The Pipe and the cross, they are all the same. There is no real difference between your and my religions."
>
> Lame Deer looked at the missionary for some time and then said, "Father, in your religion do animals have a soul?"
>
> The priest answered with a slightly embarrassed smile, "Chief, you got me there!"[5]

The spiritual ideas of Native People are based on the inherent goodness of all living beings and of the Earth that gives birth and supports the lives of all beings. Many Native American prayers express the goodness of people, of other living beings, and of nature. Native Americans do not speak about original sin; in fact, they speak about their lack of belief in original sin. Prayer after prayer expresses how all beings are unique, precious, and sacred children of the cosmos, carefully nurtured into existence over billions of years and not repeatable in time or space. For instance, Arvol Looking Horse, Keeper of the Sacred Pipe for the Lakota people, states succinctly, "A person is born sacred." The prayers of Native Americans speak about how people are pure spirits on a human journey rather than impure spirits on a spiritual journey.[6]

Native Americans frequently express how people are not more or less important than any other life form. They talk about how Judeo-Christian religions do not recognize the unchanging and unchangeable relationship between people and the environment. Pawnee John Echohawk discusses "the failure of organized religions to understand, comprehend, and include within their doctrine this understanding of the basic relationship between human beings and the universe – that they are part of it and not in control of it." Not surprisingly, many Native discourses on prayer concern life forms other than people. Oglala Sioux holy man Black Elk declared, "Perhaps you have noticed that even in the very lightest breeze you can hear the voice of the cottonwood tree; this we understand is its prayer to the Great Spirit, for not only men, but all things and all beings pray to Him continually in different ways."[7]

Similar to amen, a word used at the end of most Judeo-Christian prayers, Lakota, Dakota, and Nakota people say *Mitakuye oyasin,* meaning "for all my relations." This phrase refers not only to people's immediate families and other tribal members but also to all sentient beings. Osage-Lutheran scholar George Tinker quotes a teacher who suggests that a more accurate translation of the phrase would be, "For all the above-me and below-me and around-me things: That is for all my relations."[8]

Most Native American ceremonies express gratitude, rapture, and ecstasy for life's simple pleasures including the exquisite Earth. In prayer Native People revel in reverence and infinite wonder. They talk about life as a glorious celebration, a cosmic jubilation; their prayers celebrate the human spirit and remind people of the possibilities for boundless, unlimited joy. Prayers communicate that everyone and everything are perfumes to breathe in, treasures to share and celebrate. A typical prayer follows: "Grandfathers, this woman has nothing to ask for; she only wishes to give thanks for the Blessings she has been given." Most of the expressions of gratitude do not celebrate individual triumphs, but rather the beauty and bounty of the entire Earth. In prayer after prayer, song after song, and dance after dance, traditional Native People embrace and express exaltation for the expansiveness of the universe and voice their respect and reverence for the Creator. They immerse themselves and their lives in the grandeur and wonder of the universe, and with genuine joy and heartfelt humility, they give thanks to the Creator.[9]

In her book, *Songs of Bleeding,* written to honor women's Moon Time, Spider begins with the "Song of Each New Sun":

> With honor I greet this new day
> Great Mystery, I thank you for all of my gifts
> Mother Earth, I thank you for the honor of sleeping and walking on your breast
> Brother Sun, I thank you for returning your warmth and light this day
> Sister of the South, I thank you for the beauty and laughter you bring today
> Sister of the West, I thank you for the dreams and visions of the night
> Sister of the North, I thank you for the lessons and teachings you bring today
> Sister of the East, I thank you for the inspiration of my being here today
> Grandmothers, I thank you for your guidance as you speak through the womb cycle today
> All my relations, I honor your presence in this world we share together
> I give only kindness and love to all that I meet today.[10]

Almost all Native nations celebrate the fertility and nourishment of the holy ground. Many nations celebrate the first time a woman menstruates. Many Native women celebrate their "moon time" each month, ritualistically connecting their blood with the blood of the Earth. There are prayers to bring rain, enrich a harvest, provide good hunting, heal physical and emotional ailments, and bring victory in war. Numerous prayers express gratitude for a new day, for the ability to breathe, and for sentient beings who give freely of their lives.

Before killing animals or cutting trees, Native People express their appreciation to the particular animals and trees for giving of their lives. For example, a Kwakiutl woman gave this prayer of thanksgiving while cutting a cedar tree: "Look at me, friend! I come to ask for your dress . . . for you are really willing to give us your dress. . . . I pray, friend, not to feel angry with me on account of what I am going to do to you." Significantly, Native Americans say animals *give* their lives to people rather than their lives *being taken* by hunters. The people ask the animals and plants to give their lives; if an animal or plant responds "no," the people move on to a different animal or plant. In appreciation for animals and plants giving their lives, Native Americans give something back in return, such as tobacco or a song. For Native People, hunting is an act of worship, not an act of entertainment.[11]

Prayers dealing with hunting and food also connect speakers and listeners to the vitality of creation and to the interdependence of everything in the cosmos. Popovi Da, a Pueblo potter, explains, "Our Pueblo people eat gently, recognizing with inner feelings that the corn or the squash were at one time growing, cared for, each a plant alive, now prepared to become part of us, of our bodies and our minds, quite sacred. We reflect on the plant." Many prayers pay tribute to the soul of the prey.[12]

For Native People, part of expressing thanks involves giving. Native Americans say they receive wisdom, food, gifts, and so forth to share with others. By "others," they mean beings in both the physical and spiritual worlds. Native People say they measure people's wealth by what the people give away, not by what the people possess; this is the true meaning of "Indian Giver."

Prayer also serves to purify. Many rites of purification work like a filter for people's consciousness, purging and purifying. This clears the center of the consciousness for creative changes. Many Native American prayers try to touch parts of people that will transform them, aid awareness, free fettered souls, and open pure parts of the self. Ceremonies of fasting help purify people's minds and spirits to encourage all people to manifest clear vision and compassion. Generally after praying, Native People feel refreshed, revitalized, and closer to a state of at-one-ment with themselves and with everyone and everything on Earth.

In addition to thanking and purifying, Native Americans hold ceremonies to create spiritual unity and balance, to live in conscious oneness with other people and with the Earth. A. La Vonne Brown Ruoff, Professor of English at the University of Illinois at Chicago, says, "American Indians use ritual dramas to order their spiritual and physical world. The tool for creating this order is the power of the word, whether it is chanted, spoken, or sung." The lack of separation between the natural and supernatural worlds adds to the harmony created by prayer. For example, if Native People pray for peace, they first pray for peace, then become like peace, and then are peace.[13]

Native People express genuine confusion and disagreement with the dominant society's desire to control and dominate. Instead, they talk about the need to surrender, to flow with the waves of the universe, trusting that the waves will take them exactly where they need to go. For them religion is more like poetry than theology.

When praying, Native People rarely make materialistic requests. Rather than beseeching God for something, they generally ask for qualities such as the strength or courage to handle particular situations. They usually pray for others first and themselves last. They pray for the ability to harmonize with the Earth's energy to make crops abundant, waters pure, air clean, and fires strong. One Native individual responded to the pressure by Christian missionaries to convert him by saying, "My worship is communion, not groveling."[14]

Native American spirituality is meant to be experienced, not studied or simply recited. In general, people are active, co-creators with God. The purpose of life is to live each moment fully, vibrantly, and authentically. There is no original sin, salvation, or heaven and hell. All prayers take place in nowness, in the perpetual present, the eternal now.

Native People speak about living prayers. As people inhale and exhale, they become part of each other's prayers. And, the breath of the people praying adds to the life-giving breath of the universe. The life power of prayers adds to their intensity.

In general, Native American praying is a more engaging experience than Judeo-Christian praying. Some Native American praying also involves fasting, sweating, piercing, and/or exposing themselves to the elements of nature. Most Native American praying involves people letting down their common defenses and dealing with primal utterances, raw expressions of emotion. In many prayers they experience intense pain and suffering, joy and elation. This makes many of their prayers exquisitely painful and eloquently provocative.

Most rituals are communal ceremonies based on the cycles of the sun and moon or the movements of the stars or seasons. Ceremonies evoke kinship — a coming together. Ceremonial rhetoric serves as a means and extension of this kinship.

Other ceremonies such as vision quests are solitary vigils of nonstop praying. Native People say if they really know themselves — the secrets of their hearts, their innermost joys and sorrows — they can then empathize with others and take their place as a part of the Earth's heart. Individual consciousness recedes, giving way to an all-embracing cosmic consciousness, a peaceful union.

Silent prayers, unprepared and unrehearsed expressions of the heart, take place in Judeo-Christian religious ceremonies, but generally far more time is given for silent prayer in Native American religious ceremonies. And whereas most Westerners are uncomfortable with silence, Native ceremonies generally include soundless time. An abundance of Native American discourse concerns the sounds of silence. Whether alone or solitary in a communal experience, people try to still their minds, making themselves effortlessly aware, alert yet passive. Native Americans say that maintaining silence is an art. To really commune, people must go beyond the noise of words, beyond the noise of sounds, to a simple, serene stillness.

Most Native American ceremonies take place outdoors, on sacred soil or holy ground. The people usually go barefoot to feel the grooves and bumps in the Earth. Sometimes they wear moccasins to allow themselves to feel the ground more than if they wore other types of shoes. Walking barefoot or in soft moccasins connects each footstep with the Earth. Bowing down and kissing the ground constitutes a common wordless prayer for many Native People; kissing the Earth honors the Mother and surrenders to Her wisdom. Algonquian Tamarack Song explains how spirituality differs from religion; his explanation provides an accurate description of a Native American church: "The Forest is my Cathedral — the moss is its floor, the branches overhead are its roof, the spire of Elder Pine is its steeple. Its incense is the essence of pitch and blossom, its choral voice is the Gift of bird and Wind, its altar is the vision of Sun and Moon through stout branches." Native Americans, then, speak of the Earth as their altar.[15]

Native Americans also speak of the human body as a holy vessel. They talk about the need to revere the body and consider it a sacred sanctuary that shelters the soul. The naked body is the original holy place. They paint and adorn the body to express its sanctity. They mark rites of passage by adorning the body in particular ways, and by putting the body through particular physical trials. They speak about the need to accept the body, own it, belong to it, be open to it, and live in it. In short, they talk about coming home physically.

The sweat lodge ceremony takes place in a sweat lodge that physically resembles the womb. Many Native American prayers talk about how people enter and exit the world through the round womb of the Earth. They return to their source, their origins, the wellspring of creation. In all-male or all-female sweats, people generally participate in the nude. In contemporary mixed sweats, people often wear clothing, but one of the purposes of the sweat lodge ceremony is to help people feel the vulnerability of nakedness in order to expand the inner sanctum and carry them to heightened states of consciousness.

Most ceremonies take place in circles where people face one another. Most are highly participatory. Platforms or podiums rarely exist. Native Americans have spiritual leaders called medicine people, but these leaders generally pray in ceremonies along with everyone else.

In the ceremonies of Native People, no one is considered more important than anyone else. Native Americans have no messiahs, martyrs, saints, hierophants, avatars, intermediaries, angels, devils, or gurus. Everyone communicates directly with God. The Great Spirit speaks through vibrations with all creatures and directly hears all creatures. Virtually all ritualistic rhetoric talks about respecting a loving, tender Creator. Virtually no rhetoric talks about fearing the Great Spirit.

Of course, in all religions prayers come from people's hearts. In an oral culture, however, people say all prayers from memory. Prayer books do not exist; people do not read any prayers. Lame Deer, a Sioux medicine man, identified this significant difference between Native American and Judeo-Christian praying: "When an Indian prays he doesn't read a lot of words out of a book."[16]

Native American prayer includes and, in fact, is a catalyst for altered states of awareness, clear visions, and heightened states of consciousness. Native People make no distinction between the natural and supernatural world. The commonplace and the celestine naturally commingle. The mundane and the majestic merge, making a magical mystery. Native People speak about how people create magic every time they open their mouths and use words or even sounds. According to Native Americans, religion is about magic, miracles, and mysticism. They claim miracles occur all the time; they expect and trust them. They talk about trying to accept miracles, not understand them.

For Native People, God is a verb. They say the universe is dynamic, animate, and constantly changing, evolving, and expanding. Religion, they claim, is a process. And, like everything else, religion is divinely related to the entire web of life. Every strand in the web is a sacred path to all the other strands. Nothing lives on a strand by itself, unconnected to the rest. Nothing is wasted. Everyone and everything have their special, sacred place. Native American prayers acknowledge and express joy for the existence of the unknown. Many prayers express humility.

Most prayers of Native People, regardless of nation, are inclusive. It is difficult to disagree personally with anything found in most prayers. For instance, people from almost any religious orientation would agree with the sentiments in the following prayer, part of one given in 1975 by Fools Crow, an Oglala Sioux holy man, who became the first Native American to give the opening prayer for a session of the United States Senate:

> Give us a blessing so that our words and actions be one in unity,
> and that we be able to listen to each other,
> in so doing, we shall with good heart walk
> hand in hand to face the future. . . .
> In the presence of the outside, we are thankful for many blessings,
> I make my prayer for all people, the children, the women, and the men.
> I pray that no harm will come to them,
> and that on the great island, there be no war,
> that there be no ill feelings among us.
> From this day on may we walk hand in hand.
> So be it.[17]

Although it is difficult to disagree with most prayers of Native People, they do not present their ideas as the right way or claim to hold the totality of truth. Native American missionaries do not exist nor do attempts to convert other people. In fact, Native Americans often express how each religious viewpoint has validity. Using a pearl and crystal as metaphors, Taos Pueblo Terry Tafoya explains:

> In the Christian theology, there's the idea that Christ is a pearl. No matter how you turn a pearl, it's exactly the same from any direction. A lot of Western science comes from the ideas that if you try hard enough, you will discover that objective truth. It means this is the only way you can see, and any other way of seeing is flawed.
>
> For a lot of Native American people, there's the idea of understanding life as a crystal. A crystal of quartz has different facets. Every time you turn it you discover a new facet. But one is not more valid than another.[18]

NATIVE AMERICAN MUSIC

Without writing, Native Americans have relied on music to preserve their rich histories and cultures. Almost every ceremony includes music. Songs exist for sweat lodge ceremonies, sun dances, pow wows, and pipe-smoking ceremonies. Other songs deal with war, peace, harvesting, and healing.

Music has played a central role in the life of Native Americans, in particular, because music is basic to human nature. It comes from the center of people's beings. Tunes, melodies, vibrations, and sounds reflect people's lives and dreams. Music echoes and reechoes through the sound chambers of people's bodies, moving through them with mighty motions. Ideally the vibrations of music penetrate their core, and enter their bodies until self and sound are no longer separate, and beginning and end are replaced by a continual symphony of synchronicity. Aural soundscapes compose a language of deep feelings and thoughts, a powerful polyphony of primal sounds.

Native People release themselves in songs. They understand the power of songs to penetrate pain, sustain the spirit, and heal individual and societal maladies. Natsilik Inuit Orpingalik explained how music is the heart's native tongue: "*My* breath: This is what I call this song, for it is as necessary to me to sing it as it is to breathe." At another time, he said, "Songs are thoughts, sung out with the breath when people are moved by forces and ordinary speech no longer suffices."[19]

Just as everyone has a story to tell, everyone possesses a song. Ute Elder Charlie Knight, declares, "Everyone has a song. God gives us each a song. That's how we know who we are. Our song tells us who we are."[20]

Sacred sounds are divine, representing the seed-syllable of the universe. Through chanting sacred sounds, people develop sound bodies, minds, and spirits – one voice, in concert, creating a harmonious hymn of the universe.

Some music stirs listeners, lifting them to new levels of awareness with passionate, powerful, and soul-touching rhythms that resonate with feelings. Some music sounds melodious; some sounds discordant. Much of their music sounds like nature – earthy, steamy, alive, spirited. Some music may be described as a sensual brew – glowing, smoldering, pulsating. Much is upbeat, lively, celebratory. Some music is meditative, often with repetitive rhythms that produce a hypnotic effect. The music lends depth to the lyrics and the lyrics lend depth to the music.

The music and lyrics often concern one of the Earth's elements (earth, air, fire, water), animals, and other aspects of nature. In 1927, the Grand Council Fire of American Indians explained, "We sang songs that carried in their melodies all the sounds of nature – the running of waters, the sighing of winds, and the calls of animals."[21]

Like prayers, the songs of Native People give thanks, purify, and provide spiritual harmony. In *The Book of the Hopi,* Frank Waters talks about people and birds when sharing this song of the "Long Hair" kachina: "So they will sing together in turn with the universal power, in harmony with the creator of all things. And the bird song, and the people's song and the song of life will become one."[22]

Often songs are holophrasic, using a single word to function as a phrase or sentence. The holophrasic nature of many Native American songs makes them difficult to translate. Their precision, conciseness, and economy of style make them sound similar to Japanese haiku, as the following songs illustrate:

As my eyes search the prairie
I feel the summer in the spring. (Anishinabe)

Soldiers,
you fled.
Even the eagle dies. (Lakota)

As
I see
the earth
the whole encompass of it. (Anishinabe)[23]

Like many American songs, repetition of sound characterizes much Native American music, and repetition of words characterizes many of the lyrics. Repetition makes songs easier to remember. The repetition often creates a soothing, lulling, hypnotizing, and comforting effect. Minor changes in cadence or word choice often deepen the potential impact on listeners. Extensive use of repetition and parallel structure help make songs sound fluid and coherent. Rarely do Native American songs use antithesis, except occasionally in accompanying drumming.

Native American tunes often include vocables or meaningless words; some are remnants of languages that no longer exist. Entire songs often consist of vocables; such songs have become especially popular since different Native nations have begun to spend more time with each other. Since the people speak different languages, songs consisting of vocables constitute a language members of all nations can share.

Probably the most frequent rhythm used in the music of Native People is a four-beat sound that symbolizes the synchronicity of the rhythms of the Earth. Resembling a heartbeat, it is a primal rhythm that can transcend the moment. Drums play a major part in Native American ceremonies. Before birth, all creatures experience the heartbeat of the birth mother. Since the drum sounds like a heartbeat, drumming also connects Native People to the Earth Mother. Native Americans talk about the drum as sacred. They say that one purpose of their music is for the heartbeat of the drum, drummers, listeners, and Earth to become one.

Dancing also plays a major role in many traditional Native American ceremonies. Dancing connects the entire body to movement, form, expression, and sound. It serves as a way for Native People to rid themselves of negative emotions. Through dance, they shake feelings out, stomp them out, vibrate them out. Like praying and singing, they say, dancing serves to create and express spiritual harmony. Pueblo Popovi Da explains, "The dance expresses the union we feel between man and the whole of humanity or the union of all living things." In general, Native People dance ecstatically, completely absorbed in the movements. Dancing grounds participants to the Earth and takes them to the sky. Eventually the dancers disappear and become the dance, and the dance becomes one with the energies and rhythms of the universe. A Native American saying emphasizes the importance of dance: "We do not believe our religion, we dance it!"[24]

CONCLUSION

Traditional Native People say they pray, sing, and dance to connect themselves to the universal rhythms of the cosmos. Like their other rhetoric, their prayers, songs, and dances speak of their belief that people should flow with the rhythms of nature rather than try to control and change these rhythms. A famous American folk song written by Woody Guthrie says, "This land is your land, this land is my land," and "all of it was made for you and me." By contrast, a Cagaba Native song not associated with a particular person goes, "Our mother of the growing fields, our mother of the streams, will have pity upon us. For to whom do we belong? Whose seeds are we? To our mother alone do we belong."[25]

Because words are sacred, they have the power to create. Native People say the act of praying or singing something makes it so. Words can bring things into being or make things happen. For Native People, then, an incantatory quality exists in the use of words, which the following Ojibway song illustrates; the actions mentioned become so through the breath:

Verily
The sky clears
When my Mide drum
Sounds
For me
Verily
The waters are smooth
When my Mide drum
Sounds
For me.

The Pawnee "Ritual Song" succinctly states the assumption that the prayer has been answered: "I know now that the gifts I asked have all been granted."[26]

I conclude this chapter with my own song for the universe:

In the song of the universe, humans hum, waters whisper, doves dance. The song echoes of teachings of our ancestors and of tellings of unborn generations. The song weaves its way through the threads of the cosmic web. In the song of the universe, all hearts beat as one.

The Importance of the Oral Tradition

A word has power in and of itself. It comes from nothing into sound and meaning. It gives origin to all things. By means of words can a man deal with the world on equal terms. And the word is sacred.

N. Scott Momaday, Kiowa[1]

INFINITY AND PERPETUITY

The oral discourse of Native Americans frequently concerns two related themes – infinity and perpetuity. As shown in other chapters, Native American speakers posit these ideas and ideals in a variety of ways. For example, many speeches deal with timeless truths. Orators stress the need to live in balance with nature rather than to try to control nature. Since everything originates in nature and since everything in nature is alive and constantly changing, everything in nature is infinite. Native American speakers also talk about creation as an on-going, never-ending process. They talk about the Creator as inclusive, belonging to all creatures of the cosmos.

Native American stories encourage the imagination. Several allow the listeners' minds to go in an infinite number of ways. Most Native People hear stories repeatedly, each time understanding them in deeper ways.

Many prayers of Native People concern perpetuity, and several songs unite opposing images, making an ongoing, circular movement. Words carry the content of messages as well as a sense of continuity, history, and linking of past, present, and future. Many speeches, stories, prayers, and songs weave the old and new into one rich tapestry to preserve for generations to come.

For Native People life changes infinitely. Every beginning is an end; every

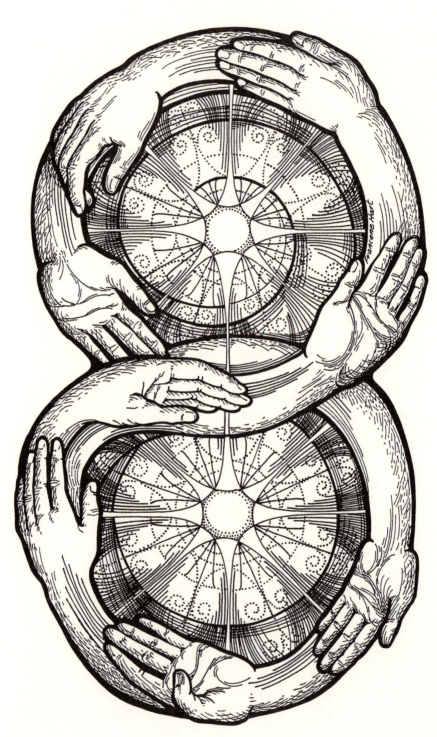

Infinity. Illustration by Francene Hart.

end is a beginning. Life is a fleeting moment in the eternal, never-ending process of cosmic oneness.

Similarly the skin does not mark the end of individuals. People manifest radiating energies that move and flow in constant, ever-changing currents. Ongoing, never-ending relationships naturally result as these living pulses connect humans to everyone and everything in the universe for always. Each person, each stone, and every other aspect of the cosmos is a relative to every other. No matter how hard people try, they cannot divorce themselves from other people, from animals, trees, or mountains, from their environments, or from themselves. People may feel divorced and they may act divorced, but, Native People say, these feelings and actions are illusions. According to traditional Native Americans, all creatures are connected in infinite interplays of energy patterns.

Unbroken circles and cycles, by definition, endlessly repeat and self-perpetuate. Circles represent eternal cycles of life and ensure equality for eternity. The cosmos can continue only if people return something to the land so life may be restored and rejuvenated. The broad perspectives the Native People take on particular problems deal with protecting the planet perpetually. Each generation considering the implications of its decisions for the next seven generations creates concern for eternity. Many Native American oral messages consider never-ending journeys and the Earth's limitless possibilities.

Dreams and visions help Native Americans transcend time and space and reconnect with the Earth. Sacred spirits, animals, places, and objects also allow them to commune with a world that many Westerners consider invisible or nonexistent. Native Americans value intuition, the inner eye, and the imagination. They talk about life as a process, and one definition of process is a continuous action.

Native American speeches, stories, prayers, and songs often include words associated with the themes of infinity and perpetuity. Words such as the following are frequently found in their varying forms of discourse: *forever, endless, timeless, infinite, perpetual, ongoing, wholeness, within, oneness, unity, circle, living, motion, process, evolutionary, continuance,* and *unborn generations*. People steeped in Western thought might call some of these terms hyperbole in part because of the analytic, objectivistic traditions of Euro-American thought.

In addition to words associated with infinity and perpetuity, much Native American discourse candidly concerns these concepts. The following example is typical: "Brothers: Let us so then act that the peace and friendship which so happily existed between our forefathers, may be forever preserved; and that we may always live as brothers of the same family" (John Ross, Cherokee, 1843).[2]

EFFECTS ON THE THEORY OF COMMUNICATION

The Native American's ideas about oral tradition and orality require a different theoretical approach to communication. Aristotle, a classical Greek theorist, viewed people as animals with the peculiar capacity to think. Rhetoric, for Aristotle, functioned as a way people persuaded others to believe in their beliefs, views, attitudes, and/or actions. As a field, rhetoric is steeped in the Western thought of Aristotle, focusing on presenting points and persuading others of their probable proof.

Kenneth Burke, a seminal American twentieth-century theorist, built upon Aristotelian philosophy, describing rhetoric as "the use of language as a symbolic means of inducing cooperation in beings that by nature respond to symbols." For Burke, symbol using was not an added power of people, but a basic part of their natures. According to Burke, speakers must identify with their audiences: "You can persuade [someone] only insofar as you can talk their language by speech, gesture, tonality, order, image, attitude, idea, identifying your way with theirs." Through identification, communicators behave in accordance with their audiences. They act together, both sides having common sensations, concepts, images, ideas, and attitudes. In acting together, the commonality makes speaker and listener consubstantial or at one with the other. Burke affirmed the importance of identification and consubstantiality as key concepts, arguing that humans are always at odds with each other. For Burke rhetoric could transcend these differences, resulting in a utopian world where all people cooperate with all other people.[3]

Native Americans would expand the scope of rhetoric even further. Like Burke, they view people not as isolated atoms who relate, but rather, as inherently relational beings. But Native People consistently talk about a natural state of interdependence, not a natural state of conflict. And, Native People say human beings are not the only creatures who relate and communicate. They believe trees talk, spirits speak, winds whisper, brooks babble, seas sing, and crops converse. To them, all creatures are symbol-using beings who possess an equal relationship with all other creatures. In other words, people engage in communicative relationships not only with other people, but also with four-leggeds, one-leggeds, and no-leggeds, with trees, plants, and rocks, with the sun, moon, and stars, and with all other components of the cosmos. Native American rhetoric focuses on relationships rather than on proving points. Their communication concerns establishing connections and negotiating relationships with the goal of living in balance or in a state of at-one-ment with all sentient beings. This oneness is not to be confused with ignoring or denying differences. As we saw in other chapters, Native Americans value differences among their distinct sovereign nations and advocate acceptance of differences between the "white man" and themselves. The idea of at-one-ment asserts that only by accepting differences can all living things live and move together as one, with one body, one mind, and one spirit.

The Native American ideal of achieving balance and harmony occurs both personally and cosmically. Native People talk about human beings as micro-cosms or miniature versions of the macrocosmic world. They speak about achieving oneness from the inside, the within, the innermost whisperings of the soul. They talk about allowing people to be continually reborn, to reach con-stantly into the womb of the Earth and emerge, grounded in nature and expressing harmony with all our relations. Native People talk about communi-cation as involving speaking with all sentient beings, not speaking to them.

The journey toward oneness takes people both inward and outward, infi-nitely contracting and infinitely expanding. As people attempt to bring their selves into greater harmony, they simultaneously attempt to consummate an all-embracing collective consciousness. As they accept their inescapable con-nectedness to and interdependence with everything outside the self, relation-ships become the focus of concern – relationships with human nature and Mother Nature. Since, according to Native Americans, the soul of the self and the soul of the Earth are one, transforming the self naturally transforms the Earth and vice versa. Individual consciousness recedes, giving way to an all-embracing cosmic consciousness.

Certainly if a car goes fast, the driver moves fast too, because the two must move together. But the Native American idea of personal and planetary peace do not happen automatically. Only by attending to acute, astute, and antiphonal awarenesses of others can people procure peace. For example, if a horse and a man know each other's minor movements, minuscule motions, and meticulous methods, the rider and horse can behave as one – a horseman is the same as a manhorse. Tewa Vickie Downey explains the importance of awareness: "Every second of our life we're studying everything around us. The sounds. The music. Outside our culture people don't have that awareness. We have to bring that awareness back. It's just being in tune with the spirit. So what people have to do now is to be in that awareness."4

Securing oneness with self and others, traditional Native People say, requires ceasing the clash for control and casting aside illusions of isolation, dogmas of division, and canons of chance. The processes require sacrifice and suffering, perils and privations. Before people's energies can connect to other energies, they must purify their bodies, minds, and spirits; clear old wounds, get rid of emotional "baggage," and release limiting emotions such as guilt and shame. Risk always precedes relief.

The Native American goals of achieving oneness with the self and everything in the cosmos constitute processes similar to Burke's concepts of Ultimate Transcendence and Ultimate Identification. Burke discussed Ultimate Transcendence and Ultimate Identification as ideals for which people, being imperfect beings, can only strive. Native Americans also talk about people as imperfect beings, but they do not separate people from other life forms. Ultimate Transcendence and Ultimate Identification involve knowing the elemental energies of all aspects of the Earth and aligning the self with the eternal flow of these primordial energies. In fact, in 1994 Tewa Gregory A. Cajete used the very words *ultimate identification:* "They experienced nature as a part of themselves and themselves as a part of nature. . . . This is the ultimate identification of being indigenous to a place and forms the basis for a fully internalized bonding with Place."5

According to Native People, the process of ultimate identification takes place slowly. Because Native Americans cannot describe their many experiences in rational terms, people in the dominant culture often discount their experiences as exaggerations, myths, or nonexistent happenings. I have had the good fortune of participating in numerous sweat lodge ceremonies and other Native American ceremonies and rituals. As a child of the Earth, my hands gently touch the ground, feeling the Earth's pulse and swaying to Her vibrations. I hear and feel Her heartbeat. I speak daily with my animal totems. As I indicated in the Preface, I have felt deeply rooted to the Earth and to all living beings ever since I was a child; well before I knew about Native American spiritual beliefs, nature served as my companion and my conduit to the spiritual world. The words *Mitakuye oyasin* (for all my relatives) are both a phrase used in all Lakota, Dakota, and Nakota prayers and a transcendent feeling of having a unique relationship with all aspects of the universe. Likewise, for me, bringing myself into greater balance has enchanted, transformed, and inspired me in ways that defy expression. The experiences have left me with a renewed sense of wonder, awe, marvel, humility, reverence, and respect for the Creator's handiwork.

An abundance of Native American oral discourse concerns living in right relations by communing with self and others that the examples below, taken from different Native nations and from different times, illustrate:

We are the spiritual energy that is thousands of times stronger than nuclear energy. Our energy is the combined will of all people with the spirit of the Natural World, to be of one body, one heart, and one mind for peace." (Chief Leon Shenandoah, Haudenosaunee, 1985)

The circle of the eagle and the circle of the human, conjoined in antiquity and mingled as one within the bosom of the Mother Earth. . . . Humans, functioning as individual species, are the creation of a community of many drawn together by the power of the interrelatedness. In turn, humans in symbiosis with their co-inhabitants create the circle of life on Earth. (Carter Camp, Ponca, 1988)

> It is lovely indeed, it is lovely indeed.
> I, I am the spirit within the earth . . .
> The feet of the earth are my feet . . .
> The legs of the earth are my legs . . .
> The bodily strength of the earth is my bodily strength . . .
> The thoughts of the earth are my thoughts . . .
> The voice of the earth is my voice . . .
> The feather of the earth is my feather . . .
> All that belongs to the earth belongs to me . . .
> All that surrounds the earth surrounds me . . .
> I, I am the sacred words of the earth . . .
> It is lovely indeed, it is lovely indeed. (Dine song)

> My words are tied in one
> With the great mountains,
> With the great rocks,
> With the great trees,
> In one with my body
> And my heart. (Yokuts prayer)[6]

Judeo-Christians might term the Native People's ideas about harmonic resonance and cosmic cooperation a messianic age. According to traditional Native People, however, the messiah is not an outside person but a force that lives inside all living creatures: Like all sentient beings, people are part of the Great Mystery, and the Great Mystery is part of people.

EFFECTS ON THE PRACTICE OF COMMUNICATION

In addition to differences in communication theory, differences exist in the practice of speaking. The rhetoric of Western thought deals with finite movements with beginnings and endings, causes and effects. Changes exist, but they are completed changes. In American rhetoric, the roles of speaker and audience are well defined; speakers actively deliver messages, audiences serve as receivers to be changed by the messages. Speakers and listeners steeped in Western culture have little tolerance for ambiguity, incompleteness, and inconsistency. They want complete, consistent messages and value clarity and precision. Speakers rely primarily on facts, figures, testimony, and other forms of logical proof to support their arguments. The structure of American communication assumes completion; listeners expect an ending. Perhaps most importantly, Americans view speakers as having control over their messages.

Listeners of Native American discourse do not assume completion or expect an ending. Rather than answering questions, Native speakers believe in letting people contemplate answers. Native Americans purposefully avoid being directive to allow receivers to glean the meanings and implications of messages. This is why many of their stories provide no definitive ending. In Native American rhetoric, roles of speakers and audiences coalesce at times since both play active roles.

Invention or coming up with ideas for American orators directs them outward to external worlds where they research topics to find the most probative proof to support their points. For Native American speakers, invention directs them inward to inner worlds. Invention means to dis-cover. They say that everything resides within people. They need only to remember. They look to their breath to see if it flows freely, expansively, and naturally. Invention involves keen concentration and a conscious cultivation of the senses. To generate ideas, they pray, meditate, observe, listen, ground themselves, seek visions, and consult the spirit world. They value dreams, visions, revelations, and prophecies. They accord heavy weight to suggestions and signs from human and nonhuman sources. For example, they intimate importance to finding a feather, to leaves shaking in a tree while neighboring trees remain still, or to seeing a color in the wrong place. They view the visible world as presenting only the surface of things, and they recognize the need to go beyond the visible world. To Native People invention or discovery comes *through* us, not *to* us.

Westerners generally cut themselves off from the invisible world, considering it suspect or unreal. By seeking logical proofs and feeling skeptical of their emotions, they deal primarily with verifiable facts. In contrast, Native Americans frequently speak about the need to listen to their instincts, senses, feelings, and emotions, to trust their inner selves. They talk about the need to listen to core sensibilities since these transcend temporal things and travel toward the truth. Whereas Westerners say answers come from outside people, Native People say answers come from both inside and outside.

The following situation involving a Native American woman and William James, a nineteenth-century scientist and philosopher, powerfully and humorously illustrates how trusting instinctive feelings differs from trusting logical evidence. The Native American woman had just finished telling a Haudenosaunee creation story about how the Earth was created on the back of a gigantic turtle.

When she was finished, James was determined to convince her that it was a fallacy to believe the Earth rested forever on the laboured shell of a turtle.

"Ma'am, I find your story very interesting, but one point is hard for me to reconcile," James said. "If the Earth is supported by the turtle, then what is it that holds the turtle up?"

"Why, another turtle Mr. James."

"But don't you see that there would be nothing to hold up the second turtle, or the one beneath it?" he asked.

To which she replied, "I'm sorry Mr. James, but it's turtles all the way down."[7]

The life power of words and the oral tradition invigorate Native messages, making them in general more vibrant, vigorous, powerful, passionate, soul touching, and evocative than the messages of their non-Native neighbors. Native American speakers frequently use word and sound repetition and parallel structure, helping messages sound fluid and making them easier to remember. As discussed in Chapter 2, Native American speakers use more sensory images than their non-Native counterparts, often involving more than one sense. Making messages vivid and intense involves listeners, and participating in the communicative act helps listeners to remember the words so they may pass them on to future generations.

To Native Americans, oral communication is what allows all living forms to relate to each other in a never-ending process. Discussing public speaking, A. P. Johnson stressed how speeches give living creatures the power to form a bond so strong that speaker and audience become one. Below is his entire speech, delivered at the First Tlingit Language Workshop, Sitka, Alaska, June 1971:

A person will often say
"I am going to speak to you."
Public speaking
is like a man walking up along a river
with a gaff hook.
He lets his gaff hook drift
over a salmon swimming at the edge of the river.
when he hooks on it, the salmon way over there
becomes one with him.
This is the way oratory is.
Even speech delivered at a distance
becomes one with someone.[8]

In addition to speakers and audiences becoming one, speakers and their words become one. Speakers become part of their words, and their words become part of them.

SILENCE

Unlike many Euro-Americans who fear silence, Native Americans talk about silence as necessary to secure oneness with themselves and with nature. Native People frequently talk about the significance of silence, claiming that the person who values silence may often be the best speaker and that in the battle of words, silence is often the best weapon. Pawnee/Otoe Anna Lee Walters explains the importance of silence:

Silence and speech at the water's edge alternated here. Remember that we need both, we are told. The totem voices took turns speaking – the Bears roared, the Eagles screeched, the Pigeons cooed – until all the clans had spoken. Silence followed. *Silence.* Then all the totem beings spoke at once. Yes, through their speeches and voices, and through the ensuing silence, the people, the clans, knew they lived. This is the power of language, but often it is not realized until silence prevails. Silence. *Remember both, we are told.*[9]

As Walters makes clear, silence does not mean absence of sound. Nature, music, and internal dialogues always provide a polyphony of sounds, ones we often do not hear because the sounds of modern technology drown them out. Sea gulls chirp, winds howl, thunder speaks with an overpowering voice. Evergreens tickle the nose with their pungent pine aroma. Pain in the body screams to be heard. Loving feelings are often expressed in sweet melodies. Music can calm, distract, evoke, stir, or stimulate. Engines rumble, power plants roar, jackhammers blast. Walking produces a stomping noise. Gorillas beat their chests and spiders drum on their webs. Animals use particular sound patterns as mating calls. Clearly sounds of all sorts surround us constantly, producing a cacophony or symphony.

Native People say silence means stilling the mind, finding solitude in the midst of busy lives, becoming attuned to inner rhythms of the body and of the Earth, and lifting themselves to new levels of awareness. They say through silence we listen; silence is a precondition for awareness and alertness. Remembering, returning, retrieving, recovering, and reawakening require this soothing and serene silence. The peacefulness that accompanies centered stillness provides a deepened awareness of the very act of living.

LISTENING

Part of the power of speaking involves the art of listening. By listening, Native people do not mean hearing in a passive placid way, but rather, participating with body, mind, and soul in the communicative act. They talk about listening as passionately as they talk about speaking, stressing how listening is active and animated, receptive and responsive. Listening means coming into a private, personal relationship that is vibrant and vigorous. It means experiencing the other's pain and joy. In "Blessing," Chickasaw poet Linda Hogan writes, "Blessed are those who listen when no one is left to speak." In an interview, Hogan elaborates, "Everything speaks. I have a friend, Flying Clouds, who one time said, 'Some people are such good listeners the trees lean towards them to tell their secrets.' I think that's true."[10]

Listening involves hearing the words spoken and the silences between the words, the sounds of drums and the pauses between the beats. The oral tradition, then, refers not only to talking but also to listening.

Sound is the first sense people experience in the womb. Darkness prevents sight, and amniotic fluid in the nose obstructs the ability to smell. The fluid presses against the eardrum, and since water is a better conduit of sound than is air, babies in the womb actually hear amplified primordial sounds. Once out of the womb, infants continually hear nature, body, and human sounds and even the "sounds of silence."

In detailing how she developed the ability to listen actively, Pawnee/Otoe writer Anna Lee Walters applies what happens physiologically to herself:

My first memories are not so much of things as they are of words that gave shape and substance to my being and form to the world around me. . . . Listening is the first sense to develop in the womb. It is not surprising, then, that I was conscious of sounds earlier than anything else as an infant. Mainly, these were the sounds of the universe, the outdoors. They included whishing bird wings rising up into the sky, rustling trees, the cry of the mourning dove, and the rippling wind. They were the first nonhuman sounds I heard because my parents spent most of the time outdoors. This awareness was followed by other sounds of life embracing me with deep sighs and measured breaths. Those human sounds became syllables, or vocables, and voice patterns with intonations and inflections. Eventually and inexplicably they turned into words.[11]

As discussed in the Introduction, Native Americans place enormous emphasis on words spoken to them. Comanche Ten Bears said in a speech in 1867, "Any good thing you say to me shall not be forgotten. I shall carry it as near to my heart as my children, and it shall be as often on my tongue as the name of the Great Spirit." Over one hundred years later, Cheyenne Henri Mann Morton advised in a speech in 1989, "Listen with courtesy to what others say, even if you feel that what they are saying is worthless. Listen with your heart." Traditional Native Americans say all people deserve reverend respect and heartfelt honor, and showing these attitudes involves, among other things, listening actively and responsively to what other people say.[12]

Active listening gives messages more power. Participating in the communicative act takes listeners to different places and new levels of awareness.

MEMORY

The strength and very existence of an oral culture depend on the memories of listeners and their willingness to teach the next generation. Without memory, the Native American oral tradition would no longer exist. Throughout time Native People have worked at making their messages memorable, listeners have worked at listening, and new generations of speakers have worked at using mnemonic devices to jog their memories. Several communicative factors may have made the oral messages easier for speakers and listeners to remember: conciseness, well-organized messages, multisensory language, and extensive use of word and sound repetition. Listeners often go into the woods and repeat messages over and over again. Native Americans use mnemonic devices to help them recall the wisdom of their ancestors.

In traditional Native American society, people revere their elders in part because the elders serve as the living memory of the clan. Not surprisingly, memory takes on extreme importance when people are entrusted to keep their history, beliefs, values, and traditions alive. The elders must remember in order to teach the next generation; the current generation must remember in order to teach the next generation, ad infinitum.

Without writing, words take on increased importance. With writing, people can be careless with language. If writers make a mistake, they can always look up the right answer and correct their mistake. If readers have a problem, they can always reread. In 1891 Oglala Sioux Four Guns contrasted the Native American oral tradition with the dominant culture's written one: "The Indian needs no writing," he declared. "Words that are true sink deep into his heart where they remain. He never forgets them. On the other hand, if the white man loses his paper, he is helpless."[13]

Writing also promotes a detached and disconnected attitude. Readers can close books whenever they want. The books are still there just as speakers are still speaking even if audiences do not listen. However, people can reopen books and read them later, but if people want to hear what speakers say, they must listen while the orators speak. Writing also encourages isolation; most people prefer to read in private. By contrast, the oral tradition encourages people to come together to listen to speakers or storytellers.

In the Native American preliterate culture, everyone held the enormous responsibility of remembering. The oral tradition enhances attentiveness. It attunes people to spoken words. There are no other. People need to know well the history, principles, and precepts of their tribal culture in order to pass them on to the next generation. An oral culture risks extinction at all times since no written records exist to help younger generations remember. Traditional Native People take this responsibility seriously. Parents and grandparents say they have the responsibility of teaching their children and grandchildren.

Today many people in Native communities know how to read, yet they talk about an intense desire to keep the oral tradition alive. This is especially difficult given the competition of television and computer games and given the rapidly expanding technology as we enter a new millennium.

CONCLUSION

An important question raised by this book involves the unique qualities of the Native American oral tradition. All cultures possess an oral tradition. For example, Euro-Americans were at one time preliterate with a rich oral rhetoric, and African Americans also possess an extensive oral tradition. To what extent and in what ways is the rhetoric of people with other oral traditions similar to and different from Native American oral rhetoric? I leave this question for future researchers.

Orality is ongoing. It refers to breathing and to sharing vibrations. Through the exchanges that ensue, people become more conscious, they get in touch with their inner selves, and they see beyond the obvious, getting glimpses into the invisible world. Rippling reverberations would result and renew repeatedly if all living beings resolved to remain in a right and reciprocal relationship with all others.

Native American speeches, stories, prayers, and songs stress the ability of collective energy to create this quintessential personal and planetary peace. Native American speakers claim that through the life power of spoken words, we can change ourselves and others. And since our words and actions have a never-ending rippling effect, we can change the world. Our collective energies could allow us to have oneness rather than oppression, compassion rather than conflict, awe rather than anguish, and prophets rather than profits. We can pioneer a planet where all creatures are family and where all beings live in right relations with everyone and everything. We can begin by celebrating creation and living love. Returning to respect and reverence of the spoken word is critical; saying the words with our breath brings the idea to life. So, let us voice this vision into existence, a new Amer-*I-CAN* Dream: All are One, whole and holy.

Nurturing Change. Illustration by Francene Hart.

Conclusion

We are touched into tribal being with words, made whole in the world with words and oratorical gestures.

Gerald Vizenor, Anishaabe

"The oral tradition is alive and well, moving and changing."

Paula Gunn Allen, Pueblo Laguna and Sioux[1]

SURVIVAL

The Native American oral tradition helps to account for the survival of their people and their rhetoric. Things do not exist until put into words or, stated differently, saying words with our breath affirms existence. Pawnee/Otoe writer Anna Lee Walters, explains, "It is through the power of speech, and the larger unified voice of oral tradition, that we exist as we do. . . They [the Pawnees and the Otoes] both had extended a pattern of life over countless generations, through the centuries, and credited their survival and continuity to the power of their oral traditions."[2]

During the past five centuries, the Native People of this country have endured unbelievably horrific acts when Euro-American newcomers to this country have tried to kill them and their way of life. To some extent the new-comers have succeeded in destroying the oral tradition by taking children away to boarding schools so their parents could not teach them. But the newcomers have not completely extinguished the oral tradition, in part, because it is an oral tradition. If Native Americans had written their teachings, their books could have been burned. Other people, however, cannot burn people's memories.

That the information resides inside people and that most of the people possess phenomenal memories have helped them to preserve many traditions, beliefs, stories, prayers, and songs.

The holistic world view of traditional Native People may also help to account for their survival. Over the past two hundred years, the indigenous people of this country have lived with cultural genocide as a daily reality in their lives. Many have become widows and orphans as they have watched their loved ones massacred and mutilated. Many have watched their lands become black and defoliated, leaving only bloody splotches and traces of remains that were once human. Daily people ostracize and discriminate against them for the "sin" of being born. Feeling alone and giving up are reasonable responses to such horrific acts. But many Native people say they have not felt alone because they view their ancestors and unborn generations as their relatives. Many say they have not felt alone because they feel embraced and enfolded by trees and related to the dazzling leaves they hear crunching under their feet, the succulent aroma of the fragrant flowers they smell, and the sun who bathes them in warmth. Not knowing the dangers that might occur tomorrow, many Native People enjoy each moment in the perpetual present.

The Native People's delicate existence gives language and the oral tradition great importance. N. Scott Momaday, a Pulitzer Prize–winning Kiowa, stated succinctly how a Native story, prayer, or song is tentative and tenuous because no matter how many times it has been told, it "is always but one generation removed from extinction."[3]

The importance of the soul may have contributed also to the survival of Native Americans. People's physical bodies may be repressed and suppressed, but many Native Americans say they will not allow their souls to be oppressed.[4]

The themes of infinity and perpetuity may also relate to survival. Most Native Americans believe Mother Earth will provide whatever they need to survive. Further, they believe they can never fully understand the Great Mystery surrounding Mother Earth. Still, they try to understand, digging deeper and deeper into their souls. But, no matter how deep people go, they can always go deeper. The paths of self-discovery and learning are endless paths. People can never fully develop; rather, human development continues constantly.

Finally, the overall optimistic outlook of the Native People may have helped them to survive. Most Native People have watched loved ones murdered, homes destroyed, children taken to boarding schools, and lands stolen; most live with the knowledge that many people in the dominant culture want to kill them and their culture. Hence, not surprisingly, much Native discourse expresses grief and sadness. What is surprising is that, given more than five centuries of genocide, their speaking is predominately optimistic: The people seem to express remarkable empathy in their discourse. I do not mean to suggest that Native People have no faults or that they all behave in the ways I describe. But, it is difficult to listen or read their rhetoric and not feel empowered about the future of our planet. Unlike many of their American neighbors, they seem to genuinely believe peace can exist on this planet if enough people pray for it and "walk their talk." Acoma Pueblo Simon Ortiz talks about the principle of compassion and love *(imih ih amoo uh haatse eh hanoh)*: "compassion and love for land, for people, for all things. It's a principle of human nature, particularly of Native American people, to love and have compassion." He continues:

As long as there's that love and compassion, you are going to keep struggling and fighting in the courts, trying to choose the right leadership for your own people, trying to find the right words for your people. You're trying to think the clear and necessary things in your counsel with young people, in realizing what your life is to be. That struggle itself, based on compassion and love, is hopeful and optimistic.[5]

Whereas Western rhetoric focuses on speakers and audiences, Native American rhetoric focuses on the power and primacy of words. Speakers are simply vehicles and audiences recipients of words. Anishaabe writer Gerald Vizenor says through one of his characters, "The speaker is not the center of the word world because words were on the earth before the talkers and tellers."[6]

Euro-Americans talk about language as representational: Words represent reality. Traditional Native Americans talk about language as presentational: Words bring reality into being or present the being of things. Viewing words as presentational may explain why Native People consider the spoken word such a solemn matter – it stands for reality. Kiowa N. Scott Momaday says, "To give one's word is to give oneself, wholly. . . . One stands for his word; his word stands for him."[7]

To Native People, words are intrinsically powerful, magical, and sacred. The oral tradition is the means by which Native People have kept alive their way of life. And their way of life has survived. Native People have been defeated but they continue to exist and to speak. The Native American oral tradition, then, has contributed to the long-range success of the rhetoric of Native People.

The spoken words of Native People move from an endless past, not gone, through the present, and into the future. With all oral communication, there is the sound, its echo, and another sound into which the first sound melts and to which it gives birth. Thus, the words of Native People continue to ripple and reverberate, sounding and resounding in a continuous procession. The procession perpetuates for eternity, never ending.

The words spoken by Native People have conferred upon me many gifts. I wish to conclude this chapter by expressing heartfelt appreciation for the magical and mystical moments I have encountered because of these words. I wrote the following piece while absorbed in nature, appreciating and admiring its splendor, sanctity, and spirit:

> We are many with different bodies, lives, and experiences.
> And we are One, inextricably interlinked with the lives
>   of All Our Relations.
>
> We are many, with different atoms, molecules, and cells.
> And we are One, breathing the same air and drinking the same water
>   as we share the Earth with all living beings.
>
> We are many, with different birth dates, addresses, and genders.
> And we are One, sharing together the grandeur of Mother Earth
>   and Father Sky.
>
> We are many, with different pasts, presents, and futures.
> And we are One, living moment by moment
>   in the perpetual present.
>
> We are many, speaking different languages.
> And we are One, possessing one language, a language of infinite love.
>
> We are many, with different traditions, cultures, and religions.
> And we are One, experiencing together the miraculous marvel
>   and mystery of life.
>
> We are many, with different words reflecting our different perceptions
>   and realities.
>
> And we are One, sharing words that reflect a deeper truth,
>   a spiritual, soul-filled certitude.

These truths and certitudes teach us that the world is a classroom and all the world's inhabitants are our teachers. From our teachers we learn that

We are the rich and the poor.
We are the master and the slave.
We are friend and foe.
We are the predator and prey.
We are the proponents of peace and the weapons of war.
We are feast and famine.
We are joy and sorrow.
We are the blades of grass and the weeds.
Yes, we are many – everyone and everything.
And we are One – one humanity sharing one planet.

Notes

PREFACE

1. In 1880, H. B. Whipple, Bishop of Minnesota, wrote, "We have not a hundred miles between the Atlantic and Pacific which has not been the scene of an Indian massacre." See H. B. Whipple, Preface, *A Century of Dishonor* by Helen Jackson (New York: Indian Head Books, 1993), p. ix.

2. Chellis Glendinning, *"My Name Is Chellis and I'm in Recovery from Western Civilization"* (Boston: Shambhala Publications, Inc., 1994), p. xii; Gerald Hausman, *Turtle Island Alphabet* (New York: St. Martin's Press, 1993), p. xvi. In his article, "The Cost of Columbus: Was There a Holocaust?" Robert W. Venables also compares the Jewish Holocaust with the Native American Holocaust. See *Northeast Indian Quarterly* 7 (Fall 1990): pp. 29–36.

3. Hausman, *Turtle Island,* pp. ix–xvi; Glendinning, *"My Name Is Chellis,"* pp. 5–6.

INTRODUCTION

1. N. Scott Momaday, "Man Made of Words," Assembly Presentation at the First Convocation of American Indian Scholars, in *Indian Voices* (San Francisco: The Indian Historian Press, 1970), pp. 49–84; Debra Calling Thunder, "Voices of the Invisible," in *A Circle of Nations: Voices and Visions of American Indians,* ed. John Gattuso (Hillsboro, OR: Beyond Words Publishing, Inc., 1993), pp. 44–45.

2. Joseph Epes Brown, "Becoming Part of It," in *I Become Part of It,* ed. D. M. Dooling and Paul Jordan-Smith (New York: Parabola Books, 1989), pp. 13–14.

3. Simon Ortiz, in *Winged Words: American Indian Writers Speak,* ed. Laura Coltelli (Lincoln: University of Nebraska Press, 1990), pp. 104 and 107–108.

4. Henri Mann Morton, in *Native American Reader: Stories, Speeches, and Poems,* ed. Jerry D. Blanche (Juneau: The Denali Press, 1990), p. 194.

5. Russell V. Boham, in Blanche, *Native American Reader,* p. 224.

6. Seattle, typescript of speech (Seattle: Seattle Historical Society) in *Indian Oratory:*

Famous Speeches by Noted Indian Chieftans, W. C. Vanderwerth, comp. (Norman: University of Oklahoma Press, 1971), p. 118; Winnebago story, in *Folklore of the Winnebago,* by David Lee Smith (Norman: University of Oklahoma Press, 1997), p. 97.

7. Louis Thomas Jones, Introduction, in *Aboriginal American Oratory: The Tradition of Eloquence among the Indians of the United States* (Los Angeles: Southwest Museum, 1965), p. xviii.

8. Edna C. Sorter, "The Noble Savage," *Ethnohistory* 19 (1972): pp. 227–36.

9. Jack Forbes, "We Can Have New Visions," in *Surviving in Two Worlds: Contemporary Native American Voices,* eds. Lois Crozier-Hogle and Darryl Babe Wilson (Austin: University of Texas Press, 1997), p. 245.

10. Ojibway prayer in *Native Wisdom,* ed. Joseph Bruchac (San Francisco: Harper, 1995).

11. Joseph Bruchac, *Lasting Echoes: An Oral History of Native American People* (San Diego: Harcourt, Brace & Company, 1997), pp. 22 and 111.

12. Old Man Buffalo Grass, "The Dine: Origin Myths of the Navajo Indians," by Aileen O'Bryan, *Bureau of American Ethnology Bulletin* 163 (1956).

13. See *How Can One Sell the Air? Chief Seattle's Vision,* ed. Eli Gifford and Michael R. Cook (Summertown, TN: Book Publishing Company, 1992), for a discussion of the difficulties and controversies surrounding the translation of Chief Seattle's famous speech.

CHAPTER 1–CULTURAL ASSUMPTIONS

1. The opening quote comes from Elaine Ramos, "Bilingual Education," in Blanche, *Native American Reader,* p. 97.

2. For a discussion of the influence of the Iroquois Confederacy on the United States Constitution and Bill of Rights, see Oren Lyons et al., eds., *Exiled in the Land of the Free: Democracy, Indian Nations, and the U.S. Constitution* (Santa Fe, NM: Clear Light Publishers, 1992).

3. Aristotle, *The Rhetoric of Aristotle,* trans. Lane Cooper.

4. Carter Camp, in Blanche, *Native American Reader,* p. 167; Vine Deloria, Jr., *God Is Red: A Native View of Religion,* 2nd ed. (Golden, CO: Fulcrum Publishing, 1994).

5. Oren Lyons, in Blanche, *Native American Reader,* p. 114.

6. Ten Bears, in Vanderwerth, *Indian Oratory,* p. 161.

7. Wa'na'nee'che' [Dennis Renault], in *Principles of Native American Spirituality,* by Dennis Renault and Timothy Freke (San Francisco: Thorsons, 1996), p. 31.

8. Wub-e-ke-niew, *We Have the Right to Exist: A Translation of Aboriginal Indigenous Thought. The First Book Ever Published From an* Ahnishinahbaeojibway *Perspective* (New York: Black Thistle Press, 1995), p. 218.

9. John Trudell, in "An Interview with John Trudell: Confronting the Spirit Eater," ed. Jose Barreiro, in *Native Americas: Ake:kon's Journal of Indigenous Issues* 15, no. 4 (Winter, 1997): 35.

10. LaDonna Harris, in Blanche, *Native American Reader,* p. 150.

11. Dagmar Thorpe, "People of the Seventh Fire," in Crozier-Hogle and Wilson, *Surviving in Two Worlds,* p. 9.

12. Tamarack Song, *Journey to the Ancestral Self: The Native Lifeway Guide to Living in Harmony with Earth Mother* (Barrytown, NY: Staton Hill Press, 1994), p. 78.

13. Harris, in Blanche, *Native Aemrican Reader,* p. 149; Morton, in ibid., p. 198.

14. Peter MacDonald, quoted by Dennis Banks, in Blanche, *Native American Reader,* p. 102. MacDonald went to jail for graft after his election.

15. Harris, in Blanche, *Native American Reader,* p. 151.

16. Hiamovi, in *The Indians' Book: Songs and Legends of the American Indians,* ed. Natalie Curtis (New York: Dover Publications, 1907), p. x.

CHAPTER 2–IMAGERY

1. Jones, Introduction to *Aboriginal American Oratory,* p. xviii; I. A. Richards, *The Philosophy of Rhetoric* (New York: Oxford University Press, 1965).

2. Joseph Rael, *Ceremonies of the Living Spirit* (Tulsa: Council Oak Books, 1998), p. 1.

3. Jone [Fire] Lame Deer and Richard Erdoes, *Lame Deer: Seeker of Visions* (New York: Washington Square Press, 1994), pp. 107–108; and Paula Gunn Allen, *The Sacred Hoop: Recovering the Feminine in American Indian Traditions* (Boston: Beacon Press, 1992), p. 71.

4. N. Scott Momaday, *The Man Made of Words* (New York: St. Martin's Press, 1997), pp. 9–10.

5. Momaday, *The Man Made of Words,* pp. 11–12.

6. Chief Elias Johnson, *Legends, Traditions, and Laws of the Iroquois or Six Nations* (Lockport, NY: 1881), p. 220, reprinted in *Cry of the Thunderbird,* ed. Charles Hamilton (Norman: University of Oklahoma Press, 1972), p. 32.

7. Michael Osborn, "Archetypal Metaphor in Rhetoric: The Light-Dark Family," *The Quarterly Journal of Speech* 53 (1967): pp. 115–26; and Michael Osborn, "The Evolution of the Archetypal Sea in Rhetoric and Poetic," *The Quarterly Journal of Speech* 63 (1977): pp. 347–63. The term "archetypal metaphor" is introduced to rhetorical scholars in Michael M. Osborn and Douglas Ehninger, "The Metaphor in Public Address," *Speech Monographs* 29 (1962): pp. 223–34.

8. Marie-Louise Von Franz, Creation Myths (Boston: Shambhala, 1995), p. 1.

9. Osborn, "Archetypal," pp. 117 and 120.

10. "Nicely, Nicely," in *Dancing Teepees,* ed. Virginia Driving Hawk Sneve (New York: Holiday House, 1989), p. 15.

11. Osborn, "Archetypal"; and Osborn, "Evolution."

12. Richard Erdoes and Alfonso Ortiz, *American Indian Myths and Legends* (New York: Pantheon Books, 1984); Rael, *Ceremonies of the Living Spirit.*

13. Phillip Deere, in Blanche, *Native American Reader,* p. 123.

14. Osborn, "Archetypal."

15. Chief Seattle, in Vanderwerth, comp., *Indian Oratory,* p. 122.

16. Michael J. Caduto and Joseph Bruchac, *Keepers of the Earth: Native American Stories and Environmental Activities for Children* (Golden, CO: Fulcrum, Inc., 1989), pp. 137–38.

17. Knud Rasmussen, *Intellectual Culture of the Copper Eskimo,* trans. W. E. Calvert (1932), p. 53.

18. Mary Leitka, in *Wisdom's Daughters: Conversations with Women Elders of Native America,* ed. Steve Wall (New York: Harper Perennial, 1993), p. 181.

19. Osborn, "Evolution," pp. 352 and 353.

20. Michael Osborn, "Patterns of Metaphor among Early Feminist Orators," unpublished essay, p. 27; and Osborn, "Evolution," pp. 347–63.

21. Washington Matthews, "Songs of Sequence of the Navajos," *Journal of American Folklore* 7 (1984): 187–93.

22. Quoted in *Trail of the Wind: American Indian Poems and Ritual Orations,* ed. John Bierhorst (Canada: Farrar, Straus and Giroux, 1998), p. 106.

23. Harris, in Blanche, *Native American Reader,* p. 155; Peacekeeper in *Wisdomkeepers:*

Meetings with Native American Spiritual Elders, ed. Steve Wall and Harvey Arden (Hillsboro, OR: Beyond Words Publishing, Inc., 1990), p. 7.

24. Camp, in Blanche, *Native American Reader,* pp. 167 and 169.

25. Vernon Masayesva, in Blanche, *Native American Reader,* p. 99; Camp, in ibid., p. 175.

26. Morton, in Blanche, *Native American Reader,* pp. 196 and 204.

27. Osborn, "Patterns," p. 30.

28. "Magic Formula to Make an Enemy Peaceful," in *Navajo Legends,* trans. Washington Matthews (Boston: American Folklore Society, 1897), p. 109.

29. Osborn, "Patterns."

30. Sitting Bull, quoted in *Touch the Earth: A Self-Portrait of Indian Existence,* comp. T. C. McLuhan (New York: Promontory Press, 1971), p. 90; Trudell, in Barreiro, "Interview," p. 38.

31. Gkisedtanamoogk and Frances Hancock, *Anoqcou: Ceremony Is Life Itself* (Portland, ME: Astarte Shell Press, 1993), p. 10.

32. Steven Crum, "How Beautiful Is Our Land," in Crozier-Hogle and Wilson, *Surviving in Two Worlds,* p. 75.

33. "The Roots of Peace," in *The Great Law of Peace of the Iroquois Nation,* reprinted in *Parabola,* 3 (Summer 1980).

34. Washington Matthews, "The Night Chant, a Navajo Ceremony," *American Museum of Natural History Memoirs,* vol. 6, 1902 reprint, (New York: AMS, 1974).

35. Tecumseh, quoted in *I Have Spoken: American History through the Voices of the Indians,* comp. Virginia Irving Armstrong (Athens: Ohio University Press, 1991), p. 43.

36. Arthur Amiotte, "The Road to the Center," *Parabola* 9, no. 3. (1984): pp. 46 and 51.

37. George Tinker, "For All My Relations," *Sojourners* (January 1991), n.p., quoted in Bierhorst, *The Way of the Earth,* p. 399.

38. Gerald Hausman, *The Sun Horse: Native Visions of the New World* (Twin Lakes, WI: Lotus Light, 1992), p. 7.

39. Herbert Spinden, *Songs of the Tewa* (New York: Exposition of Indian Tribal Arts, 1933).

40. Russell Means, "The State of Native America," in Blanche, *Native American Reader,* p. 189 and Morton, in Blanche, *Native American Reader,* pp. 195 and 205.

41. Chief Dan George, in McLuhan, *Touch the Earth,* p. 161.

42. Tecumseh, in Vanderwerth, comp., *Indian Oratory,* pp. 62–66.

43. Lame Deer and Erdoes, in *Lame Deer,* p. 114.

44. Carroll C. Arnold, *Criticism of Oral Rhetoric* (Columbus, OH: Bell and Howell Company, 1974), pp. 168–69.

45. Shabonee, in McLuhan, *Touch the Earth,* p. 115; Deere, in Blanche, *Native American Reader,* p. 121; Tecumseh in Armstrong, *I Have Spoken,* p. 46; Ten Bears in McLuhan, *Touch the Earth,* p. 147; and Camp, in Blanche, *Native American Reader,* p. 173.

46. The Zuni prayer for rain may be found in Ruth Bunzel, *Introduction to Auni Ceremonialism,* 47th Annual Report of the Bureau of American Ethnology, p. 484, quoted in Margot Astrov, *The Winged Serpent: American Indian Prose and Poetry* (Boston: Beacon Press, 1992), pp. 9–10.

47. Sarah Winnemuca [Hopkins], *Life among the Piutes: Their Wrongs and Claims,* ed. Mrs. Horace Mann (1833; reprint, Bishop, CA: Chalfant, 1969), in *Literatures of the American Indian,* by A. LaVonne Brown Ruoff (New York: Chelsea House Publishers, 1991), p. 66.

48. Osage, "Song of the Vigil," in *The Sacred Journey: Prayers and Songs of Native Amer-

ica, ed. Peg Streep (Boston: Bulfinch Press, 1995), p. 78.

49. Sia, "Rain Song," in Streep, *The Sacred Journey,* p. 31.

50. "The Song of the Stars," in Streep, *The Sacred Journey,* p. 12; the "Prayer to Introduce a Child to the Cosmos," *The Sacred Journey,* pp. 54–55. 51. Lame Deer and Erdoes, in *Lame Deer,* p. 108.

CHAPTER 3–SPEECHES

1. Neil Philip, *In a Sacred Manner I Live: Native American Wisdom* (New York: Clarion Books, 1997), p. 9; "The Lakota Family," *Bulletin of Oglala Sioux Community College, 1980–81* (Pine Ridge, SD), p. 2.

2. George Meninock in Philip, *In a Sacred Manner I Live,* p. 34; Speckled Snake in Philip, *In A Sacred Manner I Live,* p. 53.

3. Chief Joseph, "An Indian's View of Indian Affairs," *The North American Review* 78 (April 1878).

4. Four Guns in Armstrong, *I Have Spoken,* pp. 130–31.

5. Earl Old Person, in *The Congressional Record,* 1961.

6. William L. Stone, *The Life and Times of Sa-Go-Ye-Wat-Ha, or Red Jacket* (New York: Wiley & Putnam, 1841); Indians of the St. Regis Reservation, *The American Indian* 4, no. 3 (1948), in Bruchac, *Lasting Echoes,* p. 112.

7. John Echohawk, "We Are Sovereign People," in Crozier-Hogle and Wilson, *Surviving in Two Worlds,* p. 69.

8. Morton, in Blanche, *Native American Reader,* p. 198; Deere, in ibid., p. 121; Erdoes, in *Crying for a Vision,* p. 1.

9. Gertrude Simmons Bonnin, *The Earlhamite* (Earlham, IA: Earlham College, 16 March 1896), in Bruchac, *Lasting Echoes,* p. 111.

10. Young Chief, in McLuhan, *Touch the Earth,* p. 8; Kate Luckie, in *Wintu Ethnography,* by Cora Du Bois (Berkeley: University of California Press, 1935).

11. Pete Catches, quoted in Lame Deer and Erdoes, *Lame Deer,* pp. 140–41; Chief Seattle, speech given in 1854.

12. Sitting Bull, in McLuhan, *Touch the Earth,* p. 90.

13. Henrietta Mann, in *The Way of the Earth: Encounters with Nature in Ancient and Contemporary Thought* (New York: Simon Schuster, 1994), p. 416; George Tinker, in *The Way of the Earth,* pp. 441–42.

14. Asa Bazhonoodah, in Bierhorst, *The Way of the Earth,* p. 414.

15. Momaday, "The Man Made of Words," p. 54; Luther Standing Bear, *My People the Sioux* (Boston: Houghton Mifflin, 1928), quoted in Bruchac, *Lasting Echoes,* pp. 124–25; Linda Hogan, *Reclaiming the Vision: Past, Present, and Future Native Votes for the Eighth Generation,* ed. James Bruchac and Lee Francis, 1996, quoted in Bruchac, *Lasting Echoes,* p. 126.

16. Ben Black Elk, in Armstrong, *I Have Spoken,* p. 158.

17. Chief Luther Standing Bear, in *Soaring with Ravens,* by Tim Fitzharris (San Francisco: Harper, 1995), p. 23; Lyons, in *Exiled,* p. 114.

18. Kahkewaquonaby, in Philip, *In a Sacred Manner I Live,* p. 58.

19. Mathew King in Wall and Arden, *Wisdomkeepers,* p. 33.

20. Red Cloud, "Speech at Cooper Institute," *New York Tribune* (16 January 1870).

21. Tecumseh, in McLuhan, *Touch the Earth,* p. 87.

22. Means, in Blanche, *Native American Reader,* p. 115.

23. John Trudell, "Black Hills Survival Gathering, 1980," in *Stickman: Poems, Lyrics,*

Songs, a Conversation, by John Trudell, ed. Paola Igliori (New York: Inanout Press, 1994), n.p.

24. John Trudell, in Barreiro, "An Interview," p. 39.

25. Red Jacket, in Vanderwerth, comp., *Indian Oratory,* p. 45; Speckled Snake in Philip, *In a Sacred Manner I Live,* p. 53.

26. Susette LaFlesche, in *Boston Daily Advertiser* (26 November 1879), p. 4.

27. Asa Bazhonoodah, quoted in *Native American Testimony: A Chronicle of Indian-White Relations from Prophecy to the Present, 1492–1992,* ed. Peter Nabokov (New York: Penguin Books, 1991), pp. 397–400.

28. Leslie Marmon Silko, *Yellow Woman and a Beauty of the Spirit* (New York: Simon & Schuster, 1996), pp. 48–49.

29. Means, in Blanche, *Native American Reader,* p. 116; Bazhonoodah, in Nabokov, *Native American Testimony,* p. 399.

30. Four Guns, in Blanche, *Native American Reader,* p. 85; Dr. Barney Old Coyote, in Blanche, *Native American Reader,* p. 86; and Earl Old Person in Blanche, *Native American Reader,* p. 91.

31. Chief Powhatan, in Ruoff, *Literature of the American Indian,* p. 62; Tecumseh, in Vanderwerth, comp., *Indian Oratory,* pp. 62–63.

32. Red Jacket, in Vanderwerth, comp., *Indian Oratory,* p. 46; Audrey Shenandoah in Wall and Arden, *Wisdomkeepers,* p. 26.

33. Red Cloud, in Armstong, *I Have Spoken,* p. 92; Standing Bear, in Armstong, *I Have Spoken,* p. 124; LaFlesche, in *Boston Daily Advertiser,* p. 4.

34. Deere, in Blanche, *Native American Reader,* p. 128; Pastor Martin Niemoller.

35. Chief Joseph, in Vanderwerth, comp., *Indian Oratory,* p. 260.

36. Allen C. Quetone, in *Respect for Life: Report of a Conference at Harper's Ferry, West Virginia, on the Traditional Upbringing of American Indian Children,* eds. Sylvester M. Morey and Olivia Gilliam (New York: Myrin Institute, 1974), p. 151; Black Elk in Armstong, *I Have Spoken,* p. 137.

37. Little Beaver's wife, in Armstong, *I Have Spoken,* pp. 36–37.

38. For rhetorical criticisms of the American Indian Movement's protest rhetoric, see John F. Cragen, "Rhetorical Strategy: A Dramatistic Interpretation and Application," *Central States Speech Journal* 26 (1975): pp. 4–11; Tracey Bernstein Weiss, "Media Speaks with Forked Tongue: The Unsuccessful Rhetoric of Wounded Knee," paper presented at the Speech Communication Association Convention, Houston, Texas, December 1975; Edward Streb, "The Alcatraz Occupation, '69–'71: A Perceived Parody of Power Movements," paper presented at the Central States Speech Association Convention, Milwaukee, Wisconsin, April 1974; and Joyce Frost, "A Rhetorical Analysis of Wounded Knee II, 1973: A Conflict Perspective," paper presented at the Central States Speech Association Convention, Milwaukee, Wisconsin, April 1974. For a rhetorical analysis that challenges these, see Randall A. Lake, "Enacting Red Power: The Consummatory Function in Native American Protest Rhetoric," in *Quarterly Journal of Speech* 77 (1991): pp. 123–51.

39. Kevin Foley, "These Things Are Absolutely Essential," in Crozier-Hogle and Wilson, *Surviving in Two Worlds,* pp. 144–45.

40. Gkisedtanamoogk and Hancock, in *Anoqcou,* p. 29.

41. Sarah Hutchison, "The Power of Story," in Crozier-Hogle and Wilson, *Surviving in Two Worlds,* p. 127.

42. Terry Tafoya, "At the Center of the Dance," in Crozier-Hogle and Wilson, *Surviving in Two Worlds,* p. 138.

43. Dr. Gregory Cajete, in *Words of Power: Voices from Indian America,* ed. Norbert S. Hill, Jr. (Golden, CO: Fulcrum Publishing, 1994), p. 3.

44. N. Scott Momaday, "The Power and Beauty of Language," in *Native Heritage: Personal Accounts by American Indians 1790 to the Present,* ed. Arlene Hirschfelder (New York: Macmillan, 1995), p. 73.

45. Chief Seattle, in Vanderwerth, comp., *Indian Oratory,* p. 121.

46. Chief Seattle, in Vanderwerth, comp., *Indian Oratory,* p. 121; Means in Blanche, *Native American Reader,* p. 117.

CHAPTER 4–STORIES

1. Harold Littlebird, in Bruchac, *Lasting Echoes,* p. 127; Silko, *Yellow Woman,* p. 50.

2. See Walter R. Fisher, "Narration as a Human Communication Paradigm: The Case of Public Moral Argument," *Communication Monographs* 51 (1984): pp. 1–22 and Walter R. Fisher, "The Narrative Paradigm: An Elaboration," *Communication Monographs* 52 (1985): pp. 347–67.

3. Joseph Bruchac, *Roots of Survival: Native American Storytelling and the Sacred* (Golden, CO: Fulcrum Publishing, 1996), p. xi; Momaday, "The Man Made of Words," p. 57.

4. Bruchac, *Roots of Survival,* pp. 15–16.

5. Caduto and Bruchac, *Keepers of the Earth,* p. xxiii.

6. The story "Yellow Jacket and Ant" may be found in Blanche, *Native American Reader,* pp. 53–54.

7. George Copway, *Traditional History and Characteristic Sketches of the Ojibway Nation,* 1851; reprint, (New York: AMS, 1977).

8. Sociolinguist Deborah Tannen uses the terms "report talk" and "rapport talk" to distinguish between the language of men and women. See Deborah Tannen, *You Just Don't Understand* (William Morrow & Company, Inc., 1990).

9. See Blanche, *Native American Reader,* pp. 58–59.

10. "The Earth on Turtle's Back," in Caduto and Bruchac, *Keepers of the Earth,* pp. 25–26.

11. See Blanche, *Native American Reader,* pp. 62–64 and 68–69; Smith, *Folklore,* p. 93.

12. "Song of the Wren," in Streep, *The Sacred Journey,* p. 17.

13. The story "Maybe" may be found in Blanche, *Native American Reader,* pp. 35–36.

14. Erdoes and Ortiz, *American Indian Myths,* pp. 496–99.

15. For the White River Sioux story, "What's This? My Balls for Your Dinner?" see Erdoes and Ortiz, *American Indian Myths,* pp. 339–41. The Zuni story, "Teaching the Mudheads How to Copulate," may be found in ibid., pp. 279–80.

16. David Suzuki and Peter Knudson, *Wisdom of the Elders: Sacred Native Stories of Nature* (New York: Bantam Books, 1992), p. 49.

17. "The Neglectful Mother," in Erdoes and Ortiz, *American Indian Myths,* pp. 417–18.

18. For "Speela and Wood-Tick," see Blanche, *Native American Reader,* pp. 62–64. "The Sick Buzzard" may be found in Blanche, *Native American Reader,* pp. 68–69. The story of the White Buffalo Calf Woman and the Sacred Pipe may be found in Black Elk, *Black Elk Speaks: Being the Life Story of a Holy Man of the Oglala Sioux,* ed. John Neihardt (1932; reprint, Lincoln: University of Nebraska Press, 1972).

19. "Gluscabi and the Game Animals," in Caduto and Bruchac, *Keepers of the Earth,* pp. 165–71.

20. "Coyote Steals Tobacco from Crow," in *Giving Birth to Thunder, Sleeping With His*

Daughter: Coyote Builds North America, ed. Barry Lopez (New York: Avon Books, 1977), pp. 20–22; "Coyote and Buffalo," in ibid, pp. 40–42.

21. Bruchac, *Roots of Survival,* p. 16.

22. Barre Toeklen, Foreword, in Lopez, *Giving Birth to Thunder,* pp. xiii–xiv.

23. Lame Deer and Erdoes, *Lame Deer,* p. 115.

24. Dennis Tedlock, *The Spoken Word and the Work of Interpretation* (Philadelphia: University of Pennsylvania Press, 1983), p. 48.

25. Dr. Terry Tafoya, in Crozier-Hogle and Wilson, *Surviving in Two Worlds,* p. 135.

26. Greg Sarris, in ibid., *Surviving in Two Worlds,* p. 229.

CHAPTER 5–PRAYERS AND SONGS

1. Bruchac, *Lasting Echoes,* p. 20; Orpingalik, in Ruoff, *Literature,* p. 37.

2. Ohiyesa, in McLuhan, *Touch the Earth,* p. 36.

3. Betty Cooper, "Walking in Two Worlds," in Crozier-Hogle and Wilson, *Surviving in Two Worlds,* p. 120; Tafoya, in ibid., p. 135.

4. Carlos Cordero, "Reviving Native Technologies," in Crozier-Hogle and Wilson, *Surviving in Two Worlds,* pp. 84–85.

5. Erdoes, *Crying for a Dream,* p. 1.

6. Arvol Looking Horse, in Crozier-Hogle and Wilson, *Surviving in Two Worlds,* p. 36.

7. John Echohawk, "We Are Sovereign Peoples," in ibid., p. 64; Black Elk, *The Sacred Pipe: Black Elk's Account of the Seven Rites of the Oglala Sioux,* ed. Joseph Epes Brown (Norman: University of Oklahoma Press, 1953), p. 75.

8. George Tinker, "For All My Relations," *Sojourners* (Jan. 1991): n.p., quoted in Bierhorst, *The Way of the Earth,* p. 441.

9. Song, *Journey,* p. 198.

10. Spider, *Songs of Bleeding* (New York City: Black Thistle Press, 1992), p. 3.

11. Bierhorst, *The Way of the Earth,* p. 479.

12. Popovi Da, "Indian Pottery and Indian Values," in *Maria,* by Richard L. Spivey (Flagstaff, AZ: Northland Press, 1979), pp. xvii–xxi, quoted in Bierhorst, *The Way of the Earth,* p. 428.

13. Ruoff, *Literatures,* p. 23.

14. Song, *Journey,* p. 198.

15. Ibid., p. 190.

16. Lame Deer, in Philip, *In a Sacred Manner I Live,* p. 49.

17. Frank Fools Crow, in *In a Sacred Manner I Live,* pp. 89–90.

18. Tafoya, in Crozier-Hogle and Wilson, *Surviving in Two Worlds,* p. 138.

19. Bierhorst, *The Way of the Earth,* pp. 515 and 460.

20. Charlie Knight in Wall and Arden, *Wisdomkeepers,* p. 16.

21. Grand Council Fire of American Indians, in Armstrong, *I Have Spoken,* p. 146.

22. Frank Waters, *The Book of the Hopi* (New York: Penguin, 1963), p. 172.

23. Anishinabe song, in Bruchac, *Lasting Echoes,* p. xii; Lakota song in Kenneth Lincoln, Foreword, to *American Indian Poetry: An Anthology of Songs and Chants,* ed. George W. Cronyn (New York: Fawcett Columbine, 1991), p. xix; Anishinabe song, in Streep, *Sacred Journey,* p. 76

24. Popovi Da, quoted in Bierhorst, *The Way of the Earth,* p. 428; statement about dance, in Joseph Epes Brown, *The Spiritual Legacy of the American Indian* (New York: Crossroad Publishing Co., 1982), p. 123, quoted in Bierhorst, *The Way of the Earth,* p. 467.

25. Cagaba song, in John Bierhorst, ed., *The Sacred Path: Spells, Prayers and Power Songs of the American Indians* (New York: Quill, 1984), p. 111.

26. Ojibway song in Ruoff, *Literatures*, p. 31; Pawnee "Ritual Song," in Streep, *The Sacred Journey*, p. 72.

CHAPTER 6–ORAL TRADITION

1. N. Scott Momaday, *The Way to Rainy Mountain* (Albuquerque: University of New Mexico Press, 1969).

2. John Ross, in Vanderwerth, comp., *Indian Oratory*, p. 109.

3. Kenneth Burke, *A Rhetoric of Motives* (New York: Prentice-Hall, Inc., 1950).

4. Vickie Downie, in *Wisdom's Daughters*, p. 20.

5. Gregory A. Cajete, "Ensoulment of Nature," in *Native Heritage*, p. 56.

6. Chief Leon Shenandoah, "Address to the General Assembly of the United Nations," October 25, 1985, in *Meetings with Native American Spiritual Elders*, p. 108; Camp, in Blanche, *Native American Reader*, pp. 167 and 175; "Song of the Earth Spirit, Navaho Origin Legend," in Kenneth Browwer, ed., *Navaho Wildlands* (San Franscisco: The Sierra Club, 1969), p. 124; and a Yokuts prayer, from A. L. Kroeber, *Handbook of the Indians of California*, Bureau of American Ethnology Bulletin 78, Washington, D.C., 1925.

7. Caduto and Bruchac, in *Keepers of the Earth*, p. 4.

8. The speech by A. P. Johnson comes from *Haa Tuwunaagu Uis, for Healing Our Spirit: Tlingit Oratory*, ed. Nora Marks Dauenhauer and Richard Dauenhauer, vol. 2 (Seattle: University of Washington Press, 1990), p. 157.

9. Anna Lee Walters, *Talking Indian: Reflections on Survival and Writing* (Ithaca, NY: Firebrand Books, 1992), p. 13.

10. Linda Hogan, "Blessings," *Calling Myself Home* (Greenfield Center, NY: Greenfield Review Press, 1979).

11. Walters, *Talking Indian*, pp. 11–12.

12. Ten Bears, in Vanderwerth, comp., *Indian Oratory*, pp. 161–62; Morton, in Blanche, *Native American Reader*, p. 198.

13. Four Guns, ibid., p. 85.

CONCLUSION

1. Gerald Vizenor, *Wordarrows: Indians and Whites in the New Fur Trade* (Minneapolis: University of Minnesota Press, 1978), p. vii; Paula Gunn Allen, *Studies in American Indian Literature: Critical Essays and Course Designs* (New York: Modern Language Association, 1983), p. 37.

2. Walters, *Talking Indian*, pp. 11–13.

3. Momaday, *Man Made of Words*, p. 28.

4. Walters, *Talking Indian*, pp. 11 and 13.

5. Ortiz, in *Winged Words*, pp. 112–13.

6. Vizenor, *Wordarrows*, p. 94. Vizenor makes his point through the character of Matchi Makwa.

7. Momaday, *Man Made of Words*, p. 104.

World Family. Illustration by Francene Hart.

Further Reading

I am a part of all I have read.

John Kieran, Journalist

Abbott, Lawrence, ed. *I Stand in the Center of the Good: Interviews with Contemporary Native American Artists*. Lincoln: University of Nebraska Press, 1994.

Adams, Barbara Means. *Prayers of Smoke*. Berkeley: Celestial Arts, 1990.

"Affirmation of Sovereignty of the Indigenous Peoples of the Western Hemisphere." *Akwesane Notes* 10 (Summer 1978): p. 15.

Ahenakew, Edward. "Cree Trickster Tales." *Journal of American Folklore* 42 (1929).

"A.I.M.: The American Indian Movement." St. Paul: AIM National Office, undated leaflet.

Alexander, Hartley Burr. *North American Mythology*. Boston: Marshall Jones Company, 1916.

Allen, Paula Gunn. *Grandmothers of the Light: A Medicine Woman's Source Book*. Boston: Beacon Press, 1991.

———. *The Sacred Hoop: Recovering the Feminine in American Indian Traditions*. Boston: Beacon Press, 1992.

———, ed. *Spider Woman's Granddaughters: Traditional Tales and Contemporary Writing by Native American Women*. Boston: Beacon Press, 1989.

———. *Studies in American Indian Literature: Critical Essays and Course Designs*. New York: Modern Language Association, 1983.

American Indian Media Image Task Force. *The American Indian and the Media*. National Conference of Christians and Jews Minnesota-Dakotas Region, 1991.

"American Indians to Fight Sandinista Regime." *Los Angeles Times* (28 December 1985): pt. 1, p. 10.

Amiotte, Arthur. "The Road to the Center." *Parabola*, no. 3 (1984): pp. 46–51.

Angulo, Jaime de. *Indian Tales*. New York: Ballatine, 1953.

Antin, David. *Talking at the Boundaries*. New York: New Directions, 1976.

Aoki, Haruo, and Deward E. Walker. *Nez Perce Oral Narratives*. Berkeley: University of California Publications in Linguistics no. 104, Berkeley: 1989.

Aolei, Haruo, ed. *Nez Perce Texts*. Berkeley: University of California Publications in Linguistics no. 90, 1979.

Archambault, D. "Columbus Plus 500 Years: Whither the American Indian?" *Vital Speeches of the Day* 58 (1992): pp. 491–93.

Arden, Harvey, comp. and ed. Noble *Red Man: Lakota Wisdomkeeper Mathew King*. Hillsboro, OR: Beyond Words Publishing, 1994.

Armstrong, Jeannette, ed. *Looking at the Words of Our People: First Nations Analysis of Literature*. Penticton, British Columbia: Theytus Books, Ltd., 1993.

Armstrong, Virginia Irving, comp. *I Have Spoken: American History through the Voices of the Indians*. Athens: Ohio University Press, 1991.

Arrington, Ruth. "Indian Studies: Where Are We?" *ACA Bulletin* 22 (1977): pp. 34–35.

Asatchaq, Tukummuq, and Tom Lowenstein. *The Things That Were Said of Them: Shaman Stories and Oral Histories of the Tikigaq People*. Berkeley: University of California Press, 1992.

Astrov, Margot. *The Winged Serpent: American Indian Prose and Poetry*. Boston: Beacon Press, 1992.

Athanases, Steven Z. "Cross-Cultural Swapping of Mother and Grandmother Tales in a Tenth Grade Discussion of *The Joy Luck Club*." *Communication Education* 42 (1993): pp. 282–87.

Austin, Mary. *The American Rhythm: Studies and Reexpressions of AmerIndian Songs*. 1923. Reprint. New York: Cooper Square, 1970.

Awiakta, Marilou. *Selu: Seeking the Corn-Mother's Wisdom*. Golden, CO: Fulcrum Publishing, 1993.

Babcock, C. Merton. *Walk Quietly the Beautiful Trail: Lyrics and Legends of the American Indian*. Kansas City, MO: Hallmark Cards, Inc., 1973.

Bahr, Donald. *Pima and Papago Ritual Oratory: A Study of Three Texts*. San Francisco: Indian Historian Press, 1975.

Bakhtin, Mikhail. *The Dialogic Imagination: Four Essays*. Trans. Caryl Emerson and Michael Holquist. Austin: University of Texas Press, 1981.

———. *Speech Genres and Other Late Essays*. Trans. Vern W. McGee. Austin: University of Texas Press, 1986.

Balgooyen, Theodore J. "The Plains Indian as Public Speaker." In *Landmarks in Western Oratory,* edited by David H. Grover, pp. 13–43, Laramie, WY: Graduate School and Western Speech Association, 1968. 13–43.

———. "The Public Speaking of the Typical North American Plains Indians of the Nineteenth Century." Ph.D. diss., Stanford University, 1957.

———. "A Study of Conflicting Values: American Plains Indian Orators vs. the U.S. Commissioners of Indian Affairs." *Western Journal of Speech Communication* 26 (1962): pp. 76–83.

Ball, Eve, ed. "In Our Language There Is No Profanity." In *In the Days of Victoria: Recollections of a Warm Springs Apache*. Tucson: University of Arizona Press, 1970.

Barbeau, Marius, and Grace Melvin. *The Indian Speaks*. Toronto: Macmillan Co. of Canada Ltd., 1943.

Barbour, Ian G., ed. *Western Man and Environmental Ethics: Attitudes Toward Nature and Technology*. Reading, MA: Addison-Wesley Publishing Co., Inc., 1973.

Barnouw, Victor. *Wisconsin Chippewa Myths and Their Relation to Chippewa Life*. Madison: University of Wisconsin Press, 1977.

Barreiro, Jose, ed. "Interview with John Trudell: Confronting the Spirit Eater." *Native Americas: Akwe:kon's Journal of Indigenous Issues* 15, no. 4 (Winter 1997): pp. 34–41.

Barreiro, Jose, and Carol Cornelius. *Knowledge of the Elders*. Ithaca, NY: Akwe Kon Press, 1991.

Barsness, Larry. *Heads, Hides, and Horns: The Complete Buffalo Book*. Ft. Worth: Christian University Press, 1985.

Bascom, William. "The Forms of Folklore: Prose Narratives." *Journal of American Folklore* 78 (1965): pp. 3–20.

Basic Call to Consciousness. Ed. Akwesasne. Summertown, TN: Book Publishing Company, 1993.

Basso, Keith. "Stalking with Stories: Names, Places, and Moral Narratives among the Western Apache." In *Text, Play, and Story*, edited by Edward M. Bruner, pp. 19–55, Berkeley: University of California Press, 1984.

———. *Western Apache Language and Culture: Essays in Linguistic Anthropology*. Tucson: University of Arizona Press, 1990.

Bataille, Gretchen M., and Laurie Lariersa. *Native American Women: A Biographical Dictionary*. New York: Garland Publishing, 1993.

Bataille, Gretchen M., *American Indian Women: A Guide to Research*. New York: Garland Publishing, 1991.

Bataille, Gretchen M., and Kathleen Mullen Sands. *American Indian Women: Telling Their Lives*. Lincoln: University of Nebraska Press, 1984.

Bataille, Gretchen M., Kathleen Sands, and Charles Silet, eds. *The Pretend Indians: Images of Native Americans in the Movies*. Ames: University of Iowa Press, 1980.

Bates, Earl A. *Tell Me an Indian Story*. Cortland, NY: The Cortland Democrat Press, 1932.

Bauman, Richard. *Verbal Art as Performance*. Prospect Heights, IL: Waveland Press, 1984.

Bauman, Richard, and Joel Sherzer. *Explorations in the Ethnography of Speaking*. Cambridge: Cambridge University Press, 1974.

Beal, Merrill D. *"I Will Fight No More Forever": Chief Joseph and the Nez Perce War*. Seattle: University of Washington Press, 1963.

Beck, Peggy V., and Anna Lee Walters. *The Sacred Ways of Knowledge: Sources of Life*. Tsaile, AZ: Navajo Community College Press, 1977.

"Bellecourt Explains AIM Goals." *Wassaja* 1 (April/May 1973): p. 7.

Bennett, Hal Zina. *Zuni Fetishes: Using Native American Objects for Meditation, Reflection, and Insight*. San Francisco: Harper, 1993.

Benton, Thomas W. *Indian Speeches*. Pamphlet. Oklahoma City.

Benton-Banai, Edward. *The Mishomis Book: The Voice of the Ojibway*. Saint Paul, MN: Red School House, 1988.

Berman, Howard. "Resource Exploitation: The Cutting Edge of Genocide." *Akwesasne Notes* 10 (late Spring 1978): pp. 9–10.

Berry, Wendell. *Standing by Words*. San Francisco: North Point Press, 1983.

Berthouex, Susan J., and Robin S. Chapman. "Storytelling: A Way to Teach Non-Native Students." In *Non-Native and Nonstandard Dialect Students* edited by Candy Carter, pp. 37–43. Urbana, IL: National Council of Teachers of English, 1982.

Bierhorst, John, ed. *Four Masterworks of American Indian Literature*. 1974 reprint. Tucson: University of Arizona Press, 1984).

———, ed. *In the Trail of the Wind: American Indian Poems and Ritual Orations*. Toronto: Farrar, Straus and Giroux, 1998.

———. *Mythology of the Lenape: Guide and Texts*. Tucson: University of Arizona Press, 1995.

———. *The Mythology of North America*. New York: William Morrow, 1985.

————. *Myths and Tales of the American Indians*. New York: Indian Head Books, 1976.

————. *The Sacred Path: Spells, Prayers and Power Songs of the American Indians*. New York: Quill, 1984.

————. *The Way of the Earth: Native America and the Environment*. New York: William Morrow, 1994.

————. *The White Deer and Other Stories Told by the Lenape*. New York: William Morrow, 1995.

Black Elk. *Black Elk Speaks: Being the Life Story of a Holy Man of the Oglala Sioux*. Ed. John Neihardt. 1932 Reprint. Lincoln: University of Nebraska Press, 1972.

————. *The Sacred Pipe: Black Elk's Account of the Seven Rites of the Oglala Sioux*. Rec. and ed. Joseph Epes Brown. Norman: University of Oklahoma Press, 1953.

Black Elk, Wallace, and William S. Lyon. *Black Elk: The Sacred Way of a Lakota*. San Francisco: Harper.

Black, Mary E. "Maidens and Mothers: An Analysis of Hopi Corn Metaphors." *Ethnology* 23 (1984).

Blaeser, Kimberly M. *Gerald Vizenor: Writing in the Oral Tradition*. Norman: University of Oklahoma Press, 1996.

Blanche, Jerry D., ed. *Native American Reader: Stories, Speeches, and Poems*. Juneau: The Denali Press, 1990.

Bloomfield, Leonard. *Sacred Stories of the Sweet Grass Cree*. National Museums of Canada Anthropological Series no. 11, bulletin no. 60. Ottawa, 1930.

Blue Cloud, Peter, ed. *Alcatraz Is Not an Island*. Berkeley: Wingbow Press, 1972.

Boas, Franz. "Eskimo Tales and Songs." *Journal of American Folklore* 7 (1894).

————. *Folk Tales of Salishan and Sahaptin Tribes*. New York: American Folklore Society, 1917.

————. "Literature, Music, and Dance." In *General Anthropology*. Boston: D. C. Heath and Company, 1938.

————. "Poetry and Music of Some North American Tribes." *Science* 9, no. 220 (22 April 1887): pp. 383–85.

————. *Race, Language, and Culture*. New York: The Macmillan Company, 1940.

Boelscher, Marianne. *The Curtain Within: Haida Social and Mythical Discourse*. Vancouver: University of British Columbia Press, 1989.

Bolt, Christine. *American Indian Policy and American Reform: Case Studies of the Campaign to Assimilate the American Indians*. London: Allen and Unwin, 1987.

Bonvillain, Nancy. *Native American Religion*. New York: Chelsea House Publishers, 1996.

The Book of Elders: The Life Stories of Great American Indians as Told to Sandy Johnson. San Francisco: Harper, 1994.

Bosmajian, Haig A. "Defining the American Indian: A Case Study in the Language of Suppression." *The Speech Teacher* 22 (1973): pp. 89–99.

Bowers, Neal, and Charles L. P. Silet. "An Interview with Gerald Vizenor." *Melus* 8 (1981): pp. 41–49.

Boyd, Doug. *Rolling Thunder*. New York: Dell Publishing Co., 1974.

Boyd, Maurice. *Kiowa Voices, Vol. 1: Ceremonial Dance, Ritual and Song*. Fort Worth: Texas Christian University Press, 1981.

Brady, Margaret K. *"Some Kind of Power": Navajo Children's Skinwalker Narratives*. Salt Lake City: University of Utah Press, 1984.

Brandon, William. *The Magic World: American Indian Songs and Poems*. New York: William Morrow & Company, Inc., 1971.

Brant, Beth, ed. *A Gathering of Spirit: Writing and Art of North American Indian Women*.

Toronto: The Women's Press, 1988.

Brass, Eleanor. *Medicine Boy and Other Cree Tales*. Calgary: Glenbow-Alberta Institute, 1978.

Bricker, Victoria Reifler. *Ritual Humor in Highland Chiapas*. Austin: University of Texas Press, 1973.

Briggs, Jean L. "Kapluna Daughter: Adopted by the Eskimo." In *Conformity and Conflict: Readings in Cultural Anthropology*. 3rd ed., edited by James P. Spradley and David W. McCurdy, pp. 61–79/. Boston: Little, Brown and Company, 1977.

Bright, William, ed. *Coyote Stories*. Chicago: University of Chicago Press, 1978.

Brotherston, Gordon. *Book of the Fourth World: Reading the Native Americans through Their Literature*. Cambridge: Cambridge University Press, 1992.

Brown, Dee. *Bury My Heart at Wounded Knee: An Indian History of the American West*. New York: William Morrow & Company, 1985.

Brown, John Epes. *The Spiritual Legacy of the American Indian*. New York: Crossroad Publishing Co., 1982.

Browser, Kenneth, ed. *Navaho Wildlands*. San Franscisco: The Sierra Club, 1969.

Bruchac, Joseph. *Lasting Echoes: An Oral History of Native American People*. San Diego: Harcourt Brace & Company, 1997.

———. *The Native American Sweat Lodge: History and Legends*. Freedom, CA: The Crossing Press, 1993.

———, ed. *Native Wisdom*. San Francisco: Harper, 1995.

———. *Roots of Survival: Native American Storytelling and the Sacred*. Golden, CO: Fulcrum Publishing, 1996.

———, ed. *Songs from This Earth on Turtle's Back: Contemporary American Indian Poetry*. Greenfield Center, NY: Greenfield Review Literary Center, 1983.

———. *Story Earth: Native Voices on the Environment*. San Francisco: Mercury House, 1993.

———. "Storytelling and the Sacred: On the Uses of Native American Stories." In *Through Indian Eyes: The Native Experience in Books for Children,* edited by Beverly Slapin and Doris Seale, pp. 91–97. Philadelphia: New Society Publishers, 1992.

———, ed. *Survival This Way: Interviews with American Indian Poets*. Tucson: Sun Tracks and University of Arizona Press, 1987.

Brumble, H. David III. *American Indian Autobiography*. Berkeley: University of California Press, 1988.

Bryan, William Jennings, and Francis W. Halsey, eds. *The World's Famous Orations*. New York: Funk & Wagnalls Co., 1906.

Buck, Ruth M., ed. *Voices of the Plains Cree*. Toronto: McClelland & Stewart, 1973.

Buckley, Thomas. "The One Who Flies All around the World." *Parabola* 16, no. 1 (1991): pp. 4–9.

Bullchild, Percy. *The Sun Came Down: The History of the World as My Blackfeet Elders Told It*. New York: Harper and Row, 1985.

Bunzel, Ruth. "Zuni Origin Myths." *Annual Report of the Bureau of American Ethnology* 47 (1932): pp. 545–609.

———. "Zuni Ritual Poetry." *Annual Report of the Bureau of American Ethnology* 47 (1932): pp. 611–835.

———. "Zuni Texts." *American Ethnological Society*. Publication 15 (1933).

Buswell, Lois E. "The Oratory of the Dakota Indians." *The Quarterly Journal of Speech* 21 (1935): pp. 323–27.

Caduto, Michael J., and Joseph Bruchac, *Keepers of the Earth: Native American Stories and Environmental Activities for Children*. Golden, CO: Fulcrum Publishing, 1989.

———. *Teacher's Guide to Keepers of the Earth*. Golden, CO: Fulcrum Publishing, 1988.

Calloway, Colin G., ed. *The World Turned Upside Down: Indian Voices from Early America.* Boston: Bedford Books, 1994.

Camp, Charles. "American Indian Oratory in the White Image: An Analysis of Stereotypes." *Journal of American Culture* 1 (1978): pp. 811–17.

Campbell, Joseph. *The Hero with a Thousand Faces.* New York: MJF Books, 1949.

———. *The Power of Myth.* New York: Doubleday, 1988.

Capps, Walter Holden, ed. *Seeing with a Native Eye: Essays on Native American Religion.* New York: Harper & Row, 1976.

———. *Transformation of Myth through Time.* New York: Harper & Row, 1990.

Cardinal, Douglas, and Jeannette Armstrong. *The Native Creative Process: A Collaborative Discourse between Douglas Cardinal and Jeannette Armstrong.* Penticton, British Columbia: Theytus Books, 1991.

Carpenter, Edmund, and Marshall McLuhan. *Explorations in Communication: An Anthology.* Boston: Beacon Press, 1960.

Chafe, Wallace L. *Seneca Thanksgiving Rituals.* Washington, DC: Bureau of American Ethnology Bulletin no. 183 (1961).

Champagne, Duane. *American Indian Societies: Strategies and Conditions of Political and Cultural Survival.* Cambridge, MA: Cultural Survival, 1989.

Chapman, Abraham, ed. *Literature of the American Indians: Views and Interpretations.* New York: New American Library, 1975.

Chapman, John, and James Kari. *Athabaskan Stories from Anvik.* Fairbanks: Alaska Native Language Center, 1981.

Chen, Li-chu. "Sweat Lodge: Real Communication and Spiritual Rebirth." Paper presented at the National Communication Association Convention, Chicago, November, 1997.

Chief Joseph. "An Indian's Views of Indian Affairs." *North American Review* 128 (1879).

Chowning, Ann. "Raven Myths in Northwestern North America and Northeastern Asia." *Arctic Anthropology* 1 (1962).

Chronicles of American Indian Protest. Edited by the Council on Interracial Books for Children. Greenwich, CT: Fawcett Publications, Inc., 1971.

Churchill, Ward. *Indians Are Us? Culture and Genocide in Native North America.* Monroe, ME: Common Courage Press, 1994.

———. *Struggle for the Land: Indigenous Resistance to Genocide, Ecocide, and Expropriation in Contemporary North America.* Monroe, ME: Common Courage, 1993.

Clark, Ella. *Indian Legends of the Pacific Northwest.* Berkeley: University of California Press, 1936.

Clements, William M., and Frances M. Malpezzi, comps. *Native American Folklore, 1879–1979: An Annotated Bibliography.* Athens: Swallow-Ohio University Press, 1984.

Clifton, James A., ed. *Being and Becoming Indian: Biographical Studies of North American Frontiers.* Chicago: Dorsey Press, 1989.

Collaer, Paul, ed. *Music of the Americas: An Illustrated Music Ethnology of the Eskimo and American Indian Peoples.* New York: Praeger Publishers, 1973.

Colombo, John Robert, ed. *Songs of the Indians.* 2 vols. Ottawa: Oberon Press, 1983.

Coltelli, Laura, ed., *Native American Literatures.* Pisa: Servizio Editoriale Universitario, 1989.

———. *Winged Words: American Indian Writers Speak.* Lincoln: University of Nebraska Press, 1990.

Committee on Tolerance and Understanding. *Public Policy—Statements on Native Education.*

Edmonton: Government of Alberta, 1984.

Commuck, Thomas. *Indian Melodies*. New York: 1845.

Converse, Harriet Maxwell. *Myths and Legends of the New York State Iroquois*. New York: New York State Museum, 1908.

Copeland, Lewis, ed. *The World's Great Speeches*. 2nd rev. ed. New York: Dover Publications, 1958.

Copway, George. *Life, Letters and Speeches*. 2nd ed. New York: Benedict, 1850.

———. *Traditional History and Characteristic Sketches of the Ojibway Nation*. 1851. Reprint. New York: AMS, 1977.

Cornell, Stephen. *Return of the Native: American Indian Political Resurgence*. New York: Oxford University Press, 1988.

Coward, John M. "The Newspaper Indian: Native Americans and the Press in the 19th Century." Ph.D. diss., University of Texas at Austin, 1989.

Cragen, John F. "Rhetorical Strategy: A Dramatistic Interpretation and Application." *Central States Speech Journal* 26 (1975): pp. 4–11.

Cronyn, George W., ed. *American Indian Poetry: An Anthology of Songs and Chants*. New York: Fawcett Columbine, 1991.

"Crow Dog from Prison." *Akwesasne Notes* 8 (Spring, 1976): 14.

Crow Dog, Mary, and Richard Erdoes. *Lakota Woman*. New York: HarperCollins, 1991.

———. *Ohitika Woman*. New York: Grove Press, 1993.

Crowe, Charles. "Indians and Blacks in White America." In *Four Centuries of Southern Indians,* edited by Charles M. Hudson, pp. 148–70. Athens: University of Georgia Press, 1975.

Crozier-Hogle, Lois, and Darryl Babe Wilson, eds. *Surviving in Two Worlds: Contemporary Native American Voices*. Austin: University of Texas Press, 1997.

Cruikshank, Julie. *Reading Voices/Dan Dha Ts'edenintth'e Oral and Written Interpretations of the Yukon's Past*. Vancouver: Douglas and McIntyre, 1991.

Curtin, Jeremiah, and J.N.B. Hewitt, "Seneca Fiction, Legends, and Myths." *Thirty-Second Annual Report of the Bureau of American Ethnology* (1918).

Curtis, Natalie, ed. *The Indians' Book: Songs and Legends of the American Indians*. New York: Dover Publications, 1907.

Cushing, Frank. *Outlines of Zuni Creation Myths*. Washington, DC: 13th Report of the Bureau of American Ethnology, 1896.

Cuthand, Beth. *Horse Dance to Emerald Mountain*. Vancouver: Lazara Press, 1987.

———. *Voices in the Waterfall*. Vancouver: Lazara Press, 1989.

Da, Popovi, "Indian Pottery and Indian Values." In *Maria,* by Richard L. Spivey. Flagstaff, AZ: Northland Press, 1979.

Dauenhauer, Nora Marks, and Richard Dauenhauer, eds. *Classics of Tlingit Oral Literature*. Seattle: University of Washington Press, 1990.

———. *Haa Shuka, Our Ancestors: Tlingit Oral Narratives*. Seattle: University of Washington Press, 1987.

———. *Haa Tuwunaagu Yis, for Healing Our Spirit: Tlingit Oratory*. Vol. 2. Seattle: University of Washington Press, 1990.

Dauenhauer, Nora Marks, Richard Dauenhauer, and Gary Holthaus. "Alaska Native Writers, Storytellers, and Orators." *Alaska Quarterly Review* 4 (1986).

Dauenhauer, Richard. "Text and Context of Tlingit Oral Tradition." Ph.D. diss., University of Wisconsin-Madison, 1975.

Davis, Mary, ed. *Native America in the Twentieth Century: An Encyclopedia*. New York: Garland Publishing, 1994.

Deloria, Ella C. *Dakota Texts*. Publications of the American Ethnological Society no. 14. New York: G. E. Stechert, 1932.

———. *Speaking of Indians*. New York: Friendship Books, 1944.

Deloria, Vine, Jr., ed. *American Indian Policy in the Twentieth Century*. Norman: University of Oklahoma Press, 1985.

———. *Behind the Trail of Broken Treaties: An Indian Declaration of Independence*. New York: Delacorte Press, 1974.

———. *Custer Died for Your Sins: An Indian Manifesto*. New York: Avon Books, 1970.

———. *God Is Red: A Native View of Religion*. 2nd ed. Golden, CO: Fulcrum Publishing, 1992.

———. "The Question of the 1868 Sioux Treaty: A Crucial Element in the Wounded Knee Trials." *Akwesasne Notes* 6 (early spring, 1974): 12.

———. *Sacred Lands and Religious Freedom*. New York: Association on American Indian Affairs, 1991.

———. "This Country Was a Lot Better Off When the Indians Were Running It." *New York Times Magazine* (8 March 1970): pt. VI, p. 32.

———. *We Talk, You Listen: New Tribes, New Turf*. New York: Macmillan, 1970.

DeMallie, Raymond J., and Elaine A. Jahner. *Lakota Belief and Ritual*. Lincoln: University of Nebraska Press, 1980.

Dene Nation. *Denedeh: A Dene Celebration*. Toronto: McClelland and Stewart, 1984.

Deskaheh: Iroquois Statesman and Patriot. Six Nations Indian Museum Series. Rooseveltown, NY: Akwesasne Notes, n.d.

Desmore, Frances, ed. *Chippewa Music*. 1910. Reprint as Chippewa Music 1, Music Reprint Series, New York: Da Capo Press, 1972.

———. *Chippewa Music II*. Washington, DC: Bureau of American Ethnology Bulletin, no. 53 (1913).

———. *Papago Music*. Washington, DC: Bureau of American Ethnology Bulletin, no. 90 (1929).

———. *Pawnee Music*. Washington, DC: Bureau of American Ethnology Bulletin, no. 93 (1929).

———. *Teton Sioux Music*. 1918. Reprint, New York: Da Capo Press, 1972.

———. *Yuman and Yuqui Music*. Washington, DC: Bureau of American Ethnology Bulletin, no. 110 (1932).

"The Dine Nation." *Akwesasne Notes* 11 (Spring 1979): pp. 23–24.

Dippie, Brian W. *The Vanishing American: White Attitudes and U.S. Indian Policy*. Middletown, CT: Wesleyan University Press, 1982.

Dodge, Robert, and Joseph McCullough, eds. *New and Old Voices of Wah'Kon-Tah*. New York: International Publishers, 1985.

Dooling, D. M. and Paul Jordan-Smith, eds. *I Become Part of It*. New York: Parabola Books, 1989.

Dorris, Michael. *The Broken Cord*. New York: Harper and Row, 1989.

Downes, Randolph C. "A Crusade for Indian Reform, 1922–1934." *Mississippi Valley Historical Review* 32, no. 3 (December 1945): pp. 331–54.

Du Bois, Cora. *Wintu Ethnography*. Berkeley: University of California Press, 1935.

Dundes, Alan. "Texture, Text, and Context." *Southern Folklore Quarterly* 29 (1964): pp. 251–65.

Eastman, Charles A. *The Soul of the Indian*. Lincoln: University of Nebraska Press, 1980.

Edmonson, Munro S. "Narrative Folklore." In *Handbook of Middle American Indians,* edited by Manning Nash. Vol. 6, pp. 357–68. Austin: University of Texas Press.

Edmunds, R. David, ed. *American Indian Leaders: Studies in Diversity.* Lincoln: University of Nebraska Press, 1980.

Ek, Richard A. "Red Cloud's Cooper Union Address." *Central States Speech Journal* 17 (1966): pp. 257–62.

Elder, John, and Hertha Wong, eds. *Family of the Earth and Sky: Indigenous Tales of Nature from around the World.* Boston: Beacon Press, 1994.

Elder's Gathering. Ontario Federation of Indian Friendship Centres. Birch Island, Ontario, 14–17 May 1985.

Eliade, Mircea. *Myth and Reality.* New York: Harper and Row, 1963.

———. *The Myth of the Eternal Return or Cosmos and History.* Trans. W. Trask. Princeton: Princeton University Press, 1964.

———. *Myths, Rites, and Symbols.* Trans. W. Beane and W. Doty. San Francisco: Harper and Row, 1975.

———. *The Sacred and the Profane: The Nature of Religion.* New York: Harcourt, Brace & World, 1959.

Erdich, Louise. *Love Medicine.* New York: Bantam Books, 1984.

Erdoes, Richard, and Alfonso Ortiz, *American Indian Myths and Legends.* New York: Pantheon Books, 1984.

Evers, Larry, ed. *The South Corner of Time: Hopi, Navajo, Papago, Yaqui Tribal Literature.* Tucson: University of Arizona Press, 1980.

Evers, Larry, and Felipe M. Molina. *Yaqui Deer Songs.* Tucson: University of Arizona Press, 1986.

Farrar, Claire R. "Singing for Life: The Mescalero Apache Girls' Puberty Ceremony." In *Southwestern Indian Ritual Drama,* edited by Charlotte J. Frisbie. Albuquerque: School of American Research and University of New Mexico Press, 1980.

Farrell, Thomas B. "Rhetoric, Conversation, Time, and Moral Action." *Quarterly Journal of Speech* 71 (1985): pp. 1–18.

Fields, Rick, Peggy Taylor, Rex Weyler, and Rick Ingrasci. *Chop Wood, Carry Water: A Guide to Finding Spiritual Fulfillment in Everyday Life.* Los Angeles: Jeremy P. Tarcher, Inc., 1984.

Finnegan, Ruth. *Oral Poetry: Its Nature, Significance, and Social Context.* Cambridge: Cambridge University Press, 1977.

The First Americans. By the editors of Time-Life Books. Alexandria, VA: Time Inc. Book Company, 1992.

Fisher, Walter R. "Narration as a Human Communication Paradigm: The Case of Public Moral Argument." *Communication Monographs* 51 (1984): pp. 1–22.

———. "The Narrative Paradigm: An Elaboration." *Communication Monographs* 52 (1985): pp. 347–67.

Fiske, John. "Myths and Myth Makers: Old Tales and Superstitions." *Comparative Mythology Journal.* Boston (1896).

Fitzharris, Tim. *Soaring with Ravens: Visions of the Native American Landscape.* San Francisco: Harper, 1995.

Flowers, Betty Sue, ed. *Joseph Campbell: The Power of Myth with Bill Moyers.* New York: Doubleday, 1988.

Forbes, Jack D., ed. *Nevada Indians Speak.* Reno: University of Nevada Press, 1967.

Foster, Michael K. *From the Earth to Beyond the Sky: An Ethnographical Approach to Four Iroquois Speech Events.* Ottawa: National Museums of Canada, 1974.

———. *The Recovery and Translation of Native Speeches Accompanying Ancient Iroquois-White Treaties.* Canadian National Museum of Man, Ethnology Division, Canadian Studies Report 5 e–f. Ottawa (1978).

———. "When Words Become Deeds: An Analysis of Three Iroquois Longhouse Speech Events." In *Explorations in the Ethnography of Speaking,* edited by Richard Bauman and Joel Sherzer, pp. 354–67. Cambridge: Cambridge University Press, 1974.

Fox, Matthew. *A Spirituality Named Compassion and the Healing of the Global Village; Humpty Dumpty and Us.* Minneapolis, MN: Winston Press, 1979.

Freesoul, John Redtail. *Breath of the Invisible: The Way of the Pipe.* Wheaton, IL: The Theosophical Publishing House, 1986.

Frentz, Thomas S., and Janice Hocker Rushing. "Integrating Ideology and Archetype in Rhetorical Criticism, Part II: A Case Study of *Jaws.*" *Quarterly Journal of Speech* 79 (1993): pp. 61–81.

Frisbie, Charlotte J. ed. *Southwestern Indian Ritual Drama.* Albuquerque: University of New Mexico Press, 1980.

Frost, Joyce. "A Rhetorical Analysis of Wounded Knee II, 1973: A Conflict Perspective." Paper presented at the Central States Speech Association Convention, Milwaukee, Wisconsin, April 1974.

Fuoss, Kirk W., and Randall T. Hill. "A Performance Centered Approach for Teaching a Course in Social Movements." *Communication Education* 41 (1992): pp. 71–88.

Gaddis, Vincent H. *American Indian Myths and Mysteries.* Radnor, PA: Chilton Book Company, 1977.

"Ganienkeh and Now Wabanaki." *Akwesasne Notes* 8 (Summer 1976): p. 19.

Garrett, J. T., and Michael Garrett. *Medicine of the Cherokee: The Way of Right Relationship.* Santa Fe, NM: Bear & Company, 1996.

Gattuso, John, ed. *A Circle of Nations: Voices and Visions of American Indians.* Hillsboro, OR: Beyond Words Publishing, Inc., 1993.

Gedalof, Robin, ed. *Paper Stays Put: A Collection of Inuit Writing.* Edmonton, Alberta: Hurtig Publications, 1980.

Geertz, Clifford. "Ethos, World-View and the Analysis of Sacred Symbols." *Antioch Review* 17 (1957): pp. 421–37.

Gifford, Eli, and Michael R. Cook, eds. *How Can One Sell the Air? Chief Seattle's Vision.* Summertown, TN: Book Publishing Company, 1992.

Giglio, Virginia. *Southern Cheyenne Women's Songs.* Norman: University of Oklahoma Press, 1994.

Gil, Sam. *Native American Religions.* Belmont, CA: Wadsworth Publishing Company, 1981.

———. *Native American Traditions.* Belmont, CA: Wadsworth Publishing Company, 1982.

Gkisedtanamoogk, and Frances Hancock. *Anoqcou: Ceremony Is Life Itself.* Portland, ME: Astarte Shell Press, 1993.

Glendinning, Chellis. *"My Name Is Chellis and I'm in Recovery from Western Civilization."* Boston: Shambhala Publications, Inc., 1994.

Goldman-Eisler, Frieda. "Continuity of Speech Utterance: Its Determinants and Its Significance." *Language and Speech* 4 (1961): pp. 220–31.

———. "The Distribution of Pause Durations in Speech." *Language and Speech* 4 (1961): pp. 232–37.

———. "The Significance of Changes in the Rate of Articulation." *Language and Speech* 4 (1961): pp. 171–74.

Gonzalez, Ray, ed. *With-out Discovery: A Native Response to Columbus.* Seattle: Broken Moon Press, 1992.

Grace, Patricia. *Waiariki and Other Stories*. Markham, Ontario: Penguin Books Canada, 1986.

Green, Michael K., ed. *Issues in Native American Cultural Identity*. New York: Peter Lang, 1995.

Greene, Rayna. "After-Feast Speech: Contemporary Indian Humor." In *Words of American Indian Women: OHOYO MAKACHI,* compiled by the Ohoyo Resource Center. Wichita Falls, TX: Ohoyo Resource Center, 1981.

————. *Women in American Indian Society*. New York: Chelsea House, 1992.

Grele, Ronald J., ed. *Envelopes of Sound: Six Practioners Discuss the Method, Theory, and Practice of Oral History and Oral Testimony*. Chicago: Precedent, 1975.

Grinde, Donald A., Jr., and Bruce E. Johansen. *Ecocide of Native America: Environmental Destruction of Indian Lands and Peoples*. Santa Fe, NM: Clear Light, 1995.

Grinnell, George Bird. *Blackfoot Lodge Tales: The Story of a Prairie People*. Lincoln: University of Nebraska Press, 1962.

————. "Pawnee Mythology." *Journal of American Folklore* 6 (1893): pp. 113–20.

————. "A Pawnee Star Myth." *Journal of American Folklore* 7 (1894): pp. 197–200.

————. *The Punishment of the Stingy and Other Indian Stories*. New York: Harper and Brothers, 1901.

Grisdale, Alex. *Wild Drums: Tales and Legends of the Plains Indians*. Winnipeg: Peguis Publishers, 1972.

Haines, Francis. *Chief Joseph – Nez Perce*. Norman: University of Oklahoma, 1955.

Hale, Horatio. *The Iroquois Book of Rites*. Vol. 2. Philadelphia: D.G. Brinton, 1883.

Hall, Edward T. "Monochronic and Polychronic Time." In *Voices: A Selection of Multicultural Readings,* edited by Kathleen S. Verderber. Belmont, CA: Wadsworth Publishing Company, 1995.

Hallman, David G. *Ecotheology: Voices from South and North*. Maryknoll, NY: Orbis Books, 1994.

Hallowell, A. Irving. "Bear Ceremonialism in the Northern Hemisphere." *American Anthropologist* 28 (1926): pp. 1–175.

————. "Ojibwa Ontology, Behavior and World View." In *Culture in History,* edited by Stanley Diamond. New York: Columbia University Press, 1960.

Hamilton, Charles, ed. *Cry of the Thunderbird: The American Indian's Own Story*. Norman: University of Oklahoma Press, 1972.

Hammer, R. *Native Americans: Thoughts and Feelings*. Washington, DC: Smithsonian Institution, 1990.

Handy, Edward L. "Zuni Tales." *Journal of American Folklore* 31 (1918): pp. 451–71.

Harrington, John P. "Tewa Relationship Terms." *American Anthropologist* 14 (1912): pp. 472–98.

Hart, Mickey, and Fredric Lieberman. *Planet Drum: A Celebration of Percussion and Rhythm*. San Francisco: Harper, 1991.

"The Hau De No Sau Nee Message to the Western World." *Akwesasne Notes* 9 (Summer 1977): pp. 8–9.

Hausman, Gerald, ed. *Prayer to the Great Mystery: The Uncollected Writings and Photography of Edward S. Curtis*. New York: St. Martin's Press, 1995.

————. *The Sun Horse: Native Visions of the New World*. Twin Lakes, WI: Lotus Light, 1992.

————. *Turtle Island Alphabet*. New York: St. Martin's Press, 1993.

Havelock, Eric. *Origins of Western Literacy*. Toronto: Ontario Institute for Studies in Education, 1976.

————. *Preface to Plato*. Cambridge, MA: Harvard University Press, 1963.

Herndon, Marcia. *Native American Music.* Norwood, PA: Norwood, 1980.

Hertzberg, Hazel W. *The Great Tree and the Longhouse.* New York: Macmillan, 1966.

———. *The Search for an American Indian Identity: Modern Pan-Indian Movements.* Syracuse, NY: Syracuse University Press, 1971.

Herzog, George. "Plains Ghost Dance and Great Basin Music." *American Anthropologist* 37 (1935).

Hessel, Dieter T., ed. *Theology for Earth Community: A Field Guide.* Maryknoll, NY: Orbis Books, 1996.

Heth, Charlotte, ed. *Native American Dance: Ceremonies and Social Traditions.* Washington, DC: National Museum of the American Indian, 1992.

High Pine, Gayle. "The Disease That Afflicts Creation." *Akwesasne Notes* 7 (Winter 1975): pp. 34–35.

———. "Last Chance for Survival." *Akwesasne Notes* 8 (Spring 1976): pp. 30–32.

———. "This Land Keeps Us Together." *Akwesasne Notes* 10 (Spring 1978): pp. 23–24.

Hilger, Michael. *The American Indian in Film.* Metuchen, NJ: The Scarecrow Press, Inc., 1986.

Hill, Norbert S., Jr. *Words of Power: Voices from Indian America.* Golden, CO: Fulcrum Publishing, 1994.

Hill, Ruth Beebe. *Hanta Yo.* New York: Warner Books, 1979.

Hinckley, Ted C. "'The Canoe Rocks – We Do Not Know What Will Become of Us': The Complete Transcript of a Meeting between Governor John Green Brady of Alaska and a Group of Tlingit Chiefs, Juneau, December 14, 1898." *Western Historical Quarterly* (July 1970): pp. 265–90.

Hinton, Leanne. "Song: Overcoming the Language Barrier." *News from Native California* 5 (1988).

———. "Songs without Words." *News from Native California* 6 (1992).

Hinton, Leanne, and Lucille J. Watahomigie, eds. *Spirit Mountain: An Anthology of Yuman Story and Song.* Tuscon: University of Arizona Press, 1984.

Hirschfelder, Arlene B. *American Indian Stereotypes in the World of Children: A Reader and Bibliography.* Metuchen, NJ: Scarecrow Press, 1982.

———, ed. *Native Heritage: Personal Accounts by American Indians 1790 to the Present.* New York: Macmillan, 1995.

Hobson, Geary, ed. *The Remembered Earth: An Anthology of Contemporary Native American Literature.* Albuquerque, NM: Red Earth Press, 1979.

Hopkins, Mary Frances. "The Performance Turn – and Toss." *Quarterly Journal of Speech* 81 (1995): pp. 228–36.

Hopper, Paul J. "Discourse Analysis: Grammar and Critical Theory in the 1980's." *Profession* 88 (1988): pp. 18–24.

Horn, Gabriel L. *Contemplations of a Primal Mind.* Novato, CA: New World Library, 1996.

Howard, James H. "Notes on the Dakota Grass Dance." *Southwestern Journal of Anthropology* 7, no. 1 (1951): pp. 82–85.

———. "The Southeastern Ceremonial Complex and Its Interpretation." *Memoir: Missouri Archaeological Society* (December 1968).

Hubbard, J. Niles. *An Account of Sa-go-ye-wat-ha or Red Jacket and His People.* Albany: John Munsell's Sons, 1886.

Huenemann, Lynn F. *Songs and Dances of Native America: A Resource Text for Teachers and Students.* Book and tapes. Tsaile, AZ: Education House, 1978.

Huyghe, Patrick, and David Konigsberg. "Bury My Heart at New York City." *New York* (19 February 1979): pp. 53–57.

Hymes, Dell. "Discovering Oral Performance and Measured Verse in American Indian Narrative." *New Literary History* 8 (1977): pp. 431–57.

———. *"In Vain I Tried to Tell You": Essays in Native American Ethnopoetics.* Philadelphia: University of Pennsylvania Press, 1981.

———. "Particle, Pause, and Pattern in American Indian Narrative Verse." *American Indian Culture and Research Journal* 4 (1980): pp. 7–51.

Indian Voices: The First Convocation of American Indian Scholars. San Francisco: Indian Historian Press, 1970.

Indian Voices: The Native American Today. A Report on the Second Convocation of Indian Scholars. San Francisco: Indian Historian Press, 1974.

The Indians. By the editors of Time-Life Books. New York: Time-Life Books, 1973.

Inter Press Service, comp. *Story Earth: Native Voices on the Environment.* San Francisco: Mercury House, 1993.

"An Interview with John Trudell." *Akwesasne Notes* (Winter 1975): pp. 22–23.

Jackson, Helen. *A Century of Dishonor.* New York: Indian Head Books, 1993.

Jaffe, Clella Iles. *Public Speaking: A Cultural Perspective.* Belmont, CA: Wadsworth Publishing Company, 1995.

Jahner, Elaine A. "Allies in the Word Wars: Vizenor's Uses of Contemporary Critical Theory." *Studies in American Indian Literatures* 9 (1985): pp. 64–69.

———. "Finding the Way Home: The Interpretation of American Indian Folklore." In *Handbook of American Indian Folklore,* edited by Richard M. Dorson. Bloomington: Indiana University Press, 1986.

———, ed. *Lakota Myth.* Lincoln: University of Nebraska Press, 1984.

———. "Trickster Discourse: Comic and Tragic Themes in Native American Literature." In *Buried Roots and Indestructible Seeds: The Survival of American Indian Life in Story, History, and Spirit,* edited by Mark Lindquist and Martin Zanger, pp. 67–83. Madison: Wisconsin Humanities Council, 1993.

Jaimes, M. Annette. "Towards a New Image of American Indian Women." *Journal of American Indian Education* 22 (October 1982): pp. 18–32.

James, Cheewa. *Catch the Whisper of the Wind: Inspirational Stories and Proverbs from Native Americans.* Deerfield Beach, FL: Health Communications, Inc., 1995.

James, M. Annette, ed. *The State of Native America.* Boston: South End Press, 1992.

JanMohamed, Abdul R., and David Lloyd. "Toward a Theory of Minority Discourse: What Is To Be Done?" *Cultural Critique* (Fall 1987): pp. 5–17.

John Running. *Honor Dance.* Reno: University of Nevada Press, 1985.

Johnston, Basil. *Ojibway Ceremonies.* Toronto: McClelland & Stewart, 1982.

———. *Tales the Elders Told: Ojibway Legends.* Toronto: Royal Ontario Museum, 1981.

Jones, Louis Thomas, ed. *Aboriginal American Oratory: The Tradition of Eloquence among the Indians of the United States.* Los Angeles: Southwest Museum, 1965.

Joseph, Chief. "An Indian's View of Indian Affairs." *The North American Review* 78 (April, 1878).

Josephy, Alvin M., Jr. *The American Indians' Fight for Freedom.* New York: McGraw-Hill Book Co., 1971.

———. *500 Nations: An Illustrated History of North American Indians.* New York: Alfred A. Knopf, 1994.

———. *The Indian Heritage of America.* New York: Alfred A. Knopf, 1968.

———. *Red Power: The American Indians' Fight for Freedom.* Lincoln: University of Nebraska Press, 1971.

Kaiser, Rudolf. "Chief Seattle's Speeches: American Origin and European Reception."

In *Recovering the Word: Essays in North American Literature,* edited by Brian Swann and Arnold Krupat, pp. 495–536. Berkeley: University of California Press, 1987.

Kan, Sergei. *Symbolic Immortality: Tlingit Potlatch of the Nineteenth Century.* Washington, DC: Smithsonian Institution Press, 1989.

———. "Words That Heal the Soul: Analysis of the Tlingit Potlatch Oratory." *Arctic Anthropology* 20 (1987): pp. 47–59.

———. "Wrap Your Father's Brothers in Kind Words: An Analysis of the Nineteenth-Century Tlingit Mortuary and Memorial Rituals." Ph.D. diss., University of Chicago, 1982.

Katz, Jane. *I Am the Fire of Time: The Voices of Native American Women.* New York: E. P. Dutton Co., 1977.

———, ed. *Messengers of the Wind: Native American Women Tell Their Life Stories.* New York: Ballantine Books, 1995.

Katz, William Loren. *Black Indians: A Hidden Heritage.* New York: Atheneum, 1986.

Katzeek, David. *Celebration of Tlingit, Haida, and Tsimshian Culture.* Juneau: Sealaska Heritage Foundation, 1992.

Kelsey, Morton. *Dreamquest: Native American Myth and the Recovery of Soul.* Rockport, MA: Element, 1992.

Kennedy, George A. *Comparative Rhetoric: An Historical and Cross-Cultural Introduction.* New York: Oxford University Press, 1998.

Kickingbird, Kirke, and Karen Ducheneaux. *One Hundred Million Acres.* New York: Macmillan, 1974.

Kim, Min-Sun and Steven R. Wilson. "A Cross-Cultural Comparison of Implicit Theories of Requesting." *Communication Monographs* 61 (1994): pp. 210–35.

King, Thomas, ed. *All My Relations: An Anthology of Contemporary Canadian Native Writing.* Toronto: McLelland & Stewart, 1990.

Klein, Barry T., ed. *Reference Encyclopedia of the American Indian.* 6th ed. West Nyack, NY: Todd Publications, 1993.

Kluckhorn, Clyde, and Leland C. Wyman. *An Introduction to Navajo Chant Practice.* The American Anthropological Asssociation, *Memoirs.* Menasha, 1940.

Kopper, Philip. *The Smithsonian Book of North American Indians.* Washington, DC: Smithsonian Books, 1986.

Kroeber, Karl, ed. *Traditional Literatures of the American Indian: Texts and Interpretations.* Lincoln: University of Nebraska Press, 1981.

Krupat, Arnold, ed. *New Voices in Native American Literary Criticism.* Washington, DC: Smithsonian Institution Press, 1993.

———. "On the Translation of Native American Song and Story: A Theorized History." In *On the Translation of Native American Literature,* edited by Brian Swann, pp. 3–32. Washington, D.C.: Smithsonian Institution Press, 1992.

———. "Post-Structuralism and Oral Tradition." In *Recovering the Word: Essays on Native American Literature,* edited by Brian Swann and Arnold Krupat, pp. 113–28. Berkeley: University of California Press, 1987.

———. *The Voice in the Margin: Native American Literature and the Canon.* Berkeley: University of California Press, 1989.

Kurath, Gertrude P. *Dance and Song Rituals of the Six Nations Reserve, Ontario.* Ottawa: National Museum of Canada, Bulletin no. 220 (1968).

———. *Half a Century of Dance Research.* Flagstaff, AZ: Cross-Cultural Dance Resources, 1986.

LaFlesche, Francis. "The Osage Tribe: Rite of Vigil." *39th Annual Report of the Bureau of*

American Ethnology. Washington, DC: Government Printing Office, 1925.

LaFlesche, Susette. *Boston Daily Advertiser* (26 November 1879): p. 4.

Lake, Randall A. "Between Myth and History: Enacting Time in Native American Protest Rhetoric." *Quarterly Journal of Speech* 77 (1991): pp. 123–51.

———. "Enacting Red Power: The Consummatory Function in Native American Protest Rhetoric." *The Quarterly Journal of Speech* 69 (1983): pp. 127–42.

———. "The Rhetor as Dialectician in Last Chance for Survival." *Communication Monographs* 53 (1986): pp. 201–20.

Lake-Thom, *Bobby. Spirits of the Earth: A Guide to Native American Nature, Symbols, Stories, and Ceremonies.* New York: Penguin Books, 1997.

"The Lakota Family." *Bulletin of Oglala Sioux Community College, 1980–81* (Pine Ridge, SD), p. 2.

Lame Deer, Jone [Fire] and Richard Erdoes. *Lame Deer: Seeker of Visions.* New York: Washington Square Press, 1994.

LaMere, Oliver. "Winnebago Legends." *Wisconsin Archeologists* 21 (April 1922): pp. 66–88.

Lankford, George E., comp. and ed. *Native American Legends: Southeastern Legends: Tales from the Natchez, Caddo, Biloxi, Chickasaw, and Other Nations.* Little Rock, AR: August House, 1987.

Larocque, Emma. "Preface of These Are Our Voices – Who Will Hear?" In *Writing the Circle,* edited by Jeanne Perreault and Sylvia Vance. Edmonton: NeWest Publishers Limited, 1991.

Larrabee, Edward McM. *Recurrent Themes and Sequences in North American Indian-European Culture Contact.* Transactions of the American Philosophical Society, Philadelphia. Vol. 66 (1976).

Leeds-Hurwitz, Wendy. "Culture and Communication: A Review Essay." *Quarterly Journal of Speech* 76 (1990): pp. 85–95.

Lehrman, Fredric. *The Sacred Landscape.* Berkeley, CA: Celestial Arts, 1988.

Lerner, Andrea, ed. *Dancing on the Rim of the World: An Anthology of Contemporary Northwest Native American Writing.* Tucson: Sun Tracks and the University of Arizona Press, 1990.

Levi-Strauss, Claude. "The Structural Study of Myth." *Journal of American Folklore* 68 (1955): pp. 428–44.

Levitas, Gloria, Frank B. Vivelo and Jacqueline J. Vivelo, eds. *American Indian Prose and Poetry.* New York: G. P. Putnam's Sons, 1974.

Liberty, Margot, ed. *American Indian Intellectuals.* St. Paul: West Publishing Co., 1978.

Lincoln, Kenneth. *Native American Renaissance.* Berkeley: University of California Press, 1983.

Lindsay, Janet P. "Navajo Public Speaking." M.A. thesis, Colorado State University, 1954.

List, George. "The Boundaries of Speech and Song." *Ethnomusicology* 7 (1963): pp. 1–16.

Littlefield, Daniel L., Jr., and James M. Parins, comps. *American Indian and Alaska Native Newspapers and Periodicals, 1826–1924.* Westport, CT: Greenwood Press, p. 198.

———. *A Bibliography of Native American Writers, 1771–1924.* Metuchen, NJ: Scarecrow Press, 1985.

Lopez, Barry, ed. *Giving Birth to Thunder, Sleeping with His Daughter: Coyote Builds North America.* New York: Avon Books, 1977.

Lowie, Robert H. "Crow Prayers." *American Anthropologist* 35 (1933): pp. 433–42.

Luthin, Herbert W. "Restoring the Voice in Yanan Traditional Narrative." Ph.D. diss.,

University of California, Berkeley, 1991.

Lyden, Fremont J., and Lyman H. Legters, eds. *Native Americans and Public Policy*. Pittsburgh: University of Pittsburgh Press, 1992.

Lyons, Oren Lyons, et al., eds. *Exiled in the Land of the Free: Democracy, Indian Nations, and the U.S. Constitution*. Santa Fe, NM: Clear Light Publishers, 1992.

Maher, John M. and Dennie Briggs, eds. *An Open Life: Joseph Campbell in Conversation with Michael Toms*. New York: Harper & Row, 1989.

Mails, Thomas E. *Fool's Crow: Wisdom & Power*. Tulsa, OK: Council Oak Books, 1991.

Malotki, Ekkehart. *Hopitutuwutsi/Hopi Tales: A Bilingual Collection of Hopi Indian Stories*. Flagstaff: Museum of Northern Arizona Press, 1978.

Mander, Jerry. *In the Absence of the Sacred: The Failure of Technology and the Survival of the Indian Nations*. San Francisco: Sierra Club Books, 1991.

Manhart, Paul, ed. *Lakota Tales and Texts*. Pine Ridge, SD: Red Cloud Lakota Language and Cultural Center, 1978.

Marken, Jack, comp. *The American Indian: Language and Literature*. Arlington Heights, IL: AHM, 1978.

Marr, Helen Hubbard. *Voices of the Ancestors: Music in the Life of the Northwest Coast Indians*. Greenwich, CT: The Bruce Museum, 1986.

Marriott, Alice, and Carol K. Rachlin. *American Indian Mythology*. New York: Mentor Books, 1968.

Martin, Calvin. *Keepers of the Game: Indian-Animal Relationships and the Fur Trade*. Berkeley: University of California Press, 1978.

Mathews, John Joseph. *Talking to the Moon*. Norman: University of Oklahoma Press, 1945.

Matthews, Washington. "Navajo Gambling Songs." *The American Anthropologist* 2 (1889).

———. *Navajo Legends*. Boston: American Folklore Society, 1897.

———. *Navajo Myths, Prayers, and Songs*. Berkeley: University of California Press, 1907.

———. *Navajo Texts*. Ed. Pliny Earl Goddard. New York: American Museum of Natural History, 1933.

———. "The Night Chant, a Navajo Ceremony." In *Memoirs of the American Museum of Natural History*. Vol. 6. 1902. Reprint. New York: AMS, 1974.

———. "Songs of Sequence of the Navajos." *Journal of American Folklore* 7 (1894).

Matthiessen, Peter. *In the Spirit of Crazy Horse*. New York: Penguin Books, 1983.

Mattina, Anthony. "North American Indian Mythology: Editing Texts for the Printed Page." In *Recovering the Word: Essays on Native American Literature,* edited by Brian Swann and Arnold Krupat. pp. 129–48. Berkeley: University of California Press, 1987.

Maud, Ralph. *A Guide to B.C. Indian Myth and Legend: A Short History of Myth-Collecting and a Survey of Published Texts*. Vancouver: Talonbooks, 1982.

McAllester, D. P. "The Role of Music in Western Apache Culture." In *Selected Papers of the Fifth International Congress of Anthropological and Ethnological Sciences,* pp. 468–72. Philadelphia: 1956.

McKern, W. C. "Winnebago Dog Myths." *Yearbook* 10 (1930): pp. 317–22.

———. "A Winnebago Myth." *Yearbook* 9 (1929): pp. 215–30.

McKerrow, Raymie E. "Critical Theory and Praxis." *Communication Monographs* 56 (1989): pp. 91–111.

McLuhan, T. C. *Cathedrals of the Spirit: The Message of Sacred Places*. New York: Harper-Perennial, 1996.

———, comp. *Touch the Earth: A Self-Portrait of Indian Existence*. New York: Promontory Press, 1971.

————. *The Way of the Earth*. New York: Simon & Schuster, 1994.

McPherson, and J. Douglas Rabb. *Indian from the Inside: A Study in Ethno-Metaphysics*. Thunder Bay, Ontario: Lakehead University, 1993.

McWhorter, L. V. *Hear Me My Chiefs: Nez Perce History and Legend*. Caldwell, ID: Caxton Press, 1952.

Means, Russell. *Where White Men Fear to Tread*. New York: St. Martin's Press, 1995.

Merritt, Frank W. "Teedyuscung–Speaker for the Delawares." *Communication Quarterly* 3 (1955): pp. 14–18.

Midgette, Sally. *The Navajo Progressive in Discourse: A Study in Temporal Semantics*. New York: Peter Lang, 1995.

Miller, Jay. *Earthmaker: Tribal Stories from Native North America*. New York: Perigee Books, 1992.

Miller, Lee, ed. *From the Heart: Voices of the American Indian*. New York: Vintage Books, 1995.

Mohawk, John, and Oren Lyons, eds. *Exiled in the Land of the Free: Democracy, Indian Nations, and the U.S. Constitution*. Santa Fe, NM: Clear Light Publishers, 1992.

Momaday, N. Scott. *House Made of Dawn*. New York: Harper & Row, 1989.

————. "Man Made of Words," Assembly presentation at the First Convocation of American Indian Scholars. *Indian Voices*, pp. 49–84. San Francisco: The Indian Historian Press, 1970.

————. *The Man Made of Words*. New York: St. Martin's Press, 1997.

————. *The Names*. New York: Harper and Row, 1976.

————. "Native American Attitudes to the Environment." In *Seeing with a Native Eye*, edited by Walter Holden Capps, pp. 79–85. New York: Harper and Row, 1976.

————. "The Native Voice." In *The Columbia Literary History of the United States*, edited by Emory Elliott, pp. 5–15. New York: Columbia University Press, 1985.

————. *The Way to Rainy Mountain*. Albuquerque: University of New Mexico Press, 1969.

Moody, Roger, ed. *The Indigenous Voice: Visions and Realities*. 2 vols. Utrecht, The Netherlands: International Books, 1993.

Mooney, James. *Myths of the Cherokee and Sacred Formulas of the Cherokees*. Nashville: Charles and Randy Elder, 1982.

Moore, Frank, ed. *American Eloquence*. 2 vols. New York: D. Appleton and Company, 1857.

Moquin, Wayne, and Charles Van Doren, eds. *Great Documents in American Indian History*. New York: Da Capo Press, 1995.

Morey, Sylvester M., and Olivia L. Gilliam, eds. *Respect for Life: Report of a Conference at Harper's Ferry, West Virginia, on the Traditional Upbringing of American Indian Children*. New York: Myrin Institute, 1974.

Morris, Mabel. "Indian Eloquence." *Western Journal of Speech Communication* 8 (1944): p. 3.

————. "Indian Oratory." *Southern Speech Communication Journal* 10 (1944): pp. 29–36.

Morris, Richard. "Living In Between." In *Our Voices: Essays in Culture, Ethnicity, and Communication*, edited by Alberto Gonzalez, Marsha Houston, and Victoria Chen, pp. 163–74. Los Angeles: Roxbury Publishing Company, 1997.

Morris, Richard, and Philip Wander. "Native American Rhetoric: Dancing in the Shadows of the Ghost Dance." *Quarterly Journal of Speech* 76 (1990): pp. 164–91.

Morrison, Dane, ed. *American Indian Studies: An Interdisciplinary Approach to Contemporary Issues*. New York: Peter Lang, 1997.

Moses, L. G., and Raymond Wilson, eds. *Indian Lives: Essays on Nineteenth- and Twentieth-Century Native American Leaders*. Albuquerque: University of New Mexico Press, 1985.

"Mother Earth Perspectives: Preservation through Words." *Gatherings: The En'owkin Journal of First North American Peoples* 3 (Fall 1992).

Moulton, Gary E., ed. *The Papers of Chief John Ross.* 2 vols. Norman: University of Oklahoma Press, 1985.

Murphy, James E., and Donald R. Avery. "A Comparison of Alaskan Native and Non-Native Newspaper Content." *Journalism Quarterly* 60, no. 2 (Summer 1983): pp. 316–22.

Murphy, James E., and Sharon M. Murphy. *Let My People Know: American Indian Journalism, 1828–1978.* Norman: University of Oklahoma Press, 1981.

Murphy, M. N. "Silence, the Word, and Indian Rhetoric." *College Composition and Communication* 21 (1970): pp. 356–63.

Murray, David. *Forked Tongues: Speech, Writing and Representation in North American Indian Texts.* Bloomington: Indiana University Press, 1991.

Nabokov, Peter, ed. *Native American Testimony: A Chronicle of Indian-White Relations from Prophecy to the Present, 1492–1992.* New York: Penguin Books, 1991.

National Tribal Council. *The Shuswap: One People with One Mind, One Heart and One Spirit.* Kamloops, Canada: Shuswap National Tribal Council, 1989.

Native Eloquence, Being Public Speeches Delivered by Two Distinguished Chiefs of the Seneca Tribe of Indians. Canandaigua, NY: J. D. Bemis, 1811.

Nelson, Richard K. *Make Prayers to the Raven: A Koyukon View of the Northern Forest.* Chicago: University of Chicago Press, 1983.

Nowlan, Alden. *Nine Micmac Legends.* Hantsport, Nova Scotia: Lancelot Press, 1983.

O'Bryan, Aileen. "The Dine: Origin Myths of the Navajo Indians." *Bureau of American Ethnology Bulletin* 163 (1956).

Ochs, Donovan J. "A Fallen Fortress: BIA." Paper presented at the Central States Speech Association Convention, Milwaukee, Wisconsin, April 1974.

O'Connor, Alan. "The Problem of American Cultural Studies." *Critical Studies in Mass Communication* 6 (1989): pp. 405–13.

O'Connor, John E. *The Hollywood Indian: Stereotypes of Native Americans in Films.* Trenton: The New Jersey State Museum, 1980.

O'Donnell, James H. "Logan's Oration: A Case Study in Ethnographic Authentication." *The Quarterly Journal of Speech* 65 (1979): pp. 150–56.

Old Coyote, Barney. "The Issue Is Not Feathers: Legal Attacks on Native Religious Tradition." *Akwesasne Notes* 9 (Summer 1977): p. 21.

Oliver, Robert W. "The Legal Status of American Indian Tribes." *Oregon Law Review* 38 (1959): p. 200.

Olson, James S., and Raymond Wilson. *Native Americans in the Twentieth Century.* Provo, UT: Brigham Young University Press, 1984.

Olson, David R. and Nancy Torrance, eds. *Literacy and Orality.* Cambridge: Cambridge University Press, 1991.

Ong, Walter. *The Interfaces of the Word: Studies in the Evolution of Consciousness and Culture.* Ithaca, NY: Cornell University Press, 1977.

———. *Orality and Literacy: The Technologizing of the Word.* London: Methuen, 1982.

———. *The Presence of the Word.* New Haven, CT: Yale University Press, 1967.

Ono, Kent A., and John M. Sloop. "The Critique of Vernacular Discourse." *Communication Monographs* 62 (1995): pp. 19–46.

Opler, Morris Edward. *An Apache-Life-Way.* Chicago: University of Chicago Press, 1941.

Ortiz, Alfonso. *The Tewa World: Space, Time, Being, and Becoming in a Pueblo Society.* Chicago: University of Chicago Press, 1969.

Ortiz, Simon. "Always the Stories: A Brief History and Thoughts on My Writing." In *Coyote Was Here: Essays on Contemporary Native American Literary and Political Mobilization,* edited by Bo Scholer, pp. 57–69. Aarhus, Denmark: SEKLOS/University of Aarhus, 1984.

———. *Earth Power Coming: Short Fiction in Native American Literature.* Tsaile, AZ: Navajo Community College Press, 1983.

———. *Song, Poetry, and Language: Expression and Perception.* Tsaile, AZ: Navajo Community College Press, 1977.

Osborn, Lynn R. "The North American Indian: An Examination of the Communication of Cultural Identity." *ACA Bulletin* 16 (1976): pp. 22–24.

———. "Rhetoric, Repetition, Silence." In *Diversity in Public Communication: A Reader,* edited by Christine Kelly, E. Anne Laffoon, and Raymie E. McKerrow, pp. 197–203. Dubuque, IA: Kendall/Hunt Publishing Company, 1994.

Osgood, Cornelius, ed. *Linguistic Structures of Native America.* New York: Viking Fund, Inc., 1946.

Oskison, John M. *Tecumseh and His Times.* New York: G. P. Putnam's Sons, 1938.

"Our 20 Point Proposal." *Akwesasne Notes* 5 (early winter, 1973): pp. 30–31.

Overholt, Thomas W., and J. Baird Callicott. *Clothed-in-Fur and Other Tales.* New York: University Press of America, 1982.

Painter, Muriel Thayer, Edward H. Spicer, and Wilma Kaemlein, eds. *With Good Heart: Yaqui Beliefs and Ceremonies in Pascua Village.* Tucson: University of Arizona Press, 1986.

Park, Willard Z. *Shamanism in Western North America.* Evanston, IL: Northwestern University Press, 1938.

Parker, Arthur C. *The Code of Handsome Lake: The Seneca Prophet.* New York State Museum Bulletin no. 163. Albany: University of the State of New York, 1912.

———. *Red Jacket, Last of the Seneca.* New York: McGraw-Hill, 1952.

Parkhill, Thomas. "Of Glooscap's Birth, and of His Brother Malsum, the Wolf': The Story of Charles Godfrey Leland's 'Purely American Creation." *American Indian Culture and Research Journal* 16 (1992).

Parlow, Anita. *Sacred Ground: Big Mountain, U.S.A.* Washington, DC: The Christic Institute, 1988.

Parsons, Jim. "Political, Religious Differences Divide Indian Community," *Minneapolis Tribune* (20 November 1979): p. 1 Aff.

Peltier, Leonard. "An Open Letter to National A.I.M. Leadership." *Eagle Wing Press* (November 1982): pp. 17, 20.

Perkins, Sally J. "Toward a Rhetorical/Dramatic Theory of Instructional Communication." *Communication Education* 43 (1994): pp. 222–35.

Perreault, Jeanne, and Sylvia Vance. *Writing the Circle: Western Canadian Native Women – An Anthology.* Edmonton: NeWest Publishing, 1990.

Perry, Whitall N. *A Treasury of Traditional Wisdom.* New York: Simon and Schuster, 1971.

Petrone, Penny, ed. *First People, First Voices.* Toronto: University of Toronto Press, 1983.

———. *Native Literature in Canada: From the Oral Tradition to the Present.* Toronto: Oxford University Press, 1990.

Philip, Neil. *In a Sacred Manner I Live: Native American Wisdom.* New York: Clarion Books, 1997.

Philipsen, Gerry. "Navajo World View and Culture Patterns of Speech: A Case Study in Ethnorhetoric." *Speech Monographs* 39 (1972): pp. 132–39.

———. "Writing Ethnographies." *Quarterly Journal of Speech* 77 (1991): pp. 327–42.

Phinney, Archie. *Nez Perce Texts*. New York: Columbia University Press, 1934.

Pijoan, Teresa. *White Wolf Woman and Other Native American Transformation Myths*. Little Rock, AR: August House Publishers, Inc., 1992.

Porter, Frank W. III, ed. *Strategies for Survival, American Indians in the Eastern United States*. Westport, CT: Greenwood Press, 1986.

Powers, William K. "Contemporary Oglala Music and Dance: Pan-Indianism vs. Pan-Tetonism." In *The Modern Sioux,* edited by Ethel Nurge. Lincoln: University of Nebraska Press, 1970.

———. *Sacred Language: The Nature of Supernatural Discourse in Lakota*. Norman: University of Oklahoma Press, 1986.

———. *War Dance: Plains Indian Musical Performance*. Tucson: University of Arizona Press, 1990.

Prayson, Frederick. *Land of the Four Directions*. Old Greenwich, CT: Chatham Press, Inc., 1970.

Prince, John Dyneley. *Passamaquoddy Texts*. Publications of the American Ethnological Society Vol. 10 (1921).

Public Speeches Delivered at the Village of Buffalo Respecting the Part the Six Nations Would Take in the Present War against Great Britain. 1812, report, Publications of the Buffalo Historical Society. Vol. 4. Buffalo, NY: Peter Paul Book Company, 1896.

Radin, Paul. *The Trickster: A Study in American Indian Mythology*. New York: Schocken Books, 1972.

———. "Turtle Trying to Get Credit, a Tale." *Journal of American Folklore,* 39 (1926): pp. 27–52.

———. "Winnebago Tales." *Journal of American Folklore,* 22 (1909): pp. 88–101.

Rael, Joseph. *Being and Vibration*. Tulsa: Council Oak Books, 1993.

———. *Ceremonies of the Living Spirit*. Tulsa: Council Oak Books, 1998.

Raines, Howell. "American Indians: Struggling for Power and Identity." *New York Times Magazine* (11 February 1979): p. 21.

Ramsey, Jarold W. *Coyote Was Going There: Indian Literature of Oregon County*. Seattle: University of Washington Press, 1977.

———. *Reading the Fire: Essays in the Traditional Indian Literatures of the Far West*. Lincoln: University of Nebraska Press, 1983.

Red Cloud. "Speech at Cooper Institute." *New York Tribune* (16 January 1870).

Reeves, Brian O. K. and Margaret A. Kennedy, eds. *Coming Together on Native Sacred Sites: Their Sacredness, Conservation, and Interpretation*. Alberta, Canada: The Archaeological Society of Alberta, 1993.

Regier, Willis G., ed. *Masterpieces of American Indian Literature*. New York: MJF Books, 1993.

Reichard, Gladys A. *Navaho Religion: A Study of Symbolism*. Princeton, NJ: Princeton University Press, 1950.

———. *Prayer: The Compulsive Word*. Seattle: University of Washington Press, 1944.

Renault, Dennis, and Timothy Freke. *Principles of Native American Spirituality*. San Francisco: Thorsons, 1996.

Reynolds, Wynn R. "A Study of the Persuasive Speaking Techniques of the Iroquois Indians: 1678–1776." Ph.D. diss., Columbia University, 1957.

Rhodes, Robert W. *Hopi Music and Dance*. Tsaile, AZ: Navajo Community College Press, 1978.

Rice, Julian. *Black Elk's Story: Distinguishing Its Lakota Purpose*. Albuquerque: University of New Mexico Press, 1991.

————. *Deer Women and Elk Men: The Lakota Narratives of Ella Deloria.* Albuquerque: University of New Mexico Press, 1992.

Ridington, Robin. *Little Bit Know Something: Stories in a Language of Anthropology.* Iowa City: University of Iowa Press, 1990.

————. *Trail to Heaven: Knowledge and Narrative in a Northern Native Community.* Iowa City: University of Iowa Press, 1988.

Riesman, David. "The Oral and Written Traditions." In *Explorations in Communications,* edited by Edmund Carpenter and Marshall McLuhan. Boston: Beacon Press, 1966.

Riley, Patricia, ed. *Growing Up Native American.* New York: Avon Books, 1993.

Risser, Anna. "Seven Zuni Folk Tales." *El Palacio* 48 (1941): 215–26.

Robert, Elizabeth, and Elias Amidon, eds. *Earth Prayers.* San Francisco: HarperCollins, 1991.

Robie, Harry W. "Red Jacket." In *American Orators before 1900: Critical Studies and Sources,* edited by Bernard K. Duffy and Halford R. Ryan, pp. 333–39. New York: Greenwood Press, 1987.

————. "Red Jacket's Reply to Reverend Cram: A Contribution to the Anthropology of Communication." Ph.D. diss., Michigan State University, 1972.

Rockwell, David. *Giving Voice to Bear: North American Indian Myths, Rituals, and Images of the Bear.* Niwot, CO: Roberts Rinehart, 1991.

Roland, R. C. "On Mythic Criticism." *Communication Studies* 41, (1990): pp. 101–116.

"The Roots of Peace." *The Great Law of Peace of the Iroquois Nation.* Reprinted in *Parabola* 3 (Summer 1980).

Rosen, Kenneth, ed. *The Man to Send Rain Clouds: Contemporary Stories by American Indians.* New York: Viking, 1974.

Rosenstiel, Annette. *Red & White: Indian Views of the White Man, 1492–1982.* New York: Universe Books, 1983.

Ross, A. C. *Mitakuye Oyasin: "We Are All Related."* Kyle, SD: Bear, 1989.

Rothenberg, Jerome, ed. *Technicians of the Sacred.* 2nd ed. Berkeley: University of California Press, 1985.

Rothenberg, Jerome, and Diane Rothenberg. *Symposium of the Whole: A Range of Discourse toward an Ethnopoetics.* Berkeley: University of California Press, 1983.

Ruoff, A. La Vonne Brown. *American Indian Literatures. An Introduction, Bibliographic Review, and Selected Bibliography.* New York: Modern Language Association, 1990.

————. *Literatures of the American Indian.* New York: Chelsea House Publishers, 1991.

Ruppert, James. "The Uses of Oral Tradition in Six Contemporary Native American Poets." *American Indian Culture and Research Journal* 4, no. 4 (1980).

Rushing, Janice Hooker, and Thomas S. Frentz. "Integrating Ideology and Archetype in Rhetorical Criticism." *Quarterly Journal of Speech* 77 (1991): pp. 385–406.

Russell, Steve. "The Politics of Indian Identity." *Peace Review* 9 (1997): pp. 515–19.

Rutledge, Don, and Rita Robinson. *Center of the World: Native American Spirituality as Told by Plains Cree Pipe Keeper Don Rutledge.* North Hollywood, CA: Newcastle Publishing Co., 1992.

The Sacred Tree: Reflections on Native American Spirituality. Lethbridge, Alberta: Four Worlds Development Press, 1984.

Samovar, Larry A., and Richard E. Porter. *Communication between Cultures.* Belmont, CA: Wadsworth Publishing Company, 1995.

Sandefur, Ray H. "Logan's Oration: How Authentic?" *Quarterly Journal of Speech* 46 (1960): pp. 289–96.

Sanders, Thomas E., and Walter W. Peek, eds. *Literature of the American Indian.* Beverly Hills, CA: Glencoe Press, 1973.

Sarris, Greg. *Keeping Slug Woman Alive: A Holistic Approach to American Indian Texts.* Berkeley: University of California Press, 1993.

Scholten, Pat Creech. "Exploitation of Ethos: Sarah Winnemucca and Bright Eyes on the Lecture Tour." *Western Journal of Speech Communication* 41 (1977): pp. 233–44.

Seeber, Edward D. "Critical Views on Logan's Speech." *Journal of American Folklore* 18 (1925).

Sevillano, Mando. *The Hopi Way: Tales from a Changing Culture.* Flagstaff: Northland Publishing, 1986.

Shaver, Lynda Dixon. "A House as Symbol, a House as Family: Mamaw and Her Oklahoma Cherokee Family." In *Our Voices: Essays in Culture, Ethnicity, and Communication,* edited by Alberto Gonzalez, Marsha Houston, and Victoria Chen, pp. 136–40. Los Angeles: Roxbury Publishing Company, 1997.

Sherzer, Joel. "A Discourse-Centered Approach to Language and Culture." *American Anthropologist* 89, no. 2 (1987): pp. 295–309.

———. *Kuna Ways of Speaking: An Ethnographic Perspective.* Austin: University of Texas Press, 1983.

———. "Poetic Structuring of Kuna Discourse: The Line." *Language in Society* 11 (1982): pp. 371–90.

Sherzer, Joel, and Anthony Woodbury, eds. *Native American Discourse: Poetics and Rhetoric.* Cambridge: Cambridge University Press, 1987.

Shutiva, Charmaine. "Native American Culture and Communication through Humor." In *Our Voices: Essays in Culture, Ethnicity, and Communication,* edited by Alberto Gonzalez, Marsha Houston, and Victoria Chen, pp. 113–18. Los Angeles: Roxbury Publishing Company, 1997.

Sidney, Angela, Kitty Smith, and Rachel Dawson. *My Stories Are My Wealth.* Recorded by Julie Cruikshank. Whitehorse, Yukon: Yukon Native Languages Project, Council for Yukon Indians, 1977.

Silko, Leslie Marmon. *Ceremony.* New York: Signet Books, 1977.

———. *Storyteller.* New York: Seaver Books, 1981.

———. *Yellow Woman and a Beauty of the Spirit.* New York: Simon & Schuster, 1996.

Silman, Janet, ed. *Enough Is Enough: Aboriginal Women Speak Out.* Toronto: The Women's Press, 1988.

Slapin, Beverly, and Doris Seale, eds. *Through Indian Eyes: The Native Experience in Books for Children.* Philadelphia: New Society Publishers, 1992.

Sledge, Linda Ching. "Oral Tradition in Kingston's China Men." In *Redefining American Literary History,* edited by A. LaVonne Brown Ruoff and Jerry W. Ward, Jr., pp. 142–54. New York: Modern Language Association of America, 1990.

Smith, David Lee. *Folklore of the Winnebago.* Norman: University of Oklahoma Press, 1997.

Smith, Jane F., and Robert M. Kvasnicka, eds. *Indian-White Relations: A Persistent Paradox.* Washington, DC: Howard University Press, 1976.

Smith, Ross D. "A Survey of Native American Serious Drama from 1900 to 1918." *Speech Monographs* 19 (1952): pp. 39–47.

Smyth, Willie, ed. *Songs of Indian Territory: Native American Music Traditions of Oklahoma.* Book and tapes. Oklahoma City: Center of the American Indian, 1989.

Sneve, Virginia Driving Hawk, ed. *Dancing Teepees.* New York: Holiday House, 1989.

Snyder, Gary. *Turtle Island.* Boston: Shambhala, 1993.

Song, Tamarack. *Journey to the Ancestral Self: The Native Lifeway Guide to Living in Harmony with Earth Mother.* Barrytown, NY: Staton Hill Press, 1994.

Sorter, Edna C. "The Noble Savage." *Ethnohistory* 19 (1972): pp. 227–36.

Sotsisowah, "The Darkening Horizens." *Akwesasne Notes* 9 (Summer 1977): pp. 4–6.

———. "Western Peoples, Natural Peoples." *Akwesasne Notes* 8 (early spring, 1976): p. 34.

Speck, Frank G. *Ceremonial Songs of the Creek and Yuchi Indians.* University of Pennsylvania Museum, Anthropological Publications Vol. 1, no. 2 (1909–11).

Speck, Frank G., Leonard Broom, and Will West Long. *Cherokee Dance and Drama.* 1951. Reprint. Norman: University of Oklahoma Press, 1983.

Spencer, Katherine. *Mythology and Values: An Analysis of Navaho Chantway Myths.* Philadelphia: American Folklore Society, 1957.

Spinden, Herbert Joseph. *Songs of the Tewa, Preceded by an Essay on American Indian Poetry.* New York: Exposition of Indian Tribal Arts, 1933.

The Spirit World. By the editors of Time-Life Books. Alexandria, VA: Time Inc. Book Company, 1992.

"A Statement from John Trudell." *Akwesasne Notes* (Autumn 1975): pp. 7, 14.

Steiger, Brad. *Medicine Talk: A Guide to Walking in Balance and Surviving on the Mother Earth.* New York: Doubleday and Co., 1975.

Steiner, Stan. *The New Indians.* New York: Dell Publishing Co., 1968.

Stensland, Anna. *Literature by and about the American Indian: An Annotated Bibliography.* 2nd ed. Urbana, IL: National Council of Teachers of English, 1979.

Stevenson, Matilda Cox. "The Sia." *Eleventh Annual Report of the Bureau of American Ethnology,* 1889–1890.

Stewart, Omer C. *Peyote Religion.* Norman: University of Oklahoma Press, 1987.

Stone, William L. Red Jacket, *The Life and Times of Sa-Go-Ye-Wat-Ha, or Red Jacket.* New York: Wiley & Putnam, 1841.

Streb, Edward. "The Alcatraz Occupation, '69–'71: A Perceived Parody of Power Movements." Paper presented at the Central States Speech Association Convention, Milwaukee, Wisconsin, April 1974.

———. "The Rhetoric of Wounded Knee II: A Critical Analysis of Confrontational and Media Event Discourse." Ph.D. diss., Northwestern University, 1979.

Streep, Peg, ed. *The Sacred Journey: Prayers and Songs of Native America.* Boston: Bulfinch Press, 1995.

Strickland, William M. "The Rhetoric of Removal and the Trail of Tears: Cherokee Speaking against Jackson's Indian Removal Policy, 1828–1832." *Southern Speech Communication Journal* 47 (1982): pp. 292–309.

Stucky, Nathan. "Performing Oral History: Storytelling and Pedagogy." *Communication Education* 44 (1995): pp. 1–14.

Sullivan, Lawrence, ed. *Native American Religions.* New York: Macmillan, 1987.

Suzuki, David, and Peter Knudson. *Wisdom of the Elders: Sacred Native Stories of Nature.* New York: Bantam Books, 1992.

Swann, Brian, ed. *Coming to Light: Contemporary Translations of the Native Literatures of North America.* New York: Random House, 1994.

———, ed. *On the Translation of Native American Literatures.* Washington, DC: Smithsonian Institution Press, 1992.

———, ed. *Smoothing the Ground: Essays on Native American Oral Literature.* Berkeley: University of California Press, 1983.

———. *Song of the Sky: Versions of Native American Song-Poems.* Amherst: University of

Massachusetts Press, 1985.

Swann, Brian, and Arnold Krupat, eds. *I Tell You Now: Autobiographical Essays by Native American Writers.* Lincoln: University of Nebraska Press, 1987.

———, eds. *Recovering the Word: Essays on Native American Literature.* Berkeley: University of California Press, 1987.

Swearingen, C. Jan. "Oral Hermeneutics during the Transition to Literacy: The Contemporary Debate." *Cultural Anthropology* 1 (1986): pp. 138–56.

Sweet, Jill D. *Dances of the Tewa Pueblo Indians: Expressions of New Life.* Santa Fe, NM: School of American Research, 1985.

Talbot, Steve. "Free Alcatraz: The Culture of Native American Liberation." *Journal of Ethnic Studies* 6 (1978): pp. 83–96.

Tannen, Deborah, ed. *Coherence in Spoken and Written Discourse.* Norwood, NJ: Ablex Publishing Corporation, 1984.

———, ed. *Spoken and Written Language: Exploring Orality and Literacy.* Vol. IX in Advances in Discourse Processes. Ed. Roy O. Freedie. Norwood, NJ: Ablex Publishing Corporation, 1982.

Tarnas, Richard. *The Passion of the Western Mind: Understanding the Ideas That Have Shaped Our World View.* New York: Ballantine Books, 1991.

Taylor, Colin F. *Native American Life: The Family, the Hunt, Pastimes, and Ceremonies.* New York: Smithmark Publishers, 1996.

———, ed. *Native American Myths and Legends.* New York: Salamander Books Ltd., 1994.

Tedlock, Dennis. *Finding the Center: Narrative Poetry of the Zuni Indians.* 1972. Reprint. Lincoln: University of Nebraska Press, 1978.

———. *The Spoken Word and the Work of Interpretation.* Philadelphia: University of Pennsylvania Press, 1983.

Tedlock, Dennis, and Barbara Tedlock, eds. *Teachings from the American Earth: Perspectives on the Religion, Philosophy and Spirituality of the American Indian.* New York: Liveright Publishers, 1975.

———. "Towards an Oral Poetics." *New Literary History* 8 (1977): pp. 507–19.

"The Teton Sioux Manifesto." *Wassaja* 1 (July, 1973): pp. 10–12.

Thatcher, B. B. *Indian Biography; or An Historical Account of Those Individuals Who Have Been Distinguished among the North American Natives as Orators, Warriors, Statesmen, and Other Remarkable Characters.* 2 vols. New York: J. & J. Harper, 1832.

Theisz, R. D., and Ben Black Bear. *Songs and Dances of the Lakota.* Rosebud, SD: Sinte Gleska College, 1976.

Thompson, Stith. *Tales of the North American Indians.* Bloomington: Indiana University Press, 1929.

Tinker, George. "Creation as Kin: An American Indian View." In *After Nature's Revolt: Eco-Justice and Theology,* edited by Dieter T. Hessel. Minneapolis: Fortress Press, 1992.

Tobias, Michael, and Georgianne Cowan, eds. *The Soul of Nature: Celebrating the Spirit of the Earth.* New York: Penguin Books, 1996.

Tooker, Elisabeth. *The Iroquois Ceremonial of Midwinter.* Syracuse, NY: Syracuse University Press, 1970.

———, ed. *Native North American Spirituality of the Eastern Woodlands: Sacred Myths, Dreams, Visions, Speeches, Healing Formulas, Rituals and Ceremonials.* Mahwah, NJ: Paulist Press, 1979.

Trail of Broken Treaties: B.I.A., I'm Not Your Indian Anymore. 2nd ed. Rooseveltown, NY: Akwesasne Notes, 1974.

"Treaties Made, Treaties Broken: New Legal Strategies for Subverting Indian Rights." *Akwesasne Notes* 10 (Winter 1978): pp. 12–13.

Trimble, Stephen, ed. *Our Voices, Our Land: Words by the Indian Peoples of the Southwest.* Flagstaff, AZ: Northland Publishing, 1986.

Trudell, John. *Stickman: Poems, Lyrics, Songs, a Conversation.* Ed. Paola Igliori. New York: Inanout Press, 1994.

Turner, Frederick. *Beyond Geography: The Western Spirit against the Wilderness.* New Brunswick, NJ: Rutgers University Press, 1994.

———, ed. *The Portable North American Reader.* New York: Penguin Books, 1974.

Turner, Victor. *The Forest of Symbols.* Ithaca, NY: Cornell University Press, 1967.

"Two Warriors Die: But Struggle Goes On." *Akwesasne Notes* 8 (Spring 1976): p. 18.

Underhill, Ruth. *Red Man's Religion.* Chicago: University of Chicago Press, 1965.

———. *Singing for Power.* 1938. Reprint, Berkeley: University of California Press, 1976.

Unherhill, Ruth, D. M. Bahr, B. Lopez, J. Pancho, and D. Lopez. *Rainhouse and Ocean: Speeches for the Papago Year.* Museum of Northern Arizona Press, 1979.

Vanderwerth, W. C., comp. *Indian Oratory: Famous Speeches by Noted Indian Chieftains.* Norman: University of Oklahoma Press, 1971.

Van Laan, Nancy. *In a Circle Long Ago: A Treasury of Native Lore from North America.* New York: Alfred A. Knopf, Inc., 1995.

Vansina, Jan. *Oral Tradition: A Study in Historical Methodology.* Chicago: Aldine, 1965.

Vecsey, Christopher, and Robert W. Venables, eds. *American Indian Environments: Ecological Issues in Native American History.* Syracuse, NY: Syracuse University Press, 1980.

Velie, Alan R., ed. *American Indian Literature: An Anthology.* Norman: University of Oklahoma Press, 1991.

———. *Four American Indian Literary Masters: N. Scott Momaday, James Welch, Leslie Marmon Silko, and Gerald Vizenor.* Norman: University of Oklahoma Press, 1982.

———, ed. *Native American Perspectives on Literature and History.* Norman: University of Oklahoma Press, 1994.

Venables, Robert W., "The Cost of Columbus: Was There a Holocaust?" *Northeast Indian Quarterly* 7 (Fall 1990): pp. 29–36.

Vennum, Thomas. "The Ojibwa Dance Drum: Its History and Construction." *Smithsonian Institution Folklife Studies* 2 (1982).

Verderber, Kathleen S. *Voices: A Selection of Multicultural Readings.* Belmont, CA: Wadsworth Publishing Company, 1995.

Versluis, Arthur. *Native American Traditions.* Rockport, MA: Element, Inc., 1994.

Vestal, Stanley. *Sitting Bull: Champion of the Sioux.* Norman: University of Oklahoma Press, 1980.

View from the Shore: American Indian Perspectives on the Quincentenary. Northeast Indian Quarterly 7, no. 3 (1990).

Vizenor, Gerald. *Dead Voices: Natural Agonies in the New World.* Norman: University of Oklahoma Press, 1992.

———. *Earthdivers: Tribal Narratives on Mixed Descent.* Minneapolis: University of Minnesota Press, 1981.

———. *The Everlasting Sky: New Voices from the People Named the Chippewa.* New York: Crowell-Collier Press, 1972.

———. *Interior Landscapes: Autobiographical Myths and Metaphors.* Minneapolis: University of Minnesota Press, 1990.

———, ed. *Narrative Chance: Postmodern Discourse on Native American Indian Literatures.* Albuquerque: University of New Mexico Press, 1989.

————. *The People Named the Chippewa: Narrative Histories*. Minneapolis: University of Minnesota Press, 1984.

————. "Trickster Discourse." *American Indian Quarterly* 16 (Summer, 1990): pp. 277–87.

————. *Wordarrows: Indians and Whites in the New Fur Trade*. Minneapolis: University of Minnesota Press, 1978.

Voegelin, C. F. and Robert C. Euler. "Introduction to Hopi Chants." *Journal of American Folklore* 70 (1957): pp. 115–36.

Voices from Wounded Knee, 1973. Mohawk Nation via Rooseveltown, NY: Akwesasne Notes, 1974.

Voices of the First America: Text and Context in the New World. Special issue of *New Scholar* 10 (1986).

Von Franz, Marie Louise. *Creation Myths*. Boston: Shambhala, 1995.

Vonnegut, Kristin S. "Listening for Women's Voices: Revisioning Courses in American Public Address." *Communication Education* 41 (1992): pp. 26–39.

Walker, Deward E., Jr. *Myths of Idaho Indians*. Moscow: University of Idaho Press, 1980.

Walker, Willard. "Toward the Sound Pattern of Zuni." *International Journal of American Linguistics* 38 (1972): pp. 240–59.

Wall, Steve. *Wisdom's Daughters: Conversations with Women Elders of Native America*. New York: Harper Perennial, 1993.

Wall, Steve, and Harvey Arden. *Wisdomkeepers: Meetings with Native American Spiritual Elders*. Hillsboro, OR: Beyond Words Publishing, Inc., 1990.

Walters, Anna Lee. *Talking Indian: Reflections on Survival and Writing*. Ithaca, NY: Firebrand Books, 1992.

Walton, Eda Lou. "Navaho Verse Rhythms." *Poetry* 24 (1924): pp. 40–44.

Warnick, Barbara. "Leff in Context: What Is the Critic's Role?" *Quarterly Journal of Speech* 78 (1992): pp. 232–37.

Warren, William W. *History of the Ojibways, Based upon Traditions and Oral Statements*. 1855. Reprint. Minneapolis: Ross and Haines, 1957.

Waters, Frank. *The Book of the Hopi*. New York: Penguin Books, 1963.

Weatherford, Jack. *Indian Givers: How the Indians of the Americas Transformed the World*. New York: Ballantine, 1988.

————. *Native Roots: How the Indians Enriched America*. New York: Ballantine, 1991.

Weaver, Jace, ed. *Defending Mother Earth: Native American Perspectives on Environmental Justice*. Maryknoll, NY: Orbis Books, 1996.

————. *Then to the Rock Let Me Fly: Bohanon and Judicial Activism*. Norman: University of Oklahoma Press, 1993.

Weiss, Tracey Bernstein. "Media Speaks with Forked Tongue: The Unsuccessful Rhetoric of Wounded Knee." Paper presented at the Speech Communication Association Convention, Houston, Texas, December 1975.

Weiss, Richard. "Ethnicity and Reform: Minorities and the Ambience of the Depression Years." *Journal of American History* 66 (1979): pp. 566–85.

Welsch, Roger. *Touching the Fire: Buffalo Dancers, the Sky Bundle, and Other Tales*. New York: Villard Books, 1992.

Weston, Mary Ann. *Native Americans in the News: Images of Indians in the Twentieth Century Press*. Westport, CT: Greenwood Press, 1996.

"When in the Course of Human Events: An Interview with Carter Camp." *Akwesasne Notes* 5 (Autumn 1973): p. 11.

Whitehead, Ruth Holmes. *Stories from the Six Worlds: Micmac Legends*. Halifax, Nova Scotia: Nimbus, 1988.

Wiget, Andrew O. *Native American Literature*. Boston: Twayne, 1985.

Wilson, Bryan. *The Noble Savages: The Primitive Origins of Charisma and Its Contemporary Survival*. Berkeley: University of California Press, 1975.

Witalec, Janet. Critical *Essays on Native American Literature*. Boston: G. K. Hall, 1985.

———, ed. *Smoke Rising: The Native North American Literary Companion*. Detroit: Visible Ink Press, 1995.

Witherspoon, Gary. *Language and Art in the Navajo Universe*. Ann Arbor: University of Michigan Press, 1977.

Witt, Shirley H., and Stan Steiner, eds. *The Way: An Anthology of American Indian Literature*. New York: Alfred A. Knopf, 1972.

Wong, Hertha D. *Sending My Heart Back across the Years: Tradition and Innovation in Native American Autobiography*. New York: Oxford University Press, 1992.

Wood, Nancy. *Spirit Walker*. New York: Doubleday, 1993.

Woodard, Charles L. *Ancestral Voice: Conversations with N. Scott Momaday*. Lincoln: University of Nebraska Press, 1989.

Wright, Ronald. *Stolen Continents: The "New World" through Indian Eyes*. Boston: Houghton Mifflin, 1992.

Wub-e-ke-niew. *We Have the Right to Exist: A Translation of Aboriginal Indigenous Thought. The First Book Ever Published from an* Ahnishinahbaeojibway *Perspective*. New York: Black Thistle Press, 1995.

Wyman, Leland C. *Beautyway: A Navajo Ceremonial*. New York: Pantheon Books, 1957.

Young Bear, Severt, and R. D. Theisz. *Standing in the Light: A Lakota Way of Seeing*. Lincoln: University of Nebraska Press, 1994.

Zitkala Sa [Gertrude Bonnin]. *American Indian Stories*. Glorietta, NM: Rio Grande Press, 1976.

Peace Is Possible. Illustration by Francene Hart.

Index

About the Author

LOIS J. EINHORN is Associate Professor of Rhetoric at Binghamton University. She is author of *Abraham Lincoln the Orator: Penetrating the Lincoln Legend* (Greenwood, 1992), *Helen Keller, Public Speaker: Sightless but Seen, Deaf but Heard* (Greenwood, 1998), and many articles and book chapters. She has won several major awards for outstanding teaching.

ISBN 0-275-95790-X

EAN

9 780275 957902

90000>

HARDCOVER BAR CODE